Soul Exposed
Inner Guidance and Facts

A.J. Prince

authorHOUSE®

AuthorHouse™
1663 Liberty Drive
Bloomington, IN 47403
www.authorhouse.com
Phone: 1-800-839-8640

First published by AuthorHouse 6/24/2011

ISBN: 978-1-4634-1483-2 (sc)
ISBN: 978-1-4634-1484-9 (e)

Library of Congress Control Number: 2011908734

Printed in the United States of America

Any people depicted in stock imagery provided by Thinkstock are models,
and such images are being used for illustrative purposes only.
Certain stock imagery © Thinkstock.

This book is printed on acid-free paper.

CHAPTER I

Vocabulary: Terms You may start to familiarize yourself with, for not only they are new to you, but also, they are part of the vocabulary of what you are about to read

Vocabulary.

DP: direct perception

HBBs: human beings becoming

PP Life or PPL: plain physical life in correlation with essential life or soul life

PPK game=prediction\psychokinetic game or lottery

In classical theatre, the rule about one place, one time, and one action is well known. It facilitates understanding, and is relatively easy to follow in plays, movies, novels, where characters are fictive. In regard to the SOUL EXPOSED, it cannot be that way, for it deals with reality in the deepest sense of the concept. Therefore, it is related to plurality in time, place and action. With these ideas in mind, may your reading be playful and pleasant.

Sunday March 5, 2000

> DP1 In this place where I appear, I see women sitting as in an alley that starts near me and goes ad infinitum. In the scenery, there are also many red-hot iron sticks. Some of the women have horns on their heads. As I keep repeating to them that they are the devils, they leave, and while leaving, one of them throws a rock at you.

The night before the dip, I watched an episode of Zena; the television series of the same name, In that episode she was wearing horns in one sequence, represented by a skeleton in another. The meaning of these sequences escaped my conscious mind during the visioning of the series, or I was too preoccupied by the women bodies in the series to pay enough attention to the reason for the imagery. But it was meaningful to me enough to trigger the DP above.

The red hot iron sticks and the women wearing horn may be simple metaphor for men and women wanting to be together, wanting to make love to each other. The woman who throws a rock at me is my date, an expression of her wanting to be in a romantic love relationships with me or some kind of contact, an expression of my own desire of women in waking life becoming reality during the DP. In the other hand, when a woman throws a rock at you, she may be expressing her anger toward you. "God" knows that I have my share of troubles with women, having been in many relationships that I had to let go in small dosage or in which I was pushed out or relationships I had to end up squarely. We're not perfect; we make mistake. I was going out with a woman once, found another man in her apartment. I've never seen her again since that day. So she may be mad at me about that. It may be what is expressed in this DP, too.

The rock itself certainly symbolizes a rocket, missile, and even scud missile. I cherish the idea that one-day the missile technology can be used to send HBBs and things on Mars or other planets

Of course, the rock says, too, I like(pale word to describe the feeling of someone at 10 years old who had the nickname Tilan, the name of a disk-jockey) Twist and Shout, Celine Dion, LL Cool J although nowadays, I listen rather to the new rock music as in Pearl Jam, Fuel, after I've got the idea from a Britney Spears'CD .

I am discovering now that the love of rock-and-roll was not quite a voluntary, conscious, reflected upon decision. I was only of 7 chronological years old when Seradieu, after hiding behind a cactus fence threw a rock at me passing through the gate. My dead bit father had a neighbor, Eugene. Seradieu is Eugene's son. I became completely blind for several days. I can still feel a little bump on the lid and at the corner of my left eye, made by the rock that hit me. There is a link between that event and your history with rock and Roll in general.

The red-hot sticks, themselves, may be, also, a reminder of one the characteristics of DP in general that I tend to forget. Most of us know that we have DP, between other things, to clean up our psyche everyday in order to be able to function properly during the day. Most of the time for me it was about what I did wrong in the past. The red hot iron sticks suggested that DP is also about subjects that are too hot in our mind to have a free and non disturbing expression of, consequently, from which energy has to be taken off a little first, that you have to cool down.

What about saying to the women that they are Devils? It cannot be about witchcraft, the time when non-submissive women were accused of being witches and persecuted. That wouldn't be very relevant to me personally for being a man of this time. The most contact I have with witchcraft is in book (literature) and hearsay.

In certain religion the belief is that money is the devil itself. It can be about money, but it's not why I say that to the women with horns that they are the devils. I may have called them that way to say I love them. . I was reminded of that meaning after hearing it at Craig Killborn Show. He said that when you say to a woman she is the devil, it is another way of telling her that you love her.

Joseph Campbell sees "our demons as our own limitations." For him devil is god who has not been recognized."

Do I wish owning a Lamborghini? One model was called El Diablo. It could be about that too in the DP. I had Dodge Colt, a car that burst into flame in 1987. Since then, not being able to buy a car at all, I promised myself to buy a real good one when I can.

Other reason for the DP is that I am really preoccupied by woman with whom to have sexual and love relationships for not being in these kinds of relationships since 1998(4 yeats). Even though I rationalize that I cannot have steady relationships now, my body doesn't seem to see it the way you do, given that sexuality is fundamental to human life. What is expressed, then, what is being fulfilled at DP level of reality, is sexuality, in one hand. On the other hand it is a definition of what I really am, a definition of self from the infinite point of view. We are all from there Isn't it? We are all of infinite parentage, as well as everything that exists.

Jane Roberts, in her book The "Unknown Reality says; When you free your consciousness of limited concept of time and space, you begin to explore the unknown reality, that is the unrecognized self.........Each of you is part of an infinite self. That infinite self appears as series of finite self in your reality. There are different kinds of infinities, different varieties of psychological infinities that do not meet; that is, they go their own infinite ways." That may be related to the deepest meaning of the DP.

> *DP2. I have in my hands some bills. It's like they represent money that someone who reminds me of Arnold gives to me.*

Arnold is the first son of my entire family of seven children. I am the fourth. I am born from a woman who left us when I was 6 chronological years old, and a man who passed away recently and who had 27 children before changing to the state of bits and pieces.

The DP refers to a scare I had in New York once. I was living in Montreal, went to New York to visit Arnold and his family, Italien another entire brother and his family. I was very outgoing at that time. One night during my visit to Queens, New York I decided to go to Manhattan for some fun. Arnold gave me $300 cash to pay his mortgage for him in Manhattan while I was there. I had the foolish idea to go to a club with the money in my pocket. At 2 O'clock, I went to the street looking for a taxi. In the street 2 women approached me and asked if I am looking for some fun. After a few seconds I noticed that the money wasn't in my pocket any more. You grabbed the two women, yield for HBBS to call the police. I have been drinking, the time it took for police to arrive, one of the women managed to get away with the money. When they arrived, They took the one and me and to a police station near by, search the woman , she didn't have the money. They put her in jail, and asked me to go to court the next day. In Montreal a month later, I received a letter in which it said that the case was dismissed for lack of evidence.

DP3. *I have my hands full of coins.*

One of my goals is to have a foundation that I will create with 10% of all money I will have. In that sense, I need money to give money, create money to give money. I hope to help HBBs. around the globe with it, on their basic needs such as water, electricity, in poor countries, food and housing in those countries where there are victims of rather necessary structural default of capitalism.

Anyway, in the reinforcing exercises that I do once a week in order to create the foundation I make the picture of a hand full of coins to express the idea of giving.

I want to make a few children at once. I probably will not go with the technique of enriched sperm inseminated in one woman who then may give birth to sextuplet, for I find having many children at one time too dangerous for a woman. I probably will go with some surrogate mothers to give birth to one child at a time without enriched sperm, using the so-called test-tube baby technique. So it will cost some money, I could say a lot of money to have all my children the same year more or less and to raise them.

Chronologically speaking, I am not in your 20ies. I have to have the children that fast to have the time to raise them before I go to the la, la land. In theory I think I can live until I am 130 to 150 chronological years of age. There is no reason whatsoever for not being able to do that. In practice it is another matter. Nothing has been discovered yet to make sure life of an HBB can be extended that far. Psychically you will always be 25 years old; meaning will always have the body of a 25-year-old, though, because we have the body with with the age we think we have.

I need money to have the children and to create the rest of personal and public goals that I have. I would like to discover an earthquake detector and a machine capable of preventing big accident or accident where many human and animals lives would be at risk like the two planes that destroyed the two sky scrapers in New York on September 11, 2001, the Russian submarine with a latch that would not open resulting in the death of at least 300 HBBs. I feel sad when there are these events, because I know they can be prevented. I need money for this part of the goals too. I will need a small group of scientists and technicians for it.

So, I have goals, the reason why I started searching formally in 1989 the way to create them, and the reason why I am dreaming that much, writing them down, amylasing them a nit in this book I call the SOUL EXPOSED. In theory, at the end of it the goals should have been created.

It was astonishing when the title came to me on a mountain. The soul not being really visible cannot be exposed as such. However, I was preoccupied by that there is hoax in psychology. I even found afterward, that in psychology literature there is a family wearing the name SoaL whom where reported for cooking the results of their psychological experiments. There is also that there are a lot of merchants of ideologies, groups and religious groups that are trying to convince us to buy their ideas, to follow them, although they are bringing us to half of the truth or to what is not true at all sometimes. In that sense we are exposed and in many other senses.

In top of the mountain expresses the invidual and the Soul of the World. The top of the mountain may mean moves, one definition of soul.

9\11, war in Afghanistan, terrorism are direct consequence of living like a machine and our attachment to outside power (so we are at war with ourselves). Most of us know the importance of machines in human life. Yet, thinking that machine can replace the human psyche, that real power could be found outside the border of oneself is courting disaster. The SOUL EXPOSED is an attempt to bring us back to ourselves in order to recapture our innate powers, our zest for joyful living, becoming more humane, and open the door for peace on earth.

The Soul Exposed is, also, another explanation of the events of the world, about self and world therapy.

I was having a bad time, when I was writing the book, after the unforeseeable end of an employment, being forced to live with very little money. I felt miserable, vulnerable, Exposed

In one hand the reader will have the raw direct perceptions, in the other he will have an understanding of it. This sentence could summarize the book if it could be summarize in one sentence.

CHAPTER II

Wednesday March 8, 2000

DP4. I am in the same bed with Bill. It's like very close to us two there are two men loving each other.

Bed is metaphor for same philosophy, life vision or value. Although I prefer not to write last name in this book to live according to the principle "Do to others what you would like them do to you" by courtesy and to avoid all sorts of headaches, Bill Clinton is the United States president a lot of Haitians like for helping Haiti put some orders in its political affairs. Although I don't do active politics, meaning I don't belong to a political party, I share his democratic ideas by profession, for working in the teaching area for many years and for finding something very deep, and very appealing in the democratic political ideas every where in the world. That is the assumption of abundance of goods for all HBBs(Forest Gump). In the other hand I find them(Democratic politics) undisciplined, that is not appealing to you.

I have come in contact with many HBBs. with first name

Bill. One in a class at the University of British Columbia, one at a house I rented from its owner, sub rented to tenants at 3339 west 42nd Avenue, Vancouver.I think that the DP is rather about this Bill. When Bill was living in I was a renter like him. Kevin was the one who rented the house then. Yes in that house I've heard homosexual men making love to each other many times. There was Anabelle visiting her brother living in the house for a while. I started to like her gave up after I heard her brother making love with Kevin in the washroom. You don't understand my feeling about her, for she had nothing to do with her brother's sexual activities.

> DP5. The kind of factory in which I appear reminds me of Beverly Hills. Hugh Heftner comes to pick me up and brings me to his office to pay me for a work I have done for him. I think he just did something good and try to congratulate him for that. Before I am able to do that he says to me to leave him alone, runs away, playing at the same time music with very small clarinet.

Yes I have been a customer of Playboy for a long period of time. I probably will be one of the magazine readers in the future also. Nowadays, I don't indulge in this sort of consummation for fear, between other things, it could be the reason why I am not getting laid, and as my nephew Philip said to me once. I think seeing the picture of too many already good looking women , enhanced for the purpose of magazine selling, interferes with my sense of reality in that matter and renders me, then, incompetent. But, I must admit, reading Playboy is more likely to have anything at all to do with my involuntary sexual abstinence. Mental block, being too busy would be a more valid explanation.

I've never met mister Heftner, I know, though, why I would be dreaming of him. I cannot reveal at all the reason why he is in this DP yet. I may be able to do that before the publication of this volume of the Soul Exposed, or in one of the other volumes to come.

Yes I've work in factories for a short period of time while going to university. One, I even had a graveyard schedule.

Monday March 13, 2000

DP5a. I am lying in a bed with 2 women in 69 sense. One of the women reminds me of Monise. The other one opens her legs in my face. Some people are making noise outside. Both of the women get up and go to see what's happening. When they come back, they all lie down in the same sense than you.

First of all, it is important to indicate to what extent the meaning can go. For the context, kind of restraining it. Monise is my entire (in comparison to half) sister; She was born immediately after me, so the fifth of the family of six children who are alive, one in bit and pieces state. The DP emits a restraining order in regard to the meaning like I said exactly because her presence in the bed to signify that we are definitely in a metaphorical atmosphere (I learn afterward that, up to the year 700, marriage was done between family members only). In reality the other women wouldn't open her legs on my head in Monise's presence, or in any one else presence but her lover. I suppose the opposite sense refers to problem I encounter in the love department since some time.

The girl went and saw what the noise was about, came back and lied down in the same way than me. The noise may translate being famous and having lot of HBBs talking about. In other words I am going out with a woman who is famous.

Second of all, two women in the DP don't necessarily translate by two waking life women. Two parts of the same woman. As you will see in volume two of the Soul Exposed, all living things seem to have two basic functions one which operates structurally, the other one operating more loosely and transcending the first.

The two women may represent the self and the soul.

Third of all, the only time I could have two women in the same bed was when I was going out with Lorraine. I loved her very much. She loved me the same. She was not bisexual. I know that now after I went out with Tam recently. She had her period, wanted me to make love with her, using her other apparel. I refused to do that, then we don't see each other anymore. When Lorraine had her period once, she made me make love with her like that, in front.

Any way one day Lorraine presented herself with another woman in my apartment. I didn't welcome the other woman. They left together. I was naive, didn't think my love for her and hers for me could be shared any how. Today I am still like that a bit, but is sure that some HBBs. can share their partners without big damage, because most of them are not in romantic love anyway.

Last of all, Tirat nickname translates to small rat as you can guess. I've forgotten her real name, my father's niece, She used to come to my grand mother's place, in the yard, in daylight, and pulled me under her dress between her legs. that always happened in the presence of many HBBs, including my father. They all laughed at it. Then, I was small enough to be able to that without any reticence. Now I think that it was a very bizarre behavior.

It brings to the surface of my mind something I heard in the radio once. This woman was working in the street in Vancouver accompanied by her husband. They see another woman with big melons apparently. But the husband and this wife started debating if they are natural or enhanced. The big boobs' woman takes the husband hands and put them on her breasts so that he can feel for himself that they are not fake, they're real. Wow! I could believe my ears when you heard the married woman tell the story in the radio I find this behavior, too, a strange one.

Tuesday March 14, 2000

> DP5.When I arrive home I see a stranger in the front porch. Thinking he is about to make a brick and enter, I look in the yard for something with which to hit him. Then I find myself hanging on a tree; Then, I get down, pull out my belt and approach him. Then, he says" it is not I to worry about rather the person inside". When I go inside the house you see nobody.

This is more or less a recall of what happened to me once. I met this esthetician in a bus. She invited me to meet her at the beauty salon where she works. I went there with no intention to have an air cut, for it was almost time to go and start to teach a class. Ann Mary was not happy with that, but I left her anyway and proceeded to go to the school nearby. On the porch of the little mall, a skinhead approached me. The time you realized he wanted to fight with me, I was already on the floor, he on top of me. I stretched an arm, trying to grab one of his eyes. He jumped up before I could do that. Then I got up and punched him in the face about three or four times. Instead of continuing punching him until you got him down too, I went looking for something with which to hit him. That was not a very bright move on my part.

I left but did not go to the school directly, I took a long cut, the time to recollect from the incident. Then, it was like an army of policemen who joined me. You explained what happened. They let me go after I stated that I would take the matter to the court.

The incident was a trap. I was ambushed.

I was a teacher on call, meaning that I was going to many schools, sometimes one different school every day. Months after the incident I realized that, not getting off the bus at the same place all the time, Anne Marie and or her boyfriend may have thought thatI was a criminal.

The link between the DP and this incident is not clear.

Nonetheless, it is what we are inside that can cause us trouble, not the other person or outside event as it is alluded to in the DP. Everyone is little "god" beyond time, space and circumstances, if we can live with who we are.

In behavioral studies it is thought our internal sentences determine our emotion. The DP may be an allusion to that too.

The climbing on the tree reminds me of peak experiences as described by Maslow, even though I can't connect it to something related to me in waking life for now.

The house is a psychic house. DP is really saying that it is the ego to worry but not the I.

DP6. Someone is on the balcony of a skyscraper. I think that he is not *supposed to be there. As soon as I start to fix my eyes on him, he disappears. Then I find myself climbing a tree again. After you get down, a woman arrives, telling me a traumatic experience and amnesia she had once.*

In my first comment of this direct perception, I thought it was my will that makes the person disappear and that it was because of fear I went to climb a tree afterward .Now, after 2 years, the fear is still ok, but the DP was the prediction of what was going to happen in New York, I think. Obviously I didn't have a clue about its meaning when you've just made it. Climbing the tree for me is the sign of something terrible about to happen, as if there was water all over.

The woman may be Sophia the Soul of the World despite that she was in the depth of things talking about her vulnerability.

CHAPTER III

Thursday March 17, 2000

DP7. I have in my hands a quantity of bills of money, including a $ 50 Canadian bill.

In the TV show Hollywood Square last night there was a question on the origin of paper money asked to a man. Her answer was "Arabic", which was true but vague. The precise answer should have been" Chinese". I don't remember what the panel of actors and actresses thought was the right answer, but the whole thing was strange and the occasion of the DP.

In the DP I put the bunch of bills together almost the way I do it in waking life, that is to say, get them in order before I put them in your pocket. I still don't know if it's a good or bad habit or something worth mentioning, but I do that all the time.

Sunday March 19, 2000

> DP8. *Somebody who reminds me of Siliane asks if have idle money. Then she asks me to lend her some of it that she will give back after her run from the market.*

On Saturday, something similar happen with Brian, a roommate. I don't remember exactly what it was. But I am guessing now, it was as in the DP or what he did a few times borrowing your cell phone to call someone else and to ask him to lend him money when you were living in the same house than him. His behavior was a little bit bizarre.

Siliane is the form of elemental life now. In her living adult days she was a small business lady as our grandmother. She was my entire elder sister, but like a mother in replacement of my real mother in elemental life since I was 6 years old. Siliane past away when I was much older, already a self -sufficient adult?

Monday March 20, 2000

> DP8. *I hear my immediate less younger entire brother talking inside of a house. I go inside and see a few HBBs. Then I my find myself somewhere else embracing a woman. I press one leg against her pelvis. She says she is coming. I say " That's gooooooood!" Then she says again that she comes in my house to fix it but she forgot the mattress.*

I didn't see the upper part of the woman. Who knows? It could be an animal, a tree, a rock or something unsubstantial or even another man. I was not sexually active at that time, still now, in the house where I was living there were 3 other men, one man of Japanese descent, one of African descent, one of English descent. They were all pressing me for sexual encounter.

Why did the woman say in the DP " I am coming "? Women can only have an orgasm. This was not very much a lucid dream. I was in "lala state", not very rational.

Meeting women for whatever reason is not as easy for me in English Canada as it was in French Canada (or is it because I was younger, full of life in French Canada?). I was were brought up in francophone community more or less or, should we say French-African community. I was very busy and my financial situation is not the best one since I decided to live in Vancouver, but I am waiting for the big break. It will come.

It takes many adjectives to specify this brother Italien. He is living in Queens, New York. I am very closed to him; of course, although I haven't seen him since January first 1980, the day I went there to be Doris's godfather, she is 21 years of chronological age now. I don't know what she looks like. Last time I've heard of her she was trying to be a stewardess.

In the DP I heard the real voice of my brother. I was doing hearing imagining, other way if not the best way to keep this biological function, hearing, in good shape.

There is this saying in Creole " fèsè nat domi a tè", translated in French " Fabricant de lit dort sur la terre ou le plancher nu, in English " Bed maker sleeps on the row floor". Does it fit the concept according to which closeness obscures relationships then may eliminate involvement? Remind me of this saying in psychology " Be awake and fully appreciative of everything everyone"

Tuesday March 21, 2000

DP9. I am in a university. I have a lot to do and meet a student in the hall. He is going to give back his assignment to his professor. He is pressing me to give my assignment soon back too.

That period of time in my life I was not having the best time. I've just had to leave the house with 7 bedrooms on 3339 west 42nd avenue which I rented from the owner and sub rented to individuals. It was sold the reason why everyone had to get out. I lived in it from 1995 to December 1999.The misery from this house came from the fact that all the men roommate I had, about 30, were bisexual. So they were pressing me for sexual activity with them. I had to punch Adrian in his face to prevent him from coming inside my room. You had to grab another one in his neck and push him back from the door of your room.

Scarcely a few days passed after I rented a bedroom to one guy. One night at about two o'clock, I was awakened by the loud noise of a TV in the living room contiguous to my bedroom. The guy I found there just pushed his body against mine. I kind of leaded him to the kitchen with in mind to grab a knife and plunge in his chest. By the time I arrive in the kitchen with him, I chickened out of that idea, I pushed him very hard away from me, to let him know that he is in danger. He bangs his body against a wall. I went back to bed. I let him go from the house the following month, of course.

That's why when I heard in the news of a gay man killed by another man in Hollywood, I think it's a very sad situation, a misdirect anger or whatever it is that pushes someone to commit such a crime. Gay man is innocent, non-violent. They are not hurting anyone, not doing any crime. So why bother them.

In regard to bisexuality, it's a different matter. Because of the covert nature of this type of sexuality, it enhances dictator character and violent behavior in some men as we have seen above. If he was not behaving as dictator, he would try to know my sexual orientation before hand, he would find out that I am heterosexual, everything would end there in terms of sexuality.

That's the way a gay man wouldn't behave.

That's why I think there should be a law banishing bisexual men in field of work such as teaching, coaching, where children are. If the guy was physically stronger than I was, he would simply over power me.

All that to say it is the reason why I was thinking of going back to university to take some upgrading courses to go back teaching, instead of continuing in the renting and sub renting business. I had no problem at all living with women, gay or bisexual. But while renting those bedrooms at 3339 west 42nd Avenue, I noticed that it takes a longer period of time to find female roommate than it is to find male roommate. I didn't have a cent in my name in the bank, still I haven't, at that time. So I would have trouble to pay the rent most of the time waiting for roommates that are women.

CHAPTER IV

Wednesday March 22, 2000

> *DP10. These HBBs I d on't really see are walking in front of me. I am following them. They bring me near a river where a woman is taking a bath. After coming out of the water, she comes near me and sit down. You caress her body for a while. Then she says something I don't understand. I ask her to repeat it clearly. " I have no plan" Add her. I continue touching her body. I make love with her but I am not very excited.*

No wonder I was not sexually active at the time when I made that DP. U was unconsciously induced to keep away from love and sexuality for some reason. At the same time, expressing it means also that my sexual healing started since then. The energy that was keeping me away from sexual activity started to come out. All I had to do to keep the healing process was to understand this psychology behind it and let the energy comes out by catharsis. It's like it has sunk back to the unconscious, because I am still not sexually active, despite my desire to be so. I must admit that there are more factors at work in keeping me away from love and sex. Trying to keep away from bisexuality must have kept me away from sexuality too. I don't have my own house, can't afford to live in apartment alone. So I have to share houses with bisexual most of the time.

> DP11. I am sitting at a table. I have a woman friend sitting there too, Mark, a roommate, is there too accompanied by his girlfriend. She has a ticket of ppk game wrapped in a plastic paper in her hand. With a brisk gesture, she tears apart the plastic and takes the ticket out. Mark says " the way you do it shows that you use to that before." I ask if he is mad. The answer is no. Then, I start thinking that the ppkg game is like something inside of a thin layer of plastic that can be broken easily.

Mark from Australia was in an exchange work program in Vancouver. After a few days in Vancouver, his girlfriend joined him from Sweden .She spent a few days at the house and went back to Sweden. This reminds me of Andre of Quebec, roommate making his PH D at the University of British Columbia. After his girlfriend left to go back to the Orient, He said to me " My girlfriend left, now I am dry." With a low languishing voice. I can't keep myself from smiling each time I think of that. I find it so funny for him to talk like that to another man.

What if the reason I met Mark was because I often think of this?

"Few of us can stand prosperity. Another man's, I mean."

Mark Twain ?

When you don't have it, you think of it, dream of it. If I had gazillion dollars now, I would buy a big barrel of Vodka, invite all my friends and stay home for 5 days without doing a dam thing. I haven't had any alcohol in my blood since 15 days. Today I wouldn't be able to buy one ounce of vodka.

When I have so much money, it's not easy to be addicted to something. I have so many choices. Otherwise, the number of rich people would diminish very quickly to a point where everyone is average or poor money wise. But it is not the case. Rich HBBs stay rich; poor HBBs stay poor, as they say. I think that the number of rich HBBs increase across time in rich countries.

I don't understand this DP really. It may be telling me something about Mark. May be his girlfriend, the Swedish girl is still a virgin, not touched for the very first time, as would say Madonna.

Thin layer in the DP reminds me also of Yvonne a first, kind and nice looking girl I met while going home after a graveyard shift in Montreal. It was the first time I went out with a white girl. And since that day:

Ti zoizo nan bois qui ta pe chante

Ti zoizo nan bois qui ta pe chante

Hai! depuis jou ca

Moin gaingnin

Et deux pieds moin nan chain..........

It's a song known in most parts of the world created by an Haitian (as actual Canadian governor is) singer, and meaning more or less:

Little bird in the wood

Little bird in the wood

Which was singing

Hai! Since that day
I have pain
And since that day
My two feet are in chain.

Translates well my feeling except I could add ". Since that that day I have nightmares.

Yvonne was a virgin; I made love with her but didn't go all the way. She was very afraid of getting pregnant. I respected her wish.

> *DP12. I give the rent money to the woman who owns the house with her husband. She makes me think that I am too much in a hurry to pay the rent, that there must be something wrong with me. I tell her that it's because the house is not mine. It's like Mark is there too.*

It's not time to pay the rent yet. That's why allusion is made to being in a hurry to pay the rent, may be. I have been a renter for 5 years. It's been only two months since I passed from the position of renter to the position of rentee. The adjustment is not complete yet at some level in my psyche. Actually, it was not just a question of maladjustment. I was suffering physically and mentally of the demise. My feet were hurting; I was unable to move the upper left side of your body. I went to St. Paul Hospital many times.

One renter, Wayne, in 3339 west 42nd Avenue tore down part of the toilet wall, started to go out with the female roommate I had an eye on romantically speaking. Then he also was making homosexual advance to me. The following month I evicted him without giving him back his security deposit. He went to the rental office and got a hearing. I kept you initial position, no giving back security deposit to such a person. I went to that office a couple of times. When someone brought me there I loose. When I brought someone there, I loose.

He got himself a lawyer who transferred the case the small claim court. The day I went to that court the pain in my feet became more acute than ever. At my turn to speak, it was like I was going to fall on the floor. I started to tell the history of the case a little bit. The woman judge said that I should not talk about that. The pain became more acute again. I stopped talking right there. The judge said it was up to her to decide who is going to loose or win the case. But knowing that my position was not strong, having pain, I said that that was all you had to say. So, Wayne won the case, I was ordered to give him back his security deposit, what I did sometime afterward.

Then when I went to Canada Trust on Georgia and Granville streets, a woman was flirting with me. I went to the library, another woman was flirting with me, or did I imagine they were flirting with me because O felt humiliated a bit and suffering?

Not really, some thinker of love asserts that love comes after big pain (in this case pain and humiliation) sometimes. I met Jeanine on a hospital bed. She became the love of my life at that time. I met a Jordanian in Brandon, Manitoba. The same week, I have learned that my sister Siliane who practically raised me was dead.

I just rented a house from this Japanese guy, but for him I did more than that. He was not living in the same floor of the house than me, but he showed up in bedroom dressed in wardrobe only. I asked him to stay outside, by the door. He got mad and made such a big noise about belongings I had on his yard that he wanted me to get rid of. So on the first of April, I gave him notice that I was moving out in May and I did. All the other three guys who were living on the same floor than me thought his behavior with me was unfair.

The African guy disappeared in the middle of April without leaving a trace while I was still living in the Manitoba Street, Vancouver. The others moved out in June 2000.

I don't quite know why Mark is still present in this DP except that before moving out from 3339 west 42nd Avenue, he wanted me to move out with him and Sarin, another roommate. She was a small good-looking UBC student. I didn't move out with them for many reasons. The main one was the fact that I didn't know what was going to happen to me financially. I thought I might end up on welfare, and that, as a teacher, was a bad example to give to the younger ones.

Friday March 24, 2000

> *DP13. Lelio is with someone else they are inhumanly taller than I am. I tell them that I am not here for long time and that I want them to do other things...........I give to one part of chocolate cake that I had.......... I say to another "never touch the bag in which I have avocado".*

Lelio is another one of my entire brothers. I am 5'11" something tall. I do not know the exact measure of his height, but I know he his a little bit taller than I am. He was born next after my sister Monise who was born next after me. He was in the army in Haiti, living in United States of America now. I have not seen him for about a long tiime one of the reason why I have him and other brothers and sisters often in my DPs. A cousin Andre Eli has a property on which there are town houses rented to HBBs. When my cousin moved to Montreal, Lelio was the manager of the place. The cousin's wife called me once and told me that Lelio owed her renting money, that you had to pay her for him. I have never talked to the cousin since then because of that. That is the Lelio in complete life.

In this DP it's a figure may be representing other part of me at night My plain physical self being split in different parts mainly physical body, soul and spirit. In it he is inhumanly tall, sign of archetype above the human realm. He was a captain in the army. The DP may be reffering to that too.

When I move out from 3339 west 42nd Avenue January 1st, 2000, I thought I could live for a while at the youth hostel in Point Grey. The day after I found out I could not stay there, not even one more day, that the hostel is for HBBs from outside of Vancouver, I went downtown, arranged to stay in hotel there. But I had to leave the Hotel at 8 O' clock in the morning and come back 6 PM every day(Very similar ro a concentration camp . That day January 1st, 2000, I went to the Pacific Center, very close to the hotel, not really knowing what to do. I bought a bag of muffins on sale near Georgia Street directed myself to the restaurant in the second floor of the Pacific Center, left a briefcase on a table at the restaurant to go to buy a coffee. When I came back the navy colored briefcase and the bag of muffins were gone.

I did not mind the bag of muffins, but in regard to the briefcase it was like a catastrophe, for there were important documents in it including the address of Lisa Dergan. We were about to become boyfriend and girlfriend . In the briefcase there was also a picture of her she has sent to me in November.1998 with her private phone number and e-mail address. In the letter she suggested to me to go and meet her in Los Angeles. I could have gone there and stayed for at least 6 months. Lisa is very nice and very kind, very attractive woman.

I missed a huge opportunity by hanging in 3339 west 42nd Avenue, Vancouver too long meaning I should have accepted Lisa's suggestion and moved to Los Angeles, forgetting the principle:

"We bring pleasant and unpleasant events in our lives in cluster, sometimes"

In the briefcase there was books I borrowed from the library that I had to pay for.

Also another intellectual instrument that I cannot freely talk about yet.

It is probably why we have avocado in the briefcase in the DP (Edible or not yet edible, in waking life we would not think of putting an avocado in a briefcase............).

I no longer eat avocado because it gives cholesterol. Avocado in the DP it is a metaphor, should be taken in the sense of tool, as a lawyer (avocado and lawyer spells the same in French 'avocat'. For in a briefcase that's what we have, papers or intellectual tools.

Because it is a food, I have eaten a lot of it (In Haiti most of the time that's what I ate instead of rare meat) before knowing that it gives cholesterol then high blood pressure, in the DP it serves as a catharsis, or by the DP I started to solve the problem which is to accept eating no more avocado.

Sunday March 26,200

> *DP14. I see a very small girl who tells me " Hibou me"........A woman who is teaching.........*

Hibou, translated from French, means owl, but in some French communities it is also equivalent of ugliness, hence it may be about young idea like a new born baby who can be ugly. I do not know if house in Manitoba Street, or if I had or if I had the bug at the Hotel 500 on Dunsmuir street, but the first week in the house on Manitoba Street, I washed my hair with a usual shampoo. Then I've got a rash, an allergic reaction in your head, especially in the front part close to the eyes and the ears. I gave got myself some medicine and treated it.

Anyway the lesson might have been on creativity, more specifically on newborn idea. Here is what Doug Hall, author of Jumpstart Your Brain said on it more exactly:" Respect new born ideas when they first occur. They aren't full blown, finished products. New ideas are fragile like babies. They need nurtured protecting, patience, loving commitment. They require you to sit up with them at night, fret over their future, watch them grow. They can not be hurried........"

Sure that the brain is like the dynamo of the mind, but we could say it has little to do with ideas in the sense that electricity has little to do with water. Water and electricity are not the same although there can be a link between the two(Water makes the turbines turn to produce electricity but intrinsically water and electricity are not the same). The mind processes the ideas that we have. So the title of this book " Jumpstart Your Brain" is misleading. The statement on newborn idea is correct though(the brain has its own mind in the sense thatt the body has its own mind).

Then, the other interpretation would be the owl taken in other context. It has big eyes that would mean then the little girl wants to have an already developed sense of sight.

I see my self as a man; it would not make sense to conclude that the person in the DP is myself. Then who is the woman?

When I arrived in the house on Maniroba Street the first day, the Japanese woman told me to tell her if somebody bothers me. She is also teacher a driving . In this case the presence of the woman in the DP can be justified.

Beauty is in the eye of the beholder as the say. I didn't

touch a woman since 1998 in Oklahoma in a hotel. The little girl may be saying that I find her ugly or I find woman around me ugly which would not be the case, for I see beauty in everything and everyone, in a way(Remind me of Prince Philip who told me in a DP "English women are gauche".

> *DP15.From afar I see some children having a dispute around something. When I get nearer I see it is about a piece of meat. I take it in my hands, give it to Anglade and ask him to cut it in pieces and give one to each child. I send then the children to get him a knife and a cutting board. While they are away, I say to Anglade that it's because the entire piece of meet is too small that they are fighting over it. When they come back with the knife and cutting board, Anglade did as I asked him to.*

No need for a course at university to understand that it easier to find the solution of a big problem by dividing it into pieces.

Fear and our ego are what keep us from achieving our goals in short period of time. There is a process that takes some time. But because everyone has in his psyche the solution of any problem he could have, it must be fear that keeps the solutions buried in the unconscious. Most HBBs have a goal. or goals (If you are walking aimlessly in the Malls, it seems you do not have a goal; Heidegger compared that with living in nothingness). and fear. Everybody has an ego.

According to what we know now, the self of a child is

complete at about 6 years old. But at that time our selves are not very strong. Its processes are tainted of fear from infancy to 6 years old, and from there to adult life. Then we can live all our lives with the infancy self, if we don't take drastic measures to bring up the adult self. Hence, we live in fear, but it is unconscious.

Looking at it at another angle, some children do not act as if they fear something. When I was around six years I use to call HBBs names what had got me in trouble many times. I was not afraid of these who were already way pass 15 years of chronological age. Was it because of absence of fear or because of total unawareness about HBBs?

The children in the DP bring to the surface of my memory a few recent events in which children and adolescent are involved. This child is about 4 years of chronological age. There is fire in the house where he is alone with his younger sister. He goes to her room, grab her and get outside.

Apparently they were alone in the house. Someone break in his house and attack his mother, this adolescent boy find himself a knife, stabs the intruder who runs away in a hurry.

Anglade is my half brother. We are of similar chronological age we were close to each other in Haiti where he is still living now. Adolescent, I use to sleep in the same bed with him and many other brothers and half brothers. It is a custom in that country. He quit school in primary grade as all my entire and half brothers and sisters. My father and mother didn't go to school. They use row intelligence compare to me who went to school and who has intelligence just a bit sophisticated. The name Anglade is probably why I like the Shakespearian language and HBBs who speak it.

In other words, the name Anglade in the DP symbolizes Anglade my half brother and is also a metaphor. for Anglophone,

In Haiti they are still fighting between themselves all the time. The Palestinians and the Jews are still fighting against each other. In these two countries, it would be possible to say that lack of food is the contributing factor of war, according to the DP. Yes I used to think that lack of food, gas and space are the reason, but nowadays, many experiences are telling that these causes are of superficial explanations, that the real cause of war is to prevent the soul from coming out, to prevent it from being the major motivation in everyone's life.

Tuesday March 28, 2000

> DP16. *This man is hitting on the sitting woman, trying to get her to his place. She stands up, says no to the man, and asks him to calm down. Then she came to me speechless, as if she is overwhelmed by her emotion.*

It's reminds me one of my feelings, the fear of stocking accusation. I sent love letter to a few women once. Then I never wrote them again, because I don't want to be called the stocker. For me being called that way would reveal a serious hole in my character, that I have a mental disorder of some sort. Furthermore I could be dragged to court for it.

But myself I have been stocked many times.

Then there is the subtle stocking when I live in the same house than a few others. They will cut the fork I am using, make a trace on the cover of the toilet I am using, bent the bottom of the pot I am using, leaving their panties in place where I can see them as if lost by inadvertence, leaving knife on the counter in the kitchen, etc.

Why did she come to me overwhelmed by her emotion? "The cat has bitened her tongue"

> *DP17. I appear at this store to buy something. An enormous white man leans on me. I yield to make myself heard by the others and for them to come and help me get out from there. It's like the other HBBs in the store do not hear me, though. Then he let all his weight fall on me preventing me from moving, breathing, and seeing.*

I don't quite understand this DP. The notes I took immediately after having it don't help me now either. Is it about white HBBs archetype or dream body? Let say the answer is yes, then why do I do this kind of DP anyway? In the DP it is clear that it is a man, but in my notes, I mention a woman. Why? Because it happened in a store or the physical space of the DP (dream) is a store, I would adventure myself to say that it is the white business man archetype.

Is it an unconscious fear of the white man or the businessman or the white businessperson?

I perceive the white person as being very rich compare to me very poor. This would be a perception, not reality since we all born from a rich and abundant universe; therefore, we are equally rich in a way. Rich countries, rich HBBs see themselves like being rich. In poor countries, HBBs do not see themselves as being of dich inheritance, the abundant nature. The question is why don't we all see ourselves as heir/heiress of the Infinite and thus infinitely rich? Why is it only some of us see ourselves that way?

I know what I woold be buying in this store. It would be a lottery ticket. According to the direct perception there would be a fear of the game the white game. Were it the Spanish HBBs who started the game firot? However in any case it is not a white game for it is played it almost al countries in the world right now. They are bit all White HBBs. As to the second premise in the DP- the game is heavy-, it is not quite that way either for HBBs are winning in it almost everyday.I had that fear by misconception or it was created in me by society or by the dealers of the game. The problem is not knowing what we know, meaning not knowing our selves when we have one or relitivised the one we have.

CHAPTER V

DP18. I am sitting in the front seat of a car beside Fraser. He takes a paper from his pocket that he starts reading. While doing it, some bills fall from his pocket; I catch them before they completely fall on the floor.

I definitely use to watch this TV series, which is still on the air presently of the same nme as in the direct perception. He plays the character of a psychiatrist At that time when I had the DP I was preoccupied by the definition of schizophrenia: general terms for a number of severe mental disorders, involving disturbed thought processes, withdrawal from reality, and various emotional and behavioral symptoms. The four basics categories of schizophrenia are catatonic, hebephrenic, paranoid and simple.

Before moving to Manitoba street, I was living in a hotel where most of the customers were people in the street, without a permanent address. Some of them and even me might suffer a from of schizophrenia. But what excites me the most about schizophrenia and what probably triggered the DP is the name of this mental sickness itself. For "phrenia" word refers to the head, to the bones in which is the brain. It is a sign that the sickness is thought to be in the brain. And this is a big mistake. The brain has nothing to do with the mental sickness most of the time. The brain is substantial. The mental is unsubstantial, so of a very different nature. So it is a sign, also, that mental sickness was not completely understood by the pioneers of psychology and is not completely understood by the disciples of of the poineers. At the beginning of psychology there was an approach called "mentalism". The word became synonymous of craziness. I suppose first psychologists shy away from anything mental in order not to be associated with craziness which was and is a put down on the field of psychology itself. Thi is something that blocs the understanding of the psyche big time. Bizarre, isn't it?

There is something-called money sickness. I don't remember what it is exactly. I will find out. Some HBBs who are constantly broke like me may suffer from this mental sickness or simply rebelling againt a society composed in general of lost individuals. I think my problem with money is the result of my desire to create my goals by the energy of thought alone and that I didn't have enough knowledge on the psyche to do it yet. There is the theory that it can be done that way. I want to know if the theory can bring the results it predicts. So far the part of the theory that seems to be working is the one that says you can do extraordinary things with thought that cannot be done by physical effort alone, not the part on money. Then thought as well as emotion cannot be separated from action.

The allusion to the character Frazier brings to my

consciousness a psychiatrist who told me that I cannot win in the lottery game at will after counting the odds which are in the millions. It is the feeling of one person, still it signals that the psychiatry field is way out of wack, although it is composed of HBB_-human being becoming- meaning they can ameliorate the concepts of their psychology. As said above HBBs are winning almost everyday in the game in the world.

> *DP19. Gerard Delerme was at that place where I appear. We are both bare feet. He brings me at another place where they put me on a brown bed. Somebody asks: "Are you crazy?". "Everybody is" my answer is. Then, he adds that he knew I was going to answer that way.*

There was a fight between Gerard Delerme and me in Haiti. He had a school: Ecole Frere Polycarpe. I was a teacher there at the time of the fight. It was my first public work. You had a small school for three months in Haiti once. It was kind of the one eyed person teaching the blind. I fought with him because he didn't pay me one month. I thought if he was not satisfied with my teaching he would let me know but he would not keep my money. I thought also he was more interested in having money, he had a lot of it, expensive cars etc. His weight was at least 400 pounds, and 6 feet tall, I was 130 pounds. I tried to forget the incident and remind myself of him as the one who allowed me to work in a public context for the first time. It was a sad incident from which he might come out missing an eye. He was the attacker.

When I had the DP, there was a new tenant, Sherman, in the house on Manitoba Street. Somehow, I ended up in hot discussion with him many times. It started as soon as he moved in. We didn't have time to know each other yet. So, I thought he had a mild mental disorder. It was only after I move out, I figured that was his way of trying to induce me in a homosexual act with him. By remembering the way he insisted in telling me that he hasn't been with a woman for a long time. I met him at University of British Columbia, in the street. I hoped he was not following me everywhere in the city. He was so small in size comparable to mine; I would not feel threaten by him, t even if his size was comparable to mine, was it not for his homosexual propensity we could be a good friend . think the reference to craziness in the DP is related to him.

> *DP20. Qui veut se deshabiller peut avoir la maison?.......... I hear the couple upstairs having a hot discussion and the woman saying this:" It's my house".*

I only know that it is my desire to buy a house. That's the DP is connected to me. I do not know why the suggestion to the prostitution.

The French sentence means "Who wants to undress can have the house".

The house on 3339 was administered by Kevin before me. He was sleeping with some of the tenants, men and women or I heard him sleeping with a man once. He moved out with all the tenants he had in September 1995. Then I took over. The DP was telling that the way to keep the house is to sleep with tenants and the owner who harassed me for homosexual purposes a few times. The owner of the house wanted to sleep with me too. His wife wanted to move in with me in that house. In 1999 they asked me to move out with all my tenants. The DP was right.

> *DP20. My girlfriend and I are at her*

parent's. I am wearing a pair new blue jeans and the silk navy blue shirt that I have, the shirt falling outside of the pants. I am sitting away from the parents. It's like the shirt I am wearing belongs to them. They call me to come and sit down close by them to watch a film.

I used to go out with Debbie. I never had the occasion to meet her parents, but I used to stay in their house with Debbie, while they were out in vacation or in a house they had in Pender Harbor. She said her father was a millionaire. She used to buy me clothes, including the shirt alluding to in the DP. I went to a club once wearing that shirt, while standing at the bar, a lady walked up to me and said " you're wearing my shirt"(a pass I did not catch). That time I was teaching regularly, I did not have a good reason to be shy in the presence of Debbie' s parents. The DP seems to be saying that it was the reason why I didn't arrange a meeting with them with Debbie. Would that save the relationships? That is not easy to say. Do I feel not at ease in the presence of white people in general? The answer is yes, but it just because they are the unknown to me, not having been living close by them since birth, especially so 10 years ago from now.

O have been going out with a few women, one at a time across my life, since I was 18 years of chronological age. One the major characteristics of this relationships is the fact that I would be very upset in summer when she goes to spend about a month vacation in Pender Harbor with her parents. I would be emotionally so disquiet that I buy lot of pills at the pharmacy to be able to sleep, survive. The strangeness of it is that I never noticed such a need of her for the whole year, then it happened in the summer. The whole year passed again, I didn't notice that I could miss her at all. Then, summer arrived again with the same scenario. Very bizarre something I can notice when it's not there.

Not that strange after all, absence being one fundamental qualification of relationships>2 elements. 2 HBBs together the two elements become obscure, like one.

I didn't talk to her about it although I talk once in a while about other parts of the relationships. She said once, that my paper sand pelvis on her silk one is very exciting sexually. When she came back from Pender Harbor was not the time to engage in verbal relationships stuff. The behavior was rather almost carnivorous. It was as if we wanted to eat each other's flesh. We came at it with voracity.

Thursday March 29, 2000

> DP.21. Lucarne and I are together. We are visiting some places and want to talk to him about real estate property he inherited from his father. Then, I appear at a party with lot of people. I am wearing a pair of pants with pockets outside. I see some bottles of alcohol in another pocket, not knowing where they come from.

Lucarne was one of my friends from infancy. His family's house is located 3 minutes walk east of my family's houses. we've been to the same primary school, used to be the first in our classes a couple of times. So we had many things in common. They formed a club to promote the study of farming . After election wich took place in an Salvation Army's church, I became President of this club, he became Vice President. His father had a large enough property to live on.

In Canada, I always hide the alcohol I have in the house. Being a teacher most of the time I develop the habit by thinking that I should be the good model. Since 1992 there always are many HBBs in the houses where I live. I do not want to trigger the drinking habit in someone who would otherwise stay away from alcohol, which is very addictive, not very easy to control after we start drinking it. In my case, I pretend to be immune to addiction of any sort for identifying rather with nothing else but myself: Infinite supply, Eternally perfect substance,. It works until now. We will see. Any way I think alcohol is something to hide, and that's what is referred to in this DP by bottles of alcoholic beverages in outside pockets.

I must have a deep desire to have real estate property, if it is in my DPs. There is no money to make in real estate property really. The expenses are quite similar to the earnings. Then why my profound desire to own this sort of thing?

In Lucarne's name there is "Luc" which can be interpreted as luck, like in a ppk game. The DP on Lucarne is a compulsion to like luck. As a name have no problem with the magazine Luck. One of the implications of the concept luck is the theory that life comes from hazardous mutation or encounter of elements or atoms. I do not subscribe to that theory. I think rather that life is created so no place for hazard. However, There are so many bits of thing just in our universe, let alone the number of universes like ours there can be. Our minds cannot count all that bit by bit. In this case the concept luck is useful. In other words some of the events in our lives can be accounted for by luck.

Friday March 31, 2000

> DP22. This child says to another one that he did well today. The other one adds: "It's not enough to do well. Today we are waiting for the end."

The end might never comes, for we are in an infinite context, meaning that no end no beginning, meaning that everyone is fundamentally rich, being part of this infinite context, and substance being eternally perfect. That's why it is possible to call death elemental life.

I think the American adoption of democratic society is the best thing we could have done. And democratic political parties are a few miles ahead of the other parties in the sense that there they have the assumption of infinite wealth. I do not understand, though, HBBs who associate this assumption with spending money anyhow or with wasting anything. I think the foolishness in this behavior would be easy to see but apparently itis not. In the conservative parties, the atmosphere is finiteness, I think that is wrong, but fortunately this atmosphere doesn't allow the conclusion of wasting money nor anything else.

It would take books and books to make all connections with this DP. Nevertheless, I am interested in the child part or child period of my psyche, in order to recapture innocence of this period of my life. Most of the time the solution of our problem are in front of us. We cannot see, our mind being clogged by too many subjects, or it is overcooked for being on one subject too long, etc. The innocence of infancy allows us to look at the problem with fresh new eyes.

Child is not to link too childish anyhow, for it is well known that most of us are using the infancy self instead of the adult one. Then, of course, we don't make any progress in terms of solving our adulthood problems.

Some authors link the world biggest problem, namely, being mean or war, with misery suffered by the enfant in his prenatal life and the anger triggered by the non-positive state. Some authors even fused together masochistic needs and childishness in person and think that only the power of love can undo the fusion. True or false?

Despite what is said above, the DP seems to be alluding to the theory put forward by researchers in the soul field. They believe in the end of everything without falling into the path of merchant's fear. With the causal theory we aim backward, in the past. According to the finitude theory we aim forward, toward purposes and goals, so we are more interested in the future than in the past.

The theory claims that ultimately all objects will change to spirit, will change to a state closer to the Creator. The theory makes sense; there is some rationality to it. I would accept about 80% of conclusions drawn from it.

I am not a theoretician person myself as such. I am more inclined to the practical side of things. Nonetheless, it is not possible to work, to live, to do anything without being inside the frame of a theory. My theory is that we are in the middle of everything, no end nor beginning. It would not fit the finitude theory totally. My view and theirs in the soul theory are similar basically in that we both apply scientific faith in our researches and study of the psyche.

DP23. Somebody appears, insults

Gerard and escapes in a bush nearby. I go outside and say to myself that Gerard is able to defend himself, thinking that he has big arms. A few moments later, there are a lot of HBBs on the yard. They are tumultuous. Gerard reappears among them, asking someone to go to fight with him in the street. I see among them Dieujuste who decides to go to fight with Gerard also, despite his lean body.

I remember Dieujuste vaguely, one of my godmother's brothers. He and Camita, my godmother's daughter used to play with me enfant. They both past away, were the first persons who manifested affection toward me, although not related to me genetically speaking. They passed to elemental life while I was still in Haiti. Camita my baptismal sister was very beautiful. Dieujuste, was a small business person.

The DP looks like what is happening now in regard to President Bush, his fellow citizens and the rest of the world, although I had it 22 months ago from today (December 6,2002). Anyway, the war between Iraq and US can still be avoided if Saddam Hussein steps down, letting United Nations take over to organize an election controlled by many countries. This way the political democratization of this country would take off. Then the source of the terrorist phenomenon would disappear little by little in this region, as a democratic Iraq would influence other countries around. This society in Iraq would disappear anyway in 20,50 or 100 years from now. To survive it needs the free participation of all its members in all social activities. That's how we end up with the almighty US, although the demorcratic principles tend to be forgotten even in US itself.

Remember that September 11 I sent an e-mail to my nephew Philip to find out if he and the rest of my relatives in New York were ok. He called he called me back in the afternoon and said that he was working in a tower one block from the two destroyed buildings by the terrorists, that all relatives in this city were ok. But that my nephew in Port-au-Prince (Haiti) was ambushed and killed 10 days ago. It was a devastating news in many ways. So the DP was about my life that happened to be embedded with New York with GBBs the same month.

I guess that some men think it is a masculine and brave thing to do to go to war. It is not at all the case , although sometimes it might be necessary.

DP24. Beta block

So it is rather a flash than a full DP. It looks like poesy but beta refers to the brain waves: alpha> relaxed alertness; beta> intense focus, the fastest level, 26 hertz or cycle per second, the consciousness level; delta> dreamless sleep level and theta> creativity and dream level. If 26 is consciousness level, + and - 26 we are in unconscious zone. That's why Jane Roberts could write this book called THE UNKNOWN REALITY, a reality we are usually unaware of for not being at the conscious level, for being above 26 cycle/second level. Then the self, higher self and Sophia the Soul of the world, functions with a number with many more bits than we do in waking life.

In order words fastness can be a block in some occasion. Some research suggests that a child born 25 weeks after conception or before is not going to survive, is born prematurely. It is the same for a concept or a goal or a project, if created too fast it is premature and unlikely to survive. Is it an explanation for the successful HBBs like

Elvis Presley who die young? Is it where our fast world is going if we do not slow down, take sometimes to get closer to ourselves and the Creator? Down the drain.

I had a not very positive experience with the School Board in Delta (alpha, beta, delta, theta) suburb of the greater Vancouver where I was treated like dirt and dismissed from teaching as if I as nothing, without reason or explanation. The flash reminds me of it. I am still trying today to resolve the matter using the means I have. It happened in 1991. the DP may be alluding to that too. But, in the depths of things it means that the soul practice is a slow affair. One person said that soul = unhurriedness, although in life in general there are the element, faster than light, some structure slower than the turtle, slower than can be perceived by us.

> DP25. I am with a group of students whom I am tutoring. One of the students refuses to be tutored by me and leave. I follow him until he arrives in front of his house. Then I realize that I am wearing a kind of dress with a window in front where your sexual apparel can be seen. The student enters into his house and sends someone to tell me that he cannot receive me. Then I reappear on a terrain near his place where I see lots of foods, including a whole stem of bananas.

May be the robe is for symbolization of profession. The DP is bizarre in appearance. I use to tutor a couple of students. It might be those students and the rest of them who may consider teachers who tutor them as being hungry (or as I am of black color I am supposed to be hungry). Some students used to put their telephone numbers in the pocket of my jacket. Some followed me at home. Some insist that I go out with them, to teach them in the sexual area too. They get mad at me when you don't. Therefore , there has never been something sexual between me and student. It's not like I would want to sometimes. Some sixteen and seventeen year-old are so grown up for their age, so beautiful, so sexy and intelligent. But they were student under age and possibly emotionally not mature enough for sexuality especially with an adult. I do not want to bore the reader, but there is nothing unusual about me in regard to student, although in adolescence I had sex with a much younger female.

In this DP this student was the person to guide me to where the foods are, although there is connotation of pornography and even prostitution and food. May be that what some students would like me to do. One of the male roommates I had came to my room once, started to talk about the belt of money and displayed $50 bill. It's like they were offering me money for sexual gratification in many more occasions.

In Haiti, I thought I was intelligent and that almost everyone around was ignorant and farmers. At that time farming did not sound right to me(although the farm we die), probably because of the false association between farming and ignorance, although all my parents and grand parents were farmers. Nevertheless, I had a little garden of bananas once. It was my first experience with cloning. It is the same way more or less bananas is grown. Small banana starts to grow from the banana tree's root. I cut it from there and plant it.

I would not want to try to clone part of me even if I become elements before having children. Cloned children have little chance to survive for not having a mixed pull of genes to fight sicknesses according to the scientific knowledge we have about it for now. The purpose of having children, keeping part of me alive in the future, would be cancelled that way for me. Contrary to cloning, I prefer mixed blood children to create strong children themselves and so on. So because time is not in my favor, I might have to rely on test tube babies to be able to have them all at once and on time.

Is the DP about some future wife who is a star but who shows her body? May be.

Sunday April 2, 2000

> *DP26. I see a kind of electrical rocking horse going down the river quickly and coming up as quickly. Then I think about the Swedish HBBs.*

Bizarre, bizarre. The horse makes me think of polar bear swim not electrical rocking horse...... But in Vancouver it is done January first not April first. At the English Bay, that day, HBBs. enter into the cold, near zero degree Celsius water as quickly as possible, get out of it as quickly as possible, At a pinch one may coalesce Swedish and furniture and the rocking horse. I do not know yet if there is a polar bear swim organized in Sweden each year as in Vancouver, or if Swedish HBBS just like water extraordinarily, or if the event is organized in April.

I had Swedish sofa, table and two chairs in storage. While moving my belonging from a storage company to the house in Manitoba Street, I passed by a thrift store to give the furniture I would not have space to store. I forgot on the side walk the 8 feet of the two chairs. When I remembered, went back there to get them, they were already gone. The HBBs in the thrift store said they knew nothing about them.

Strange to steal the feet of the chairs without the rest of the chairs" I still have the chais, but without feet

Haitians have in their mind that the Swedish HBBs, especially the Swedish women, among white people have something positively especial about them. Why? Haitian people may adore Mr. Nobel and think they could have one by liking Swedish HBBs, not like they are not likable, but the same as in other group, some likable some not.

I live in Quebec for 6 years. They also like Swedish HBBs. Haitians Quebec HBBs have French language in common. So do French HBBs like in a particular way everything Swedish too? But I guess Swedish are liked in Quebec because of the social democracy type of government they have. It surfaced in political parlors many times when I was living Quebec.

CHAPTER VI

Tuesday April 4, 2000

> *DP27. I have a Parrot in my left shoulder, another one on my right shoulder. The one on my right shoulder says something like: "Remember Angelina Jolie and her film Something Like that; do we call that tele, tele, and telepathy?": "Sean kicks off the "stowed" .Something else happen to the animal on my left shoulder that I push back to the unconsciousness.*

I know now who Sean is. It was about what Sean Penn did just before the war in Iraq courageously challenging the warriors there, June 6, 2003 way after the beginning of the war, However in December 2002, when I rewrote the DP didn't know. There was another Sean among the first groups of tenants I had at the house on 3339 west 42nd Avenue. Before he left he was kicking all over the place. The word is probably towel or serviette in French, except in French it's used to say, also, briefcase. Sean was the business type person. I lost a briefcase while moving, but I know Sean had nothing to with it. He is not this type of person, although he is not perfect. Reminds me of another violent encounter with animal. This time it was a dog that bit me and let me with a scarce for life. Reminds me again of Darwin who said more or less that animal, crazy HBBs and children have one thing in common. It is that they rely heavily on emotion to function. They don't rationalize and can be very dangerous, even to themselves(too much emotion may be bad as well roo much rationalization.

My ex friend Muriel (ex because she would like more with me, I would like more with her, and more means sexual encounter; I suspect her husband was sleeping with other women; I still prefer becoming an ex with her because of the principle, when the application is not stupid "do the other what you would like him to do to you" sort of thing, or I just do not want to get mix up with married couple) had a parrot. I went at her place to bring her a work to computerize for me once. Murielle's parrot flu toward me, entered inside my shirt through the gap of two buttons, bit me very hardly and quickly on your belly, as if it knew what was going on between me and her owner, as if it knew about the unsatisfied sexual tension between Muriel and me.

Although the DP seems to be alluding to the paradigm in psychology once, that is, left brain, right brain. Now the idea appears to be of minor importance, if there any importance at all.

Is the woman in the previous DP has a son named Sean?

A.J. Prince

Wednesday April 5, 2000

> DP28. A few persons and I am having a conversation. At the end, a woman approaches one man to whom I am talking and says to him "What did he tell you?". Instead of answering the question, the man adds "I speak to the reporter /counselor".

That was one of the compulsions I used to have in order to take some courses in psychology at University. At the time of the DP I was thinking of going back to University of British Columbia for "recertification" in Education. I was never really interested in academic psychology after the first courses at University of Quebec in Montreal. I've read a lot books on psychology, Freud, Andrew Young and Maslow, and so on. When I was in France at a language and literature course at University of Quimper in La Bretagne, one teacher mentioned the fear of psychology and psychologist by the members of the government of that time . They did not like scientist-taking picture of their psyche, trying to conceptualize it. I have heard also of HBBs like Pavlov who did not take a stand in political ideas and activities of his time and his country, what might have save them time and human lives, etc.

Yesterday, I was too tired to come back home right away; I went to the library to rest. At the same time I thought it was better for me to read something while resting. So I picked any book, that happened to be psychology. The author mentioned in the last chapter that academic psychologists are playing a dangerous game, for not taking a social place, and at the same time for letting powerful tools in the hand of politically and economically bias social decision takers. True in regard to political activity the vacuum will only serve the strong ones, the ones with big political and economic ambition and muscles. But, according to me psychology must try to empower the individual so he and she can find their way through political and economic forces. So in the end psychology is doing what it is supposed to do by staying in the sideline a bit.

Is the DP referring to me and the SOUL EXPOSED, because it is written on the form of a journal?

> DP29. *While going somewhere I fall in a pit. Then I become very emotional, and am having negative thoughts. After coming out of the pit, I appear somewhere with a tall woman wearing a silk dress, smoking cigarettes. I only see part of her who reminds me of Fran. Then, I appear in front of a house. It's like there is a class of children inside. Then again I appear seating in front of a piano.*

Fran was the neighbor living in the house facing mine in this part of Vancouver closer to point Grey and west Marine Drive street, inhabited by middle class human fellows, when I was living at 3339 west 42nd Avenue, she invited me at a Christmas party in her house once. She has many kids and a husband that Christmas eve day, her and her husband relatives were at the party to, plus a teacher of piano. I had a good time but were a bit shy with these HBBs to whom you use to say hi only. I was shy also because of the children. I thought the parents had already enough responsibility, I should not drink their drinks, eat their foods.

I was not in good terms with these neighbors for many reasons. First of all, I didn't mixed with them very much. Each year there used to be a street party when they all meet.I didn't go to these parties. At a certain point of time, they started spreading bad news about me. Second of all, it was the first time I had tenants. I made mistakes by renting bedroom to HBBs who were not supposed to live there, quite residential area. One guy had a girlfriend. It's like they were both prostitutes also. They were making lot of noise when they arrived home from one to four AM. I slept through it all, never noticed, until they neighbors start to talk about it and let me know that the noise had to stop.

The DP is not a lucid one, for in it I fall into a pit, which can mean having a bad time in one or many aspects of my life. In a DP, I suppose to do everything perfectly by the simple use of my will. Falling into a pit(catharsis) is reproduction of what happened to me in waking life. It's not supposed to be like that. You must admit that it's not easy to remember to have lucid dreaming every night. When I do not remember memory takes over and activates the simple reproduction of waking life. So the waking life feeds the psychic life and vice versa. That way we are not really using our psyche to live a life reflecting the perfection of the universe. We are not really solving our problems. We live mostly like a machine.

> DP 30 I appear somewhere with a briefcase. There are some HBBs sitting in a porch. I leave the briefcase at one end of the porch in order to take it at the other end while leaving. During that time I worry about someone going away with the briefcase inadvertently. Then I appear again near a terrain on which there is only grass. I sit on the part of a baton as suspended in the air. Pretty soon, the baton becomes

a sort balustrade. A pen falls on the floor from my hand inadvertently. A child who is standing in the street picks up the pen and gives it to me so I do not have to go down the street to pick it up myself. Then I see two boys passing in the street. One says to the other something in which there is the word "abrument". I correct him by saying" abriment". Then I correct it again by adding that it is "habillement"(dress) he should have said.

In front of the house in 3339 west 42nd, there is a porch and a kind of whole in the wall to live newspapers. In summer time I used to sit there. There were some small trees with nice reddish colored leaves I liked to look at it while being in the outside fresh free air. One thing is that between the porch and the street there is a big bush fence, a side walk, a portion terrain planted with grass. So the DP isn't about this living situation in which I was.

I was worried about the briefcase I have lost in the Pacific Center and the teaching profession when I was living on Manitoba Street. I wasn't teaching at that time. So the DP must be triggered by this nostalgic state of being then.

I can not help but to point out the most despicable act of violence that happened in Vancouver in the last few years and which is in the mind of many human beings right now although in the history of man kind there are many cases of individual or group violence. I am thinking of the pig farm court process, and Picton the man who is accused of killing 52 prostitutes, a number, according to police, that can be very much higher. Nobody in his right mind will do that. This person is deranged somehow. The pig farm crime reminds us to take a stand against violence. It is said that there are two things all human beings should be against. They are violence and poverty. It seems also when I take a stand against one, I automatically take a stand against the other. Those two seem to go hand in hand. Life is dynamic; things are moving and changing all the time. That is a potential for violence. Most of us are not able yet to take advantage of the opulence of the universe. Some HBBs, as me, sometimes aren't even able to feed themselves for one reason or the other; etc.

Then, there is the tendency to associate sexuality with pig. I do not quite see the link. Pig is one ingredient of alimentation. Why associate it with sexual indulgence? There is association of sex with pig, but not sex with violence. Why did Picton do what he did then? Some of us think that criminal are raised that way. Also there would be a big feeling of guilt created by the cocktail of pig farm and the sex"

In other words Picton is not an Island. He is part of a society

where a tag of shame is clipped on certain sexual conduct understandable when it is to keep the population at a certain level. If on the entire planet too many HBBs were engaged in sexual activity for recreational purpose only, the population would decrease rapidly and who knows where that could end up? The problem is that the shame tag attached to sexuality is artificial, can be exaggerated and have very negative consequences. If Picton felt proud to have as many prostitutes as he wanted, would he have any compulsion to kill them? You bet the Picton phenomenon wouldn't happen in Holland, and other countries where prostitution is "institutionalized". The past Prime Minister of Canada, Pierre Eliott Trudeau hinted to that when he said the state has nothing to do in the bedroom of its citizens.

Why banish something, which is in itself not a crime? Do not legalize prostitution, you will have many more Picton to come. The rationalization of this thought seems to be simple and clear for everybody. Why, then, prostitution is still illegal in some countries? It is over my mind. I cannot understand it. Nevertheless, it reminds me of this Greek or Latin author who said more or less that "A human being is not an angel nor a beast, but unfortunately who plays the angel, plays the beast".

I've heard of a woman who creates an organization that collects fund to same gender in transition between prostitution and "normal life". There is also a song that is being sold now to collect fund for the same purpose. It's a good start, but it is not enough. That is not going to allow the avoidance of the repetition of the Picton phenomenon. We must go to the root of the problem. Prostitution must be lrgalized. It's the only way to erase this social discomfort related to sexuality and crime.

Yes, everyone is responsible for him/herself. So education is the way to go, also, after the right thinking about sexuality becomes law that is reflected in social structures that individual can pick up

The children, the baton or macaque, the terrain the briefcase are in the DP indication of sexuality, crime, police the pig farm and lawyer(avocat in French close to avocado). My psyche was on it almost 3 years before it becomes clear to everyone. Or does it have to do with the fact that I am sexually inactive since 1998?

Macaque, used for baton in Creole, is the name of a kind of monkey. Do some African people look like monkey by the nose? Sometimes, I have a tendency to think so(Really). Anyway, I was a very shy child and adolescent, because some HBBs around me were making fun of my nose. There were many names to qualify my nose (nes vonvon= insect that makes a noise while flying in hot countries like Haiti, nez large, etc.). This unconscious background makes me the person am are today, a bit shy in regard to body parts, and ehich probably influences my relationships with other HBBs.

I think it is clear for everyone now that humankind does not come from monkey as we used to believe in the past. At the beginning, there were animal and Homo sapiens.

The thing to remember from this DP seems to be, though; criminal persons are raised that way.

Does the woman have two boys? Who can have 2 boys in April 2000?

> *DP31. Sitting in the back seat of car, I am going to a party. It stops in the middle of a street corner, the door beside me wide open. Other cars pass by avoiding the one in which I am. One of them comes close to hit the open door. Then I move in front of the car and get out from there.*

There is this law of accident where a number of HBBs having a very bad time in their life, in general, united in a vehicle at the same time. This plane or bus or car or boat will have an accident, according to the number of the group and the intensity of their negative feelings. That's partly how I come to conceive the possibility of a machine capable of preventing big accidents. I still do not have time to research it. I am barely surviving, financially speaking. But it's a date without a date, as soon as I can dispose some time to it. The machine will be able to tell what will happen before it happens, if there going to be an accident due to the group of passengers or engine failure or not.

In October 2000, a black truck while crossing a street did hit me. I saw the car coming, I continued to cross

Blenheim street anyway, thinking the truck (Black SUV) was going to stop at the red light in that way, for the green light was in my way. When I realized it was not going to stop, I started to run for my life, but too late. It hit my left leg; you fell flat in the middle of the street, projected a little away from the front of the car. I was given $ 4525.37 from which I got $ 2632. Lawyers had the rest of the amount.

So this DP (direct perception or perception without the use of rational process, what is usually referred to as dream) was predicting something, a few months before the waking life accident.

It is saying that when we do not claim our place in life, when we are not in the front seat, the leader seat, we risk having some accident. Many times HBBs become paraplegic, or lost one part of their body, or they are constantly sick, because they aren't at their right place, they are performing below their abilities. Being in the driver sit of ouselves is not an easy task, we fall off many times. Then according to the archetype theory, we dould not have will. According to me without will no driver sit, we can be run even by our enemies.

I had this car, a Dodge Colt. I think a person working in a gas station forgot an oil and gasoline- soaked-rag on top of the engine while putting oil in it. After a few kilometers of driving , I saw smoke coming from the engine. I stoped the car, opened the hood and saw a bowl of fire all over. At the insurance company they gave me the choice between getting the car fixed or having 21 hundred dollars for it. I chose the latter. It was the mistake of my life, for I was not able to give that amount for down payment and buy a new car. The dealer offered me an old station wagon for the money. At that time I did not know the good reputation of the Swedish car, Volvo, I did not take it, another big mistake. I needed a car to go to teach in Delta, I was and are still am leaving in

Vancouver. Some day I will be able to buy all sorts of cars, expensive, inexpensive ones.

At the time of the DP, Brashier, one of the roommates I had when I was living on Manitoba Street, was working in a company where they sell cars. One day he was caught driving one car under the influence as you say, but I will say under the influence of drug and alcohol and was fired. This incident is another trigger of this DP. He is of African descent like me, was forcing himself in my bedroom when I just moved in the house, I had to fight with him a bit to get him out.

Friday April 13, 2000

> *DP32. I hear a noise in the hall of the house where I am sleeping. I get up to go in the kitchen. While passing by I see each of the other 3 men lying in front of the door of their respective bed-room. You speak to them a little and come back to MY bedroom-room. One of them follows ME at the door and tries to kick me with his foot. I catch his foot but decide to do nothing to him. I want to bring him back to his bedroom, then I see many tall men in the hall.*

This DP is describing three more or less similar waking life incidents. The one with Brasgier is already said in the previous DP

Another incident this DP refers to is what took place between a West Indies black guy (Trinidadian or Jamaican) and I about Lorraine in Montreal. I met her at a Mexican bar. She was going out with me and Ashouin at the same time. It was not my preferred thing to do to go out with a woman already in a relationships, but we were attracted to each other, the time I know she was going out also with a married man, it was too late. There was a party at her sister's place. I went with her there. After that I went with her to her apartment. She wanted me to leave at the door without going inside. I had a hot discussion with her about that. Suddenly a man rushed out and punched me in the face. You punched him back. He tried to kick me with his foot. I catch the foot and pulled him behind me thinking if am going to just push him three floors down from the hall with no fence. You decided not to do that and let him go.

The third incident happened in Vancouver at 3339 west 42nd Avenue. There was only three of us in the house that afternoon, Daniela, Adrian and me. There used to be a telephone set on the kitchen table for all the other 7 tenants to use. I look on the table and do not see the telephone. I followed the cord until Adrian's bedroom in the basement. I asked him to put it back where it was, then went back upstairs in the kitchen. He came up get mad at me. Then I went back to my bedroom. He followed me until the door. When I realized he wants to enter, I punched him in his face. He punched me back. Then I run in the bedroom to get a baseball bat. Adrian flu so quickly he fell down the stairs. I called the police; he called the police too. He told them that I stole his ring, that they have to look for it in my bedroom to justify his presence at my bedroom door. The police came back later and told me to leave the place, because Adrian is mad. I said to them that I would not leave the other tenants alone with him. Adrian had a girlfriend who collected shared houses to manage. He tried to get mine by the fight for his girlfriend. He told me that later more or less afterward.

Bizarrely, I was going to be engaged with Janine a Haitian girl once. Problems developed in the relationships later. I gave it up and wanted to sell the ring, Pancho, the cousin of one of my sisters in law said he was going to sell it for me. I gave it to him and that was the last time I saw Pancho.

For Adrian to accuse me of stealing his ring after I punched him in the face is still a mystery to me. How does he know of this part of my life occurred years ago? Did the fight cause it because of the intense emotion of the moment? Or he simply read my mind during DPs the night before? In this case I can speculate that the general knowledge might have been the cause of the fight too, because it was only general, not a specific knowledge. In other words war can be the consequence of unspecified information that we have about each other. Bizarre.

Actually the DP is only about the second incident, for the description, leave my bedroom, and go the kitchen, passing by the door where the other guys lived, fits the house on Manitoba Street only. This incident itself reminds me of the other two.

Saturday April 8, 2000

DP.33 A few schools

Is that to say there are not enough schools. To that I would say no, that there are too many Schools. For after grade 12, schools kind of spoiling place for most of us. So I would say to developing countries not to do the same mistake as I did in believing that I needed to go school for ever. I would encourage these countries to push their kids to go to work in the field(not just farming), to develop their natural skills. Anyway, everyone cannot be a doctor, we need the garbage collector too.

In the other hand some society, like Haitian society, 80% of HBBs have great intuitive skills, but are able to read and write., are illiterate. We are no more advanced like that either. We need an our rational abilities developed enough, to combined with intuitive abilities to be able to create on a regular basis. Illiteracy will not do it.

Also, DP is suggesting that there are different kinds of school, that Psychic Faculty and Research ,the name of my company with one person for now, is a school too, that the Soul Exposed is a school too. That is true.

> *33a. At that appearance a few fellow and I are discussing one thing or the other. Among them there is a woman. For a reason that I ignore, somebody takes a five cents off his pocket. Then me too, I take out some changes from my pocket. Someone else makes a comment on the woman. Then get closer to her, I pass my arm around her waste, telling her jokingly that it's her that I have.. Later, she smokes a cigarette, and I feel very good about myself.*

It is like there is a making love session in this DP; made by the imaginative I or about my past life, for I was not sexually active when I had it. The DP does not mean that I made love in the presence of school comrade. Although I met Didier in psychology class, we became friends later. He arranged with her girlfriend for me to touch her sexually in his presence once. I did not really make love with her.

Another time a friend and I went to a club. There he met a girl, because he was married, he brought her to my place. I arranged that with him; he made love to her first and I staid outside while he was in session. After he left, then I made love with her, . I didn't like the experience, didn't do it again.

It would simply means that the woman with whom I made love in the DP is a school comrade. I do not recall having had such experience either. Today, December 19, 2002, I will go to hook up a cable for Amanda, a roommate I have since last September. At that time she said she was going to start to go to University of British Columbia the following month. I had never talked to her about it since then. In other words I don't know if she will go to school or not, although I have no solid reason to doubt her. I do not know either if the invitation to fix the cable is also an invitation for love. I find her attractive, but do not know her at all. I do not know if the DP I had in the past have anything to do with her, although it could.

There could be the explanation of what is happening between Heather and me She is the previous roommate before Amanda. She is in a course program at University of British Columbia. You went out with her a few times when she was living in the same house on 16th Avenue. Last September I went out with her once thinking that the relationships would continue from there. I have not seen her since then. I have to have a female roommate here to avoid too many troubles with a male, if it is possible. The week before Thanks Giving Day in Canada, a woman called supposedly for a research for Global Television Company. She asked me all sorts of questions. She asked questions, including if I am sexually active. I think only someone who knows me would ask me those questions, that it should be Heather who told those things to the marketing researcher? Of course I am not sure of the conclusion. Then someone called a couple of times, but does not talk. I think that too should be the act of Heather. She is only 22 years of chronological age. She is allowed to make mistake. The problem is I do not know yet how to deal with what occurred recently between me and her. Not knowing it prevent me from calling her more than once since September, call she didn't bother to answer anyway if she had received it.

Heather might, also, not like the fact that I have a female roommate now. And, before the summer I told her I was going to publish Kickitwell, a book I wrote on getting rid of addiction. I thought I could do it before the summer, but I still can not do it. I would have to pay someone to edit it, and would have to have have at least $ 1000 to make the first few copies to be able to test it. I will be able to do all that later. The first time I talked to her in September, she mentioned the book, questioned me on why I did not publish it. Because of that she may think I am unreliable, unworthy of her love, thinking that I never had a book to publish in the first place.

Even if I had it a long time ago (The gap in chronological time is not very relevant. Are we not in infinite space and time when we are dealing with our DPs?) I wish this DP meant that I am going to make love with a woman shortly.

Another reason for not seeing Heather is a lack of financial means. I will have that later, plenty of it. I just choose to live that way for the moment, not consciously, though.

In Haiti, I had a friend, Max. we went to the same secondary school, at the same time. And we were teaching at Ecole Frère Polycarpe at the same time. He encouraged me to go to prostitute women, what I did a couple of times. As anything else it's very chip in Haiti. In Montreal, I saw one prostitute twice. That's the only history I have with prostitution.

DP34. I appear standing at the entrance door of this house. There is an escalator that goes down. A woman appears at the door too, but let herself slide down the escalator.

rail right away. Then I follow her. Down there I find a kitchen. I sit down at the kitchen table a little bit. At the other side of the wall I hear some people calling my name. I tell them that it's me who is in the kitchen and say my name, and that I come from Haiti. Then they say that it is not really me they are looking for. Then I let some gas out that makes a noise. I move and sit away from the smell. Then the house becomes a classroom with a lot of food and an important person who comes to talk. Later, the director of school appears at the door and says that it is almost 2 o'clock. I think it's time for me to go.

This house is a psychic house of course. I have to present myself to the HBBs behind the wall. There are two similar situations in waking life I can associate this DP with more or less. First one was when I was living in a building in Montreal on a street called Villeray. I was there for some times before I started to share the apartment with a certain a Haitian man. Georgette was living behind the wall I had never noticed her. As soon as Francois arrived in my apartment, he noticed Georgette, went to her apartment many times. Then I met her, found her very attractive, went out with her and lived with her for sometimes.

I think this DP is putting the emphasis on a feature of my character which does not make me a very effective person in regard to making friends, meeting new HBBs. In other words I do not meet new HBBs, make friends easily. It is may be explainable by looking at my infancy when I was hit with a rock by Seradieu hidden behind a fence, when I was bullied by one student in primary school, and another one in secondary school. So, deeply, I mistrust strangers and neighbors. Seradieu (identified in first chapter) was a neighbor lot older than I was. Then in Montreal I had a few friends who could have got me in serious trouble, if I did not leave that city on time. Then again, my financial situation is not the best for years. I do not want my friends to always feel obliged to help me in that sense. All these minuses in my character and negative encounters impair my ability to make new friends.

I went to Manitoba from Quebec to work as French Monitor in Pelly Trail School District. Something very bad happened on the first night. It is already described elsewhere in the book. Besides that, because I went there to work the day after my arrival there, I was welcome everywhere I went in that province. I made lot of friends right away. I became very good friend of Michael Totté, Stuart Robottom, and Joseph Poitras, all three teachers in the School District. Presently I'm working at creating my goals that are, of course, relevant to me only. That situation, also, impair my ability to make new friends especially in Vancouver where I arrived after being laid off from work.

The second similar situation the DP prompted in mind is that that time when I went to a party with Lorraine. As soon as I entered into the house there was a man from Morocco there who started something with Lorraine or a flirt. I got mad and left the house leaving Lorraine there. There was an outside escalator with two rails. I went down on it fast. A nail or a dent in one rail ripped apart some flesh of one of my hands. Instead of staying there and punch that guy in the face if I had to, I left the place. That was so brilliant. Wasn't it?

When I was living in Haiti I knew some HBBs who

were gay, but I did not hear of bisexuality. The HBBs behind the wall in the DP may over generalized by thinking that HBBs from Haiti are not bisexual because I am not and I come from there. That one way to explain what they say in the DP that they're not looking for someone like me after I told them I am from that country.

And, Haiti may have a bad name in America. They came in as slaves, later; they took the country from the French at the same time causing a breach in the slavery mentality. And then they helped a few countries get their independence in North and South America, country such as Bolivia, a name coming from Simon Bolivar (Bolivia), one of the Presidents of Haiti. That may be another reason why the HBBs behind the wall said that they are not looking for me after I said I come from Haiti in the DP.

After all there is the psychic phenomenon "being in the world as I, the specific individual in comparison to other individual. In this DP I might have started to be like that being in the whole world as the specific me via Sophia, the Soul of the world, via the Creator, my body, my soul and my spirit

> DP35. I am looking in muddy water. There is a man who is trying to start an engine in the muddy water too. I tell him how much I dislike looking for something in that kind of water. Then I think the water might have passed through toilet in open air before arriving where I was looking for something.

This muddy water is probably referring to the unconscious. There is the saying that Knowledge is a consciousnrss. It may also refer to the unknown and the fear of the unknown(instinctive reaction: the unknown is the ennemi, no ratioalization at all there). To create my goals, I am using some techniques. One of them daily declarations in which there are some thoughts I brings up to the surface of my memory everyday. One of these thoughts is the courage in front of the experimental aspect of knowledge, exposition, unknown, institution, nature, others reaction to what we do or say, to our individuality. Some of these fears, such as fear of exposition, fear of the unknown are universal. Anyone can suffer from them. Only I suffer from some of the other fears, such as les institutions, la nature?

The engine wouldn't start in muddy water, it depends. If the muddy water were in the engine, it would not start. But I can pump the muddy water out by putting an engine with a mouth to suck it out. In general when it rains in the mountain, the water in the rivers flowing toward the sea is muddy and has a reddish color. The result of that natural and physical process is desert, for the fertile soil is drained in the sea. So, muddy water can be seen as being fertile water or as erosion.

During the DP I had a negative reaction to the muddy water. One reason of that is because I was unconscious, unable to rationalize. Other reason would be that the muddy water repulses me for echoing impurity and dirtiness. This reason would not be related to any of my values, would rather be of influenced by some religious belief where matter is considered impure and dirty, where sexual activities are considered impure and dirty. According to me, matter and life cannot be separated. The puritan interpretation of this DP is not applicable here. Creation is creation, every part of it is necessary.

In Haiti and probably in other countries nowadays or in the past, they use mud and small log to make wall of ajoupas (mud house). White layer of lime covers the mud. The holly week and Easter Sunday is big deal for Haitians especially the ones who live in the backcountry part. When I arrived in some villages during this period of time I saw white everywhere. It was a pleasure for me to redo the walls of my grand mother's ajoupas every year while you was going to elementary school.

The rice that some HBBs like to eat is planted in the muddy water. First, grains of unpeeled rice are planted in small portion of fertilized and dry soil. Second, the newly grown plant of rice is taken of that soil and replanted in much bigger portion of muddy watered soil.

For the final thought on this DP we will say that it is about the soul and the spirit as you say in English. Working with soul as a conscious element among the various tools you may have is like working in a muddy water in the sense that you do not necessarily needs to be an expert in a particular domain of work. You can go at it with your feelings, your rationalization. You will quickly learn how to get through it.

The engine, of course, refers to engineering, engineer another name for soul. In another words in this DP there is a sort of marriage between the individual soul and the Soul of the World or interpenetration of the two.

CHAPTER VII

Sunday April 9, 2000

DP36. I am in France, while walking in the street a woman appears in front of me and it's like she gives me a t-shirt..........Rousseau.

While I was there I met a couple in a restaurant. I remember vaguely what happened next. I remember them better because of the t-shirt they gave me. Too small for me, I do not wear it so I still have it in my briefcase somewhere. I do not remember their names anything else about them. Why, then were they in my my space of the psyche since then(we all have access to each others space of the psyche in a latent way)? April kind of announces summer. I met them in summer. I probably was comforting myself with the memory of lavish summer experiences when I had the DP at the end of the winter hibernation.

Of course Rousseau reminds us of the nature in all his intellectual activities, his writings, especially with Les Rêveries du Promeneur Solitaire, and this statement: "People are born good, the society corrupt them". May be Rousseau was grand parent of one of the couple I've met in France. Do native HBBs in France like nature like Rousseau did? Are they more romantics than the rest of us in the planet? Do the hug three? I would not be able to answer these questions without falling into stereotyping, or race profiling?

Yes I had a good time in France when I went there. But I may say that the circumstances of my life at that time were such that I was predisposed to have good time. Knowing the language a bit and having an emotional history with the French GBBs eased my time in that country when I went to France.

While in France I met a woman from Switzerland. I visited her country for a month after Bretagne where I was in vacation and studying. I visited Geneva And swam in the lake for a few minutes. I staid in Zurich most of the time you spent there. I found Switzerland a very nice country and I compared it with Vancouver that you used to see on TV almost every day while living in Canada. The trip to Switzerland was probably one of the strongest arguments of the decision for me to live in Vancouver.

The woman, who was studying French at the same university than me, was married. I could have met a girl who was living in Canada. I was with her because she promised more days of vacation and the rest of my expenses. She was sending me money even I came back in Canada. After a while I cut all communication with her, wondering why I did such a thing now. It's like I was with her just for what she was able to do for me, something I cannot be proud of, of a bad boy, worst, something which happened many times. I had an apartment in Russell Manitoba where I was teaching, but did not want to go back there for one bad experience. I had a new girlfriend in Winnipeg, Angelika,the sweetest of sweetest woman I have never met, could not go to stay to her place the time I got set up in Winnipeg after what I have done in Switzerland with Ursula. I had a very rough time in Winnipeg for a short period of time. after the trip.

Rousseau reminds me of nature in its entire splendor, its huge and nice landscapes. His writings, especially Les Rêveries du Promeneur Solitaire, and some his statements like" The individual is born good, but corrupted by the society" reflect his taste for what is natural and were one of the parents of romanticism of his time and after him.

They accused Freud of putting the individual in opposition to the society. I bet HBBs like Rousseau were also accused of standing the individual against the society, of causing revolution. I define the individual as being a social unit. In sociology the social aspect of the individual is what mostly studied, the reason why I think in psychology the individual aspect of human being should be what mostly studied for a balance, keeping in mind that the individual and the social in the human being cannot be separated without causing a damageable rupture, what has been demonstrated by misery and suffering caused by autocratic and communist society across human history.

So the reader cannot say he doesn't know my political philosophy, quite similar to social democracy as applied in Sweden and probably in more countries in this part of Europe. I do not know how they arrive at the adoption of this kind of political thinking. Mine is from the definition of the individual as being a social unit and I think it would do all humanity great service to adopt this kind of political thinking. It's not necessary to change political parties to integrate the social democracy philosophy. It can exist inside of the Democratic Party, liberal party, and the Conservative Party. The essence of it is to promote individualism(the inner world of the individual) as much socialism in any political denomination. Without that consciousness, you are bound to be out of track.

Liberal party in Canada doesn't seem to be conscious of this necessity. There is a hole in their political philosophy anyway- the essence of the hole is a laissez faire attitude. For the liberal promotes benefits only the rich HBBs who have money to invest take advantage of. In this political context the poor can only become poorer. I can cite the example of the liberal in power in British Columbia presently. Not only the flaw in their philosophy disadvantages the poor, but also their economic "restructuration" is directed toward taking money from the economically weak. HBBs on welfare are getting up to $200 less than what they were getting a month before the liberal took power in this province of Canada.

Economic "restructuration" makes sense in any political philosophy. But, it should not at all be done to the disadvantage of a group of HBBs in the society. The "restrucration" should rather be done creatively which is lacking in all political parties in Canada and in the United States presently, part of the explanation of violence at the OPEC meetings. A creative committee is not something you hear in politics nowadays.

Tuesday April 11, 2000

> *DP37. I find myself a position in a school as a research teacher. I take the metro to there, I realize I don't know where it is located.*

I probably were so happy to find that position that I forgot to find out where it is before I took the metro. What was it to propel someone toward working so much, to the point where his thinking is impaired? Since September 11, I always thought that if the firemen hesitated a few minutes before going to these burning buildings, their life would be spared while they would not be able to save the HBBs in the buildings anyway. I know that it's almost asking the impossible, asking to hesitate in that circumstances, but these building would fall before they get in. It is sad to contemplate the case where HBBs already inside the building would die without the firemen, but the number of victim would be reduced significantly. Anything you identify with controls you as they say, then becomes a danger to your life. It's better to identify with yourself only.

In my notes it is written that I made an application for a teaching position in Douglas College. I remember now that at that time I was making application a little bit everywhere for various sorts of work, including teaching, Teacher on call and tutoring.

That brings up to my memory DP 33 and Debbie, the woman I was going out with. In the first years after I met her, I was teaching fairly regularly. She decided to take a course at Langara College. After one year she became a social worker. She started to work right away. She is a very outgoing person. It easy for her to find help to succeed her enterprises. As for her assignments I help her sometimes. When she was looking for a position, someone already employed there, or one of her interviewers told her before hand what the questions where going to be. Life is definitely easier for some of us because of who we are, the way we were brought up. Before our relationships were undone, she was having a good time at work, I was struggling ro survive. Is there something in women that make them more adaptable than men? I want you to tell me.

Anyway searching for a place and not being able to find it in DPs is interpreted by me as a big change in that kind of reality. The DP was telling me that there was something wrong with working the way I used to, that I should make a big change, that I should become like a researcher(What I am now).

Wednesday April 12, 2000

> *DP38. In this group of HBBs that I see there are some musicians. Far from there I hear the accute sound of clarinet and other music instruments. Then, the musicians near me decide to leave. It's like Arnold appears after they left and he is speaking of competition.*

Is this DP saying that the one who makes the louder noise wins

the competition? I have already mentioned universal and personal fear that can prevent someone from creating his goals. In the analysis of that DP there is a list of them. In that list we might add the fear of competition(anyway competition sometimes serves the ego which is already an overpowering entity in our psyche). I do not know yet if it's universal or personal. I know that the first time I had a fight with Michelet, another boy in the grade one class we were attending, I sent him a a jab that goes directly to a gravel wall. It hurts very much. I didn't think very much. I was so overwhelmed by the emotion caused by Michelet's assault to my personhood. I was much more vexed than being mad, and lost control. In higher grade school it was the same scenario. When a bully attacked me, I became too emotional to act properly.

The DP is indicating that my fear of competition is rooted there, and that it's the explanation of not having been able to find a permanent teaching position. The sister I had told me a history about Arnold, elder brother. He and Gerard, a far cousin, were playing card together which end up in a fight. Gerard were strangling my brother. My sister had to knock him senseless in his back with her fist for him to let go of our brother's neck. Although, he could have killed Arnold that way without the help of Siliane, it was a fight, nothing really extraordinary. But because I was too young when I learned the story, it left an indelible mark in me, in my inner world. So I would be ready to say that violence and children do not mix inconsequentially, especially when it is not between the children themselves. Am I thinking of TV, cinema? You bet.

The DP reminds me also that it is a genetic feature of mine, that other members of the family are like that too, emotionally overwhelmed by others' physical attack. That reminds us of this saying" the interpretation override genetic imprint, causing a change in the body transformational field of Mister Chopra. In other words, we do not have to be submitted to all the inherited imperfections, physical/ and or emotional. We can change things around within a certain limit. We can change the genes by "refocusing" our lives, by having our own goals, by following our own calling. Nowadays many kinds of psychologies are of the same advice, meaning the gene's traces are not absolute.

DP38. I am asked to work for two days.

I was looking for work and for a place to stay in this period of time. But I don't recall having been offered a position in which I would work for 2 days. Then, that was a compulsion to work for two days in order to be able to work at the research at the same time. While I was a teacher on call, I used to be called at least three days a week.

The psychologist author has the idea that to sit on a subject for two days at a time, writing during the whole time, the way he wrote his books. I don't write that way. It depends on how many things I have to do the same day and on a lot more factors. I write one to 4 hours a day, but at night I wake up to write DPs many times the . When I dlept at Debbie's place I wrote first off in the morning.

Friday April 14, 2000

> *DP39. It is a dance club. Bodies are moving very quickly, energetically and smoothly, at the same time. After that I appear in house. Many things happen to a man that I don't remember. At the end I find myself sitting on a sofa between a child and the big ass of a woman who lean her head on a man's shoulder supposedly her husband or her boyfriend,*

I like dancing, although I never really learned to dance. In Manitoba, I went to dance class for a few weeks. From there I move to Comox, British Columbia where I went to work for the government of Canada. Even if I wanted to continue the dancing activity, even if there was a dance club in Comox or Courtney, I wouldn't be able to do that right away. I had no car when I just arrived there. Later I became too preoccupied by too many things to be able to put some time for leisure activity like dancing. There are two dance clubs at one bloc from where I am living now. It is an opportunity to start dancing again before I move out this house. It looks like one of them is a flamenco dance club. When I pass by I hear a huge noise made by the sole of shoes of many feet hitting a hardwood floor.

I like dancing music since I was in elementary school. In the village, Dieurond, where my parents are born and those villages in the surrounding environment, they used to have dances for adult once in while. They used to have school dances too, but you did not go to those. I went to the ones closer to were I was living: LaBoule and Dieurond, Galette Roche Blanche. The adult HBBs there, living without any schooling, did not mind children dancing among them, because in this natural type of life marginal sexual behavior against children is unusual. Anyway, my taste for music and dancing started there and it is still alive in me now. Sometimes in Montreal and in Winnipeg I went dancing every night, even though I was working full time.

I've never been married. Around 22 years old, I was going to have a child that was subjected to abortion. I will get married some day and have some children. But often in my DPs. Children refer rather to the act of making children(making love as in the song of that name). In this DP the child is the metaphor for the birth of relationships between members of a couple, I suppose, which is other parts of me. I have been in a relationships for six years that has started at Pelican Bay, a club in Vancouver.

This DP reminds me of "lean On Me" of Boys2men, the singers and "Married with Children", the popular TV series.

In the final analysis, The DP suggests that after the dancing I went back home with a woman and made love with her, thing that occurs to me a couple times in CLLR complete physical life.

DP40. She appears near my house. I say "Are you looking for someone?" She doesn't answer me and look confused. Then I see a few bottles close by. In one of these bottles there is some oil. It makes me think that it is Mercida sho is looking for. I tell her that Mercida is not home at this moment. After telling her that I notice a few small white rocks around the house, a few pea trees and a pot in which there are some cabbages growing.

The person who comes to my mind first while typing this DP is someone I cannot describe yet for some reason. I remember she said she likes cooking and grow her own vegetable. It was a surprise to me. She looks so beautiful. I couldn't associate her with garden and cooking. She may be living in a farm or something. In the DP there is green peas. So it's about women with beautiful green eyes(All eyes tha see are beatiful in a way. Let say she has colored). I crave that in a woman, probably because Debbie has beautiful blue eyes, and that I loved her. Color of eyes will not be a determinant factor in my choice of woman, but it will be a plus. We are lame, are we not?

Mercida is one of the other women with whom my past away father was living, with whom he has children. Anglade, their first boy together is already introduced in a previous DP. She has big influence on me, for instead of my own mother who is now in elemental state (dead bits) which started when I was around 6 years old, it is Mercida that I knew when I was growing up. There were 15 minutes walk between her house and the one in which I was living with my father, brothers and sisters. I used to go Mercida's house very often. Was she a beautiful woman? My father had thought so to include her in his small harem.

Later, when I was a young adult, I used to have DPs. in which I make love to Mercida or want to make love to her. So the idea of incest has some truth to it, but not at all the way it is described by Freud disciples. In my waking , infant, adolescent and adult life I never had the desire of her, for one thing. For the second, Mercida is not my mother. In life there are a lot of possibilities, but not all possibilities are fulfilled.

It looks like an intuition on the house in which I was going to live when I had the DP, in other words the house in which I am right now. In the back of the house on Manitoba Street where I made the DP, there was a bit of mud. In that mud a dog was attached to a leach. I did not have to walk in it to get in the house, but I kind of resented having to see the picture constantly each time I came back home. It was what triggered the DP at the time when I was looking for another place to stay. In the house where I am writing now, there is Barbara, Todd her husband, Jake and Brianna, their little boy and daughter. They are living in the first floor. Amanda is living in the same floor than me, the ground floor. She is a roommate I found for the bedroom beside, because I rented the whole floor with two bedrooms and sub rent one. There are many trees on the West Side of the house. There is also a vegetable garden there. In the back of it there are berry trees. one apple three, and some rocks, almost like in the DP, except the vegetation which is typical to hot countries such as Haiti where I was born and living for some times.

I am not sure if someone else would ever be able to make sense of these DPs without the comments I make on them. They are necessary sometimes.

The soul we have, the individual soul is the same that grows plant and the trees around us. This DP may be alluding to that. It may also telling us about the future, wimen and Roch and Roll, singer of Rock and Roll.

DP41. I see a man waiting somewhere in the yard of the house. The woman that accompanies me climbs on my back and says: "I did nothing with him". Then, I start thinking of the

meanings behind the words she spoke.

The problem I had with my lungs, especially the right lung, was already thing of the past. That it started again when I moved in the house where I had the DP suggests there is a connection between the two. After all, I do not quite know if it is my left lung that was hurting in that part of my body. In the house on 3339 west 42nd street where I was living a few months before moving in the house on Manitoba Street in Vancouver, there was some smoking inside. I tried to prevent it but I didn't succeed. I always included " non-smoker preferred" in the advertisement when I am looking for a roommate. But the one who hides the smoking fact to have the bedroom always argued that they allowed smoking outside of the house. Sometimes they did smoke inside.

Nevertheless, the problem in the right side of the body was may be the consequence of hand writing DP at night. I have been doing it for so long. That part of the body may be tired. I was sick before I moved out from the house on 3339 west 42nd Avenue, but did not feel any sickness in the upper part of the body before moving in the house on Manitoba Street. Why there? Why did it nott happen before? In the house on 3339 west 42nd Avenue, I did something like 800 dumbbells(90 KG) moves at a time. That was excessive, could have caused the problem in the right side of the body. I went to hospital for it, but the diagnostic was not clear.

I don't really know what this DP is about yet. Women with me who slept with musician. not very dignificant in my life for the moment.

CHAPTER VIII

Saturday April 15, 2000

DP42. She appears with her hands full of bills that she counts and gives to me . There are 300 of them. I am happy. Before she appears with the money, I was with her and left her with a toy in her hand.

So, I left her with the toy, she comes back with the money there is a kind of exchange. It doesn't appear to be so, but we are somewhat in the germination stage of a theory of money, or toy for money. It would not be in favor of money to say that it is good only to buy toy. If it said food for money, then it would be in favor of money as an important item in a market economy. In this DP then there is a trace of communist economic theory (where money is not important, not as important as it is in the capitalist economic theory) that is forced down on the throat of everyone who has been to metaphysical universities.

Bizarrely, on Friday January 3rd I gave Barbara $300 to

pay my rent, all in 50 $ bills. I should have given her 375, but I didn't have that much last Friday. That time. Actually, I should have given her $ 395. Obviously, I did not have that much either that time. You use to give her a few $ more while paying the rent of January so she can buy something for Jake her son. I mention it because of the toy in the DP. $ 300, it's amazing how precise an intuition can be! It may still about goals of mine, the future. Do DPs apways have a future dimension in them? I bet.

That's why in my mind, an economic theory in which the idea of abundance for all who want is included, is a very sound one according to me. It's not in the Marxism theory for they have to take from the rich to give to the HBBs even kill the rich for the poor. Who said the earth turns from west to east, the eun rizes on west diappear od east? It's a very negative consequence of Marxism that has cost us many killings and destructions. This idea is not in the market theory either. In the market theory the will to restructure ends up being taking money from the poor to give to the rich. Also a negative consequence of market theory. So, capitalism, communism very similar in the action they prescribe. Similar in theory too. They are both very much marked by excessive and restrictive materialism which prevent them any freedom in regard of abundance of goods or whatever for everyone who wants on the planet. We are not out of the wood yet.

I insist on the idea of freedom(but not laissez faire arrirude only the rich can take advantage of) being part of a theory that should not degenerate in doctrine. Some HBBs will choose to live with very little, the strictly necessary. They should be free to live like that too. It is the explanation of some kind of poverty in the rich countries. And individual freedom in general is more important.

Someone would say:" If you had good ideas, why would not you have enough money to pay your rent?". To that I would answer "Lack is just appearance transcended by ever-present available substance" as they say. I know that in the deep down of things it is My choice not to have a lot of money this time. For the sake of waking life explanation, last year (2001) I was kind of forced to quit the university and spent all my time in the researches that I am doing. I thought that of one of my ideas would already fructify to allow me to live on my own, or to finance my own needs. I was wrong on that. It doesn't happen yet.

I don't have money now despite my good ideas in order to be able to expand my horizons.

DP43. She is wearing a silk nightgown, rubs her body against mine. finding that sexually attractive ,I say:" what do you want to talk about today?"..........Then I see the picture of the roof of an old red truck.

It did not happen like that in complete life. Nonetheless, I find myself in situations where human beings rub their bodies against mine many times, and sometimes in forbidden situations. Sometimes I find that her very attractive, sometimes I find that repulsive. One day at lunchtime, she rubs her legs against mine under the table. She was teaching in that school. I was a monitor of French, in Winnipeg. Because she was married or because I was too naive in the domain or too preoccupied, I did not bring the courtship further although I found her very attractive.

The first time they called me from British Columbia Teachers Federation to go and tutor a couple of adolescents in a house. They were alone in the house. The ones I was tutoring was a young boy and her sister. In the middle of the tutoring, the sister who were sitting at the same table than us, rub her leg against mine, you pulled them away, right away, my heart beating after a sexual suggestion very upsetting between me and student, under age, etc.

At 3339, when I just moved there, there was a very nice group of HBBs living in that house. They are very humane and very educated. I could be their friends for the rest of my life if there was not an important difference of life choice between them and me. I moved in April. They organized a couple parties from April to September when all 7 of those men moved out. In the summer, at one party they get a big round plastic tub full of water in the back of the house. Many of us were in the tub wearing bathing suit, men and women. One male tenant rubs his leg against mine. I was so choc and speechless. I got out of the water after a while never talked to him about it.

Sometimes, I think they think it's because of shyness I do not engage in such activity, for I never talked about it with them. It's because I think they are free to be who they want to be as well as I am.

I am proud for having been a tutor. Most of the time the service was badly needed. Without counting all the new immigrant families who decide to establish themselves in Canada, who have kids in Canadian schools but who do not speak a word of French. So the parents are not able to help their kids with their French homework. That when I came into the picture to redress the situation.

I remember this adolescent woman who contacted me for French, after reading my advertisement in the newspaper. Nicole does not have immigrant parents, though. They live in the West Side of Vancouver, not very far from me. She finished her grade twelve, but failed the provincial French exam. I pushed her a little bit for two months. She went to the exam; she passed, moved to Montreal to pursue her studies there. She needed to be tutored badly. She is English.

Another tutoring experience I am proud of is related to a family born in Philippine. They immigrated first in a place close to Syria, then to Canada. They had with them a son in grade 11 for whom French was a very trouble some matter. I worked with him for about three months. By that time, all his marks were A in French.

Tam was a professor in Vietnam her country, spent a few years doing her master degree in another country in Asia where they speak English. From there she found a bursary to do her PH D at University of British Columbia in Environmental Economy. She was staying in one of my bedrooms on 3339 west 42nd. She understood English, spoke it a little bit then. I spoke with her constantly, very slowly at first, increasing the speed progressively. Before long she was speaking English fluently. And she passed the international English Test required by the University. With love, I can make anything happen. Is it what you say?

I find the last tutorial experience funny. I was living in the West End in Vancouver. He is working for the government of Canada as a chemist, making sure food product is safe to be consumed. After a few sessions of French lessons, I said to him to keep his French Knowledge alive in his mind, he has to listen to the radio in French everyday, read French books as often as possible, and go for interaction in French communities once in a while. At first, it will be difficult, keep it like that until you break the barrier of strangeness in the foreign language. He stops coming for French lesson from me. Wayne, born in Lithuania, knows how to do it, himself alone, he doesn't need me anymore. However, I lost the money I was getting from him for the lessons. In other words I tried to be a good tutor. That destroys the tutoring. That's why it's funny.

It is not quit clear to me yet the meaning of the truck. The color of the only car I had and which I was driving while tutoring was white or off white. When that car burnt, you got $ 2100 for what was left of it. A car dealer wanted me to get an old station wagon Volvo (I didn't know that Volvo was such a popular Swedish Car in North America) for that amount of money. I think its color was yellow but it was may be a mistake. Its color might have been red. I declined the deal, because I went there to buy a new car, and that I thought it was possible even if it was not that particular car dealership. I was wrong on the last assumption, what I discovered later in life. It was a huge mistake; I needed a car to do my job, which was teacher on call, to go to a different school almost everyday. Is that sotory already told here ? May be.

My father was a heavy-duty machinery worker. I was practically born in cars, machinery parts, and dark dense oil. I do not know if that creates a kind of car repulsion in me. I do not know either if the car I would like to drive is too expensive; I have not been driving for years.

Lamborghini is one of the cars I like. One model is of red color. The DP may be suggesting that. It might be suggesting also that it is my dark skin color more reddish as Marvin Gay's), my chronological age that are the problem with car dealers and the school Board. The effect of that kind of racism would be not having a car, neither a permanent teaching position. Before I left Montreal, I was driving many sorts of cars without having to buy one. I was younger, in another community.

> DP44. On top of a roof I am fixing an electrical cord, then I plug a telephone. I am about to finish it,

when someone calls me from down there to let him finish it for me.

It touches a subject already discussed before, I think. The DP seems to be about theory and practice in the sense that some of us are more inclined on the side of theory, some others on the side of practice. It is, also, about transcendence, climbing on top to have a better look at the truth? The problem is after the climbing, we tend to want to stay there, and Life seems to be easier up there, void of everyday obligations in the life down there. It seems that's what is wrong with certain religious beliefs, too much on the up not enough on the down side of things.

> *DP45. Home is near the sea. I am back there, before I go inside, I decide to take a walk along the sea. After half a kilometer about, I meet Samuel, turn around, following the same trace to go back home again. A few women run and catch up with me with their hands full bills(money). They keep some for themselves, give me some. One of them reminds me of Yvette Amante's daughter. Suddenly a small man appears among them asking me money he has given to me. I ask him if he needs it.*

It is not clear for me now if it was many women or one woman in the DP. After reading part of the note, it says in a paragraph " I bring you money. I know you do not have, for if you had, you would bring me a gift". The DP reminds me of Heather whose is speaking, although I did not meet her yet when I had the DP in April 2000. I met Heather in August 2001, the day I rented her a bedroom in this house on 16th Avenue. I was not living here yet when I had rge DP.

I know it is her because last year I gave her a gift, a bottle of perfume for a Christmas present . I have not even talk to her since October of last year. Before last night and yesterday evening I tried to get in touch with her unsuccessfully.

I've already described something she was doing that I did not understand. She called me but did not talk. I had read a book: "Dreams of Love, the Power of Romantic Passion and Fateful Encounters", written by Ethel S. Person. In it what Heather was doing is described as one of the effects of love on the lover who is unable to speak in the presence of the beloved, even when he\she is a loquacious in all other situations in his\her life. So now I understand what she was doing but still unable to reach her. I find that a bit childish despite what Person said.

Samuel, a doctor, may be, is Jacqueline's husband. Jacqueline is Anne Marie's sister. Anne Marie is my sister in law. Just before they met I was in some kind of relationships with her. It was in Montreal, I was meeting a new woman almost every week. The relationships with Jacqueline didn't matter much. I was too busy with too many women. But it s like I expected it would develop to a stable relationships sometime. It was after she met Samuel I realized that. We all were living close to metro station Berry. Gerard, someone I met at secondary school in Haiti became one of my best friends then. I used to sleep over at his family's place in Port-Au-Prince. I helped him with accommodation when he immigrated to Canada, went to set up in Montreal. He is the one who met Samuel in a protestant Church or he knew Samuel before hand. They both are active members of a protestant religion. Samuel met Jacqueline through Gerard. Because I had a little bit of something for her, I resented to have welcomed Gerard at my place. It was partly why I left Montreal.

While I was still living in Montreal, I moved closer to the north part of the city. Jakeline did the same. They invited me to a party just before I was about to leave Montreal. Samuel asked why why was I living? I could not tell him the whole truth. I said it was because I wanted to live in a province where I can earn more money, which was partly true also. The small man who appeared after I received the money is again Samuel, although in complete life I didn't not borrow money from him. 2 other men lend me money in Montreal. May be Samuel was representing them in the DP.

Is it pimping that is alluded to in the DP? It looks like these women were prostituting themselves for me. I do not know if that was the case in my childhood. I myself never engaged in such practice, never consciously had women given me money from 'meat market" despite the allusion in the DP?

Amante, was one of the women in my father's small harem. So, Yvette, Amante's daughter is my half sister. She has a slender figure, slim and tall. She reminds me of Amanda, the roommate who is living in this house presently on 16th Avenue. She pays the rent to Barbara, not to me. That prompts in my mind the other possible meaning of the dream. I expect to be able buy a house near the sea. I expect also to have two or three tenants there. It cannot be males with whom I would have too many homosexual innuendos to deal with. They would not accept me being different, heterosexual. So, these women were giving me rent money. This meaning is more likely. And it sounds as a prediction. It's like, I will buy that house near the sea, move in with Amanda, as one of the tenants. Isn't it? I wish.

Yvette awaken in me an elementary school teacher of the same name. I went to elementary school most of the time without money or lunch. Yvette used to give me part of her lunch. I liked her also as person. She was of very light colored woman, something of value in Haiti. She was also very gentle, and, of course. good hearted, generous.

She triggers in me also a minister in the government of Quebec who was demoted on question of popular vote. She said something derogatory about women of low economic status, which Yvette symbolizes in Quebec. In other not to loose votes they had to let go.

All in all this DP is about my wishes and my struggles to live.

Dp46. Wile putting some order in my business, I throw away an old shoe that I had.

It makes me think of some of my goals. I would prefer to have mixed blood children. I think they would inherit two different pulls of genes, what would make them stronger for future generations. So I tend to neglect women of my race, avoid going out with them at all, for fear of difficulty to disengage from such relationships when the time comes to have those children. Then, I am not very young chronologically speaking; not being sure if sperm can spoil I tend to go rather toward chronologically younger women to compensate. As nothing like that happens yet, I do not know what it is really going to be. I do not throw away anyone. I need everyone for one reason or another.

So, I will have trouble with women of the chronological age I have, with women of the race in which I came into the world, and with men.

In a shoe there is a sole, so the DP is referring to soul more specifically to the Soul Exposed. In the past I was very reticent in relation to the concept soul thinking that it was a religious concept. I is only while writing the book in 2000

I realized that the concept does not belong to church. The DP may be referring to that too.

> *DP47. Seeing this woman sitting in a bench, I say to her "what are you doing here?" As she does not answer my question in French, I start a conversation with her in English.*

In the notes from the date of the DP, I was wandering who is the woman, thinking it might be Barbara to whom I pay rent of this house on 16th Avenue or Jane Doe to whom you paid rent of the house on Manitoba Street where I made the DP. She is a new immigrant from Japan to Canada, doesn't speak French at all, and speaks English a little. I thought that Barbara might have been worrying about the security deposit that I did not give to her yet. Her parents are from Germany. She is born in Canada. By that time I knew already that I was going to come to live here.

I do not recall having been in the situation described in the DP, not able to say who that woman was, or if it were important at all to ask that question.

Although it does make me think of Pierre Eliott Trudeau. The bilingualism is in Canadian mind for years before Trudeau, yet he is the one who promoted it to the point that bilingualism is attached to him. In history when we think of him we will think of bilingualism in Canada certainly. The woman may be a person I am going to meet in the future.

> *DP48 In this School or university, there are many cakes. I have the desire to eat some, but I leave the school without eating any for not having money to buy some.*

Cake is definitely associated with a part of the woman

body in my mind. It is true that Barbara is woman who would like to eat the cake and having it too. I do not remember exactly how I came to that conclusion about her. But it is related to her strange behavior toward me, when the other bedroom will be empty and there will be prospective renters coming to visit it. She us jealousm says ri her husband ib front of me that she loves me.

When I go to school to teach, or to university to learn, I have a bit of money usually paid to me for teaching or loan from governments and bursaries. So this DP cannot be taken in for face value in regard to me. It may be alluding to the fact that students are generally poor. I eat muffins, drink coffee sometimes in the morning. That day may be I did not have money to buy muffins.

To eat the cake I would have to have money to buy some. Despite the subjacent meaning that I don't need money to have the cake, I have no quarrel with a society where money is the device of exchange of good. Some HBBs call money: the energy that connects you with the outside world. At University of Quebec in Montreal, where I had my first experiences with that level of schooling, the accent was on Marxism-Leninism, however money was not really contested. Some theories within the market economy advances that it is possible to have money for exchange of good with other countries, and a voucher for goods and foods for the inhabitants. It is kind of twisted, a "torticoli" as I call it; but it is a possibility.

Noble persons in the sense of king, queen family and entourage might find money a vulgar device. For it, in a way, it eliminates social ranks . Anyone with the same amount of money can have the same kind of service, the same kind of goods, etc. However, it is that my last name is Prince. The DP is probably saying the problem I encounter with money has its origin from the name. For me consciously it is just a name. Sometimes, I think it was given to slaves brought to Haiti at the time of the commerce of slavery . But memory does not rationalize. It may process Prince as a noble name, therefore, with disdain for money.

> *DP50. Somebody finds a dime, gives it to me. Then I see another dime on the ground. I bent my body to pick it up. And then, you see gold watches coming from the ground as if ad infinitum. One of the men with me picks up a few watches, while saying that they are collector's watches and so minimizing their value.*

The waking life experience to link to this is that one day I was passing beside Eaton's, on Robson Street. There is a vendor sitting behind trunk opened and full of watches. A few HBBs circle him looking at the watches. The vendors gave a watch to about four of them. I stand there thinking he was going to give you one too. He did not, but made a comment that sounded like" He too thinks he deserves one." Everyone laughed. I left them there feeling humiliated. Now I have a different point of view on the event, I have the idea that the watches might have been stolen that he didn't owe me a watch, even when I was were in same group.

In complete life, I have long time forgotten about it.

But this little incident is important enough in my memory to trigger this DP in which I performed a multiplication. So this is the good side of the incident. Multiplication in dream is not something one does everyday, despite the wish to do so.

I have a Casio watch of 23 years, still giving me the exact time of the day. I also have a pair of Xavier watches that I want to get rid of, because they are not precision watches. They are only for decoration. The other time I went downtown and try to sell them to a jeweler. He didn't buy them. They are out of battery, not functioning presently. May be that was why, he did not buy them. It was a buy and sell store.

Of course, more would like to have more and better watches.

DP reminds me of the body of human beings in which there are a multitude of watches.

DP51 *these tall friends and I leave the school together. In the middle of the street they disappear.*

Some of the friends I met at school in Haiti were disappearing like flies at one time. What happened to them?

Then, you moved to Canada, went to university of Quebec in Montréal, moved again to Manitoba, went to university there. Last year I started to go the University of British Columbia, something happened that made it impossible for me to pursue that study anymore (You were sexually harassed by the three professors of the three courses I was attending from September to December 2001, two men, one woman, by other male employees, and by other males students. I filed a complaint, but didn't pursue it. If they were female students who were sexually harassing me, I would be happy. Simon Fraser University is too far from where I am living now. It would take too much from the research time. In Montreal there were 50000 Haitians when I left. In Vancouver there are may be a 100. So it's a bit difficult for me to meet and be with the right friend. So, be advised my friends of the whole planet Earth, it's better to live in the city where you went to school, if you do not want to meet with the teeth of loneliness(lonelines in complete life that is). They are going to bite you, if you are not careful enough in big cities (It might be my own experience, not to be generalized).

I had the DP in April 2000, When I was thinking of going back to the university for some refresher courses. The DP was saying that it was a good idea makes to make friend at that level of schooling in Vancouver.

That said, it is amazing how accurate a DP could be. I did it in 2000, but there is a kind of scandal about the Premier of BC presently. It started last weekend when he was caught driving while drunk.If he were not Premier of a Province no one would ever noticed what happened. It is an important issue for human beings; life is involved, but at the same time very banal also. It happens all the times. It even happened to me once. I was working in a Canadian forces base. There was an October feast night with salamis and alcohol in abundance. I drank too much, took the car, crossed the gate of the base, I was stopped right there. The policeman asked me to go back home.

I do not know, but it seems like we have to behave with friend carefully. Mister Clark was the Premier of British Columbia 2, 3 years ago. His friends got him in trouble. He had to resign, to leave the premier position. This Mister Campbell went to see some friends; he got himself in trouble that may be costly politically speaking. What a strange phenomenon friendship(is it friendship or escaping self?) can be sometimes? It can cost you.

> DP52 *The woman gives me some work to do for her. I do it well and fast. Because of that, it is like, she asks me to do the same work again. While walking near the place where she is selling things I find many loonies and "twonies".*

Once I found a 20 $ bill on Davie street at a time when there used to be prostitutes there. It cannot be the trigger of this DP, for it's about money in coins.

I was reading an article in Money Saver, a Canadian magazine, in which there is an article on Canadian $ or its diminished value compare to American $, the Japanese yen and Euro, above all. When I immigrated in Canada in 1971, our $ was higher than the US $. May be I brought the bad luck to the Canadian $ from Haiti with the gourde, a fifth of the American $ when I left. It went down and never climbed up again. I think it was the arrival of a separatist government in power in Quebec that was the cause of the slide down, donot know if it could be the same cause that keep it down.

Loon is the name of common bird in Canada. But one cannot prevent one self from going to lunatic after hearing the name of he bird. It's not clear to me if that connotation is in the mind of every Canadian and if that would cause the recent descending value of the $. Canadian economy is more stable than the United States now. The latter is in a kind of jigsaw period for a while. This year, 2003, the Canadian economy gains 3% in BNP better performance than any other country in the G7 group.

Although, it is question of loonies and twonies in this DP, I have never been really interested in pennies. Or in my goals there is a lot of money. As it said before I see myself as being rich, for opulence is the nature of my universe . That's why I feel wealthy and think rather of million of $.

There are also a sexist and a feminist issue in it. It is as if I am not supposed to work for a woman, let alone work well and getting promotion from her(this woman in the DP may represent Sophia, the Soul of the World). For when I go where she is, all I find are loonies and twonies, in other words small amount of money. There is the meaning: working for women, I will earn only small amount of money. There is some truth to it given that in most societies and most cultures they are not making the policies, taking the decisions in regard to economy, finance, or money of their country, their families. Their contribution to the wealth of the society is rather done through menial low paying jobs(but important job as well). Indira Gandhi, Margarett Tatcher, Benazhir Buttho created a phenomenal event in history. . In Canada women were allowed to vote only recently. Fortunately, this situation has changed for the better nowadays.

If I have worked for women, you wouldn't pay attention to it enough to remember it. Therefore, working for a woman in the DP may mean that I am a woman fan.

Sunday April 17, 2000

> *DP53. A boy shakes my hands many times and says:" They need to have a doctorate." At the end of the handshake, he leaves a few coins in my hand.*

The boy is happy to see me. When I create my goals, I will take 10% of they money in them to put together a foundation. I have been thinking about it for sometime, since I started to structurally celebrate my goals everyday in order to create them, in 1989. I will hire someone to take care of it. It will be there for human beings in any country in the world. I will try to help where help is needed. I have a "quit smoking" project designed and written in 1973. . Unable to find money to execute the first conception, I redesign and rewrite it last year, thinking that the new conception would be easier to execute, for I do not have a lot of money to start it. It still sitting in one of my drawers for lack of financing. With the foundation, I will find out those who are in that kind of situation in order to help them getting out of it.

I will not try to play God. I know that everyone is responsible for himself, for everything that happened in her life. I know also that, sometimes, a little push by someone other than self creates the spark to unravel a project. I have this DP many times. I see the sky with so many stars; it scares me(A view of the whole may be) . I think itis about abundance, infinite opulence of the universe, I see myself and everybody else as having rich potential. I equate myself to all that exist.

Last April, Heather finished her courses at the university for the year. She was about to go back to Calgary where her parents are. So I found myself another roommate, Shugo, a Japanese student in Japan where he comes from. He came here to study English. I was looking for another female to replace Heather. Because Shugo, a young man, said he was going to stay here until September only. I thought that even if there were problem with homosexuality with him, there would not be time for it to degenerate into something impossible to live with. I accepted, therefore, to have him as roommate. There was a little bit of negative tension between us two at first, but nothing really worth detailing. The day of his departure, I went to see how he was going to leave his room, started a conversation with him. At the end we were happy with each other, I shake his hand a couple of times. Then. Before he left you gave him a cheque of $ 187.50 to return to him his security deposit. He never cashed it.

I behaved like that with him knowing that it was OK, meaning it would not have negative consequences, given that he was about to leave. I knew if he were going to stay here more it wouldn't be a wise gesture to shake his hand like that. I had another male roommate at another time. At first there was very negative tension between us. He was in an intensive campaign of seduction toward me via subliminal messages. After he stopped doing that, I started to relax, to show him friendliness, to be myself. He then, restarted the homosexual campaign right away.

The boy is part of me or is my ego telling me that I have to have a doctorate in something. But my experiences are telling the opposite, that I don't need a doctorate to be able to create your goals.

The use of the pronoun "they" to signify that HBBs around me want me to have a doctorate.

> *DP54.Where I appear there is a woman wearing a very short skirt that let me see the shape of an enormous vagina. I am chocked to see it like that. I am tempted to tell her to go back home put a longer skirt.*

I do not have any particular interest in the way women dress themselves. Mini-skirt make them look attractive sexy, but women dress themselves that way for especial occasions as going to dance or working on the beach in the summer. If they were to dress like that all the time they would put themselves at risk, I suppose. In winter in the north it's not very convenient anyway.

The DP is bizarre for presenting a vagina as if it were a breast. A vagina cannot be seen that easily. Then, we are getting its meaning. It kind of diminishes the importance of breast compare to vagina. There is the Western men love affair with big breast (Look at the number of words they have to describe it: "boobies, boobs, cantaloupes, casabas, fun bags, globes, maracas, melons, racks, tits". If it is not an obsession with breast, I don't know my name The DP is may be saying that it is a misplaced appetite, that that kind of appetite should be directed toward the vagina. How to understand the appetite for breast? It's the mark of a woman, the visible mark of the women's feature that distinguishes her from me, a man, a woman in a sexual context. From the appetite for breast derived the love affair with big breast, which is going to be exaggerated in a whole culture. But what is really important sexually speacking according to the DP is the cake or the vagina.

Obviously there is pornography in this DP. When I was chronologically younger I would devour with my eyes a woman picture in pornographic magazine. Actually, it was something I was doing in recent past. The reason I stop now is that I think it might be interfering with myr active sexual life. Or, because I cannot explain clearly why I am not sexually active since 1998, I stop entertaining yourself with fictive females I see in magazines and TV. I will not be able to meet them; so, they are only pictures for me .

I received playboy for a long period of time. I never watched unusual pornography. You received pornographic e-mail on children and homosexual men a couple of time in the computer. I deleted them without opening them.

Then, there is also a little bit of jealousy, or little bit of possessiveness. I am tempted to ask the women to dress differently. I want to be the only one to see her beautiful and attractive body according this DP. Again when I was younger I was a very jealous person. All my life, I have been a romantic monogamist. I went out with one person at a time. There was intensity, possessiveness and jealousy in me. I started thinking recently that my mode of loving might also be responsible for the too long recent period of love and sexual abstinence. Then, reading some books on romantic love makes me realize that it is y my romantic love kind of love. For, like the sun, it is an agent of change, of self-realization, self liberation, all things that are necessary for me.

In a final analysis the DP may be just about Sophia the Soul of the World who is exposing herself for me to see, tempting me (individual and Soul of the World), etc. After all the title of the book is The Soul Exposed(little woman in Hollywood exposed herself, is then the Soul of the World reprensative in complete life(how about Barbara she may have a big vagina she is tall, she open her vagina once for me to see in amother DP)

The DP may be also linked to that I am not going out with a woman.

CHAPTER IX

Tuesday April 18, 2000

> *DP55. It's like a lot of human beings are running after me for some reason. I am running away with fear.*

Is it the fear of exposition it is about? The fear of becoming very popular, having many human beings running after me all the time. I wish or I expect to have a lot of money. The DP may be suggesting that what will happen, when I have a big amount of money. A lot of human beings will run after me for it. In other words that was the block preventing me from creating that goal. I start to unblock it by its expression in the DP. <u>It is at the same time an advantage to use DP as tool in life in general. Anything can have an expression in a DP, without any damage to the psyche. Instead, sometimes it heals(catharsis).</u>

> *DP56. The person is still playing volley Ball without a top. I have seen her doing it before. This time I say to*

her:" Quite ca ", Creole for: " Give it up".

I used to see groups of human beings playing volley ball without shoes, and yes, some men without a top in the English Bay. Nevertheless I do not do sport enough to be dreaming of it. It must be about the noise emancipated women were making a few years ago in Canada in order to be able to take their top off in public without breaking the law in the same measure than men. They have won in that their demand became a law afterwards. This subject is not very hot in the era of Internet where complete nudity is available for everyone to see, even if you are not curious.

The DP is probably about the power ball game, the game I play on a fairly regular basis. Haitians like playing lottery(all human beings apparently), I started playing when I was living in Haiti, gave it up when I immigrated to Canada, took it up later, when you started to have money problem.

The DP may be a compulsion not to play it anymore, as if it is the cause of anything bad that happened to me , although, I know that it's me who are the cause of everything that happened to me, nobody else, nothing else. I suppose society attaches a stigma of immorality to any game for money, because there is no production of goods in those games. Human beings live with clothes, houses, and food. Nothing like that is being directly created in those games. So in order to keep the gross national product growing, any unproductive activity must be forbidden, according to society. In psychology, they advise against it. A psychiatrist, I saw for a couple of weeks advised against it. Rhona, the talk show woman, advised against it. I have negative vibration about it in this DP. Like Simpson the comic character would say: "What a man to do?" with a big voice as if he is crying.

These moral codes are no longer relevant in 2003. A lot of qualified human beings are unable to find a public work. Low or high, there is a percentage of unemployed HBBs in all countries. Besides, without all the sports games, unemployment would be a lot higher than what it is. Sports games are very similar to PPK game(Lottery). I decided to call it like that, because when we win I can not determine if it's a prediction or a psychokinetic move, or action at a distance, by our will.

Where I was brought up, the sport game everyone was playing was soccer. So soccer game is part of me . I even right a book to help quit smoking that I call Kickitwell Or Else. I like soccer that much, even though I have not been playing it very much in Canada. I like the other sports games too. In that book there is a famous paragraph where I mentioned the name of Gretsky and Jordon. Something happened later related to a research I am doing that makes the paragraph famous. Unfortunately, I can't give more detail on it yet.

I plaid volleyball a little bit. I am always very busy with researches, I do flex, cardiovascular, and strength exercises 2 times a week(3 hours). I used to do a lot of walking. Since do not drive, I do not walk for sport, but by necessity.

I think volleyball, baseball, tennis, running, jugging are among the most healthy sports, because they are good for a healthy heart. The cells of the heart, of the back bone or what is in it, the nerves, do not renew themselves. So, physical exercises related to these body parts are more important. However I think commercial sport, in the long run, is unhealthy.

DP57. When I come back home, I find Monise in the room with a very small neighbor of ours. I think she is going to make a mess of my reputation again. I say to her " What are you doing at her place?"

This DP is about a subject I do not want to think of very much. A thin fence of cactus separates the house of my mother from the house of a neighbor named Charite (Charity in English). She was already in her sixties chronologically speaking, when I was a child. The name of that person has such an influence on me that I am still dreaming about it after years and years. It is probably because that period of one's life is very impressionable. The impressions we form at that time last a life time, is the original motivation for the rest of our lives sometimes.

I am struggling to get my economic independence, but instead of that I find myself rather dependent of the state on minimum salary. I have been working for five years before I had the DP. When I had it I was on minimum salary. I did not succeed in preventing that from happening, from a conscious point of view. Deep down, I chose to live like that for some reason or another. In the process of attaining financial independence, there may be something I must learn by being on welfare. It is a puzzle to my conscious mind, but that what it is for Woopi many HBBs. There are the author of Harry Potter, a successful black actress, the person who created Wendy's were they sell hamburger, another person who has a chain of buy and sell electronic devices with one store on Dunbar street(Dunbar and 10th), a few blocs from where I am living, and who knows how many more. They have been in the same situation than I am, before being successful. Hence there must be some real reason why they had to take that road in their way to financial success. The same is probably true for me too.

When I deal with welfare, each time I talk to a person at her office there, or each time someone from there talks to me, it is about money. To get rich I may need this kind of practice, that is to say, speaking about money all the time to activate it in the mind program. Then what is happening to me now, what happened to this two famous human beings that we know about is no longer as senseless as it appears to be at first. Not everybody on welfare are trying to wake up the money part already in their psyche, their mind in order to bring it in their lives, but some are definitely, willingly or not, consciously or not.

Then now I can speculate that many money crises are in fact richness crisis. <u>Translated, some human beings on welfare, the so-called poor, are experiencing richness crisis. Imagine. No wonder it is a phenomenon of Rich countries, rather.</u>

I have already noticed a similar phenomenon in the health system. Many human beings believed to be crazy thrown in an asylum, are in fact having a health crisis, are in fact healthier than before, than many of us.

I was physically and mentally sick all the time because of what I considered at the time of the DP being a descent to hell. I think living close to Charity in my infancy is the fundamental motivation of the minimum salary aspect of my financial situation, although according to the DP it is the fear of character assassination that is keeping me in the red financially speaking9 (before I came to Vancouver, first year after my certificate in education I was earning $22 000 a year, at Delta I was hired for $40000 a year) .

> DP58. *The woman says to another that a younger woman can do the same work while still sleeping at regular time, and that from now to five years later she will have the best results.*

While living a 3339 west 42nd Avenue, I went to bed during the week at around midnight and got up at 5 AM. I adopted this kind of schedule from teaching. I had to be at School at 7:30 AM, class started at 8 o'clock in most schools I used to go to. At 42 Avenue, I was not teaching, but besides researching, I also had to take care of the whole house and big yard surrounding it: trimming the bush fence, mowing the lawn, cleaning the common rooms etc. So I had to have some kind of schedule to be able to amalgamate the two tasks(research and tasks related to the house).

At the beginning of the year 2000, I lived at a youth hostel for one day. Then I lived at 500 Dunsmuir, a hotel. There I had to vacate the place after breakfast at 6 o'clock AM, come back for lunch, and got out again until 6 PM. So I spent most of my time during the month of January 2000 in the Vancouver Public Library, not far from the hotel, and read lots of books. It's like all the torments of the time was to bring me close to the library and to read, exactly what I did, without reflected upon it(500 is also related to one my goals). Then I moved in the house on Manitoba and 63rd Avemue . So I was a little bit disorganized. I had just two bags and some cloths with me at first. Everything else like alarm clock, bed, TV, radio was still in a storage house.

By this DP I was keeping myself on my toes, not to react to the wild situation, to keep a schedule for creative stimulation of consciousness no matter what, going to bed and waking up at any time causes sleep disorder anyway.

I will have to wait until 2005 to see if the best results in the DP will materialize. I was living at 500 Dunsmuir; 5 years in DP may mean that. In my goals there is an amount of money I would like to have starting by number 5, the DP may be referring to that too. We will see. 5 is also the number of children I want want to have.

While the younger woman is already explained a few

DPs before this one, explanation is related the mix of old sperm with younger ovule.

> *DP59. I am driving a Mercedes; I try to do some exhibitions, playing with the car as if I was in a racetrack, as if I was Michael Mikanen or Shumaker. Then I find myself on foot, climbing a mountain with difficulty. It is icy; I am sliding back down, on the rails of a train.*

Strangely enough, On January 27, 2003 they reported at Global Television that Billly Joel had an accident in his Mercedes that was completely wrecked. Fortunately, Billy himself got out of it without a scratch. I tend to think that there is no coincidence, that everything is explainable, even when we cannot find links to so many things. On April 2000 when I had the DP I might have been predicting what was going to happen to Billy recently. In my analysis of the DP last week, I know him as being inspired, as a singer who draws material for himself from his own dreams, the only link there would be between Billy and this work.

What a way to describe an accident? What would be a good thing was to understand the DP on time and not having the accident I had in October 2001. The meaning of the DP escaped me totally. As I was not driving a car at that time, I did not go in that angle, not thinking that it could be a car driven by someone else which were going to hit me.

A sub-part of one of my goals is about discovering an accident "preventor" I have many goals on a continuum. I do not know if I will be able to reach that sub-part while living, but I really want to do that too. The point is it is why accident is in my DP, not because I am meanly spirited. There are so many accidents happening everyday in a city, let alone a country, a continent, the whole world. The "accident alarm" I have in mind will not be against all those. It will be only against big accident where many human lives would be involved.

Someone I already met in my reading journey Gerard Delerme had a Mercedes. In Haiti when U was there it was the symbol of someone in possession of a great wealth, a wealth equivalent to what a big movie star would have. For, in that country at that time and probably here and now too, possessing any car was already a sign of richness.

That reminds us, also, of the human beings that used the street in big cities as a racetrack sometimes. What are they thinking? They do kill some pedestrians that way. Apparently, in Vancouver mostly rich oriental kids do it. Their parents leave them in the city alone to go to school, while they are busy at home, in Hongkong, Taiwan, etc., that is. These parents are placed in the dilemma of raising their kids, and earning their lives at the same time. I would like to place an ad in a paper to put myself at their service in regard to this particular problem. I still do not have a chance of doing it yet. It would be for the higher goods of both parties as they say, the correct way. A few minutes a day, or a few times a week, or month, or whatever, would not disturb my research so much. And I would do a real a service which would help avoid preventable accident in the street of some cities.

I do not go to car showroom recently, do not have a clue what the Mercedes of this year looks like, but it is one the best machines human beings have made for themselves. It is not for anything it was so prestigious in Haiti when I lived there. I am sure it would impress some women if I had one now, and so, quit being in the jail of celibacy as it is for me now. I would use it to go to Stanley Park, to go downtown today that I need to go there, to go to promenade with the beautiful girl with whom I would be in these times. In order words a car is very useful, and important tool for human, according to me. Imagine having to put 200 years to go from a city to another on foot, definitely not the way to go.

While traveling from Liancourt to Port-Au-Prince in Haiti when I was about 7 years old in a bus with father sisters and brothers, another bus hit the one in which we were from behind. It came close to fall on one side. Everybody had to get out of it. We waited there for at least 2 hours before another bus picked us up to continue the voyage. It was almost a banal accident, but at this age everything like that is seen with bigger proportions.

I think that may be the basis for my dwelling in this subject in my space of the psyche.

> DP60. Sitting at a table facing someone who reminds me of Lelio, they bring him his lunch, but he is not happy. I say something like:" That's enough. I want to start the lesson now" thinking that the other person at the table does not realize how little time I have.

My life is quite different now than what it was three years ago in regard to eating. Before, I used to sit at a table to eat, something I do not do anymore. I eat while watching TV, probably a common behavior in North America. Then this DP is a compulsion to do the same thing again, that is to sit at a table to eat. At the house on 3339 west 42nd Avenue, I was still sitting at a table to eat. I helped one roommate practice her English that way. After she left the house to go to live in US, little by little I lost the habit. The male roommate wanted me do that with them, I did not. For one reason, I think that they are homosexuals. I would feel very uncomfortable in sitting at a table and eating with them.

Another reason is that I associate eating with love with family (Lelio is the name of a younger brother). In other words, I would not sit at table to eat with someone else even if that person is a woman, or a heterosexual male. I left some food on the table for a few minutes once; a male roommate put some torn grocery bags close to it. When I came back and saw that, I was not happy, but did not say a word to him. He is a very tall, at least 200 pounds body, but very young. I did not say anything to him, because, after all, he was my roommate, I had to minimize the incident to keep the relationships stable. He probably has heard from other roommates that I would not give them food, would not eat with them. You could not explain to any of them why I was behaving like that, finding the subject too delicate, too intimate.

This incident had probably contributed the change of my eating habit. In the house on Manitoba Street, there was a table, which were dancing a little bit. In this house on 16th Avenue, there is a very small table between two walls in a passage to a storage room. Two HBBs can sit and eat at that table. I never sat and eat at that table yet, meaning that I have not fall in love in this house yet.

In infancy, I was very mad very often. I thought that Mercida(Is there a connection with the Mercedes and a certain celebrity in the previous DP?), the other woman with whom my past away father have children was giving the nice food to her own children, I was given less food of a lesser quality at least that was what I was thinking in my little psyche of infancy. I resented that very much, and refused to eat at all, many times. In fact what I really resented was to see her serving food to her children with love, what I was deprived of, not having a mother of my own. My contention with food was one with a lack of love at an age when it is very important to have it. Those too explain my attitude now toward food and love, love the nourishment of the psyche.

I tutor a lot in my lifetime. To do that, most of the time we sit at the same table.

> *DP61. In a trance like state talking about philosophy in a classroom, a man who becomes agitated kisses me. I feel uncomfortable, say to the class something like "he is very much mixed up". Someone in the audience rises up to tell it's because in my race they do not do those sorts of thing.*

He just arrived from Maroc, rented a bedroom from me, stayed for one month. After a while, he used to come and sit in my bedroom for a few minutes. The night before his departure he did the same thing. Just before living, the entrance door, he embraced me, gave me a kiss on the cheek, I did the same too. I thought it was because it is the custom in that area of the earth where he comes from. He was about to live that gesture could not cause any nuisance later.

Some human beings just like to kiss. I met Claude another teacher, another Haitian in Vancouver. He probably still is living here in Vancouver. He looks a bit like Fred Astaire. I met him on the street again. He kissed me on both cheeks. Later I learned that he was going out with a woman From Israel. That may explained his behavior. True, it's not common in Haiti. It something I become accustomed to in Canada. But Claude may have exaggerated the custom. He was teaching at school, very shortly after he started to work at that school, he was fired. When I asked him why, " It was a girl's birthday in one of my classes, I kissed her" was his explanation. I did not ask for the details of the kiss. I imagined it was not on the chick. I think he tried to bring to himself the sympathy of all his students to keep his position by doing what he did, but it backfired.

I still find that a very bizarre behavior.

CHAPTER X

Wednesday April 19, 2000

DP62. " My name indicates my age".........."14 months me"..........

The 2nd flash is written like this in my notes "14 mois me", partly in French, partly in English. The only weak link I can make between my life and this DP is related to a Chinese family, Which were living on 43 Avenue and Cambie Street. They were new in Vancouver. I started to tutor French to 3 of their kids at first. One girl quit. You continued with a brother and sister who were 14 year old at that time. Then their father died. The mother sent the boy to finish his high school in Victoria. I left with the girl. I was a little bit affectionate with her for having lost her father. Older sister may have sensed my emotion and misinterpreted it wrongly. When you was enclosed with her in the room assigned to tutoring in the house, older sister, or less younger sister used to go in the street facing that room to see what was happening there through the window. She might have not thinking straight either because of the lost of her father, they were all in grieving mood, sort of.

The first Flash may be referring to Arnoux, one of my first names. It sounds old in English, French? I do not know. In the other hand, I thought that it would be easy to pronounce by an Anglophone, because all the sounds exist in English, Surprisingly, when an Anglophone says it sounds different. Apparently the letter n before the sound u as in book, changes u to o as in oak. The sound u or "ou" in French is made in the very front of the mouth with the lips pointing forward. After all it might not exist in English. There is a sound u very similar to it but not quite the same. In pronouncing it in my name, they kind of round it up. So the way they sound Arnoux in English is not the same as it is sound in French. It doesn't matter anyway. I would like everyone in the world to call my name with all different accents.

I know that the results of some researches indicate that mental factor plays a determining role in a person's body staying young or aging. I am not obsessed by chronological age in any way. I think my body is the same as the one of an HBBs who is 25 years old. I will think that way all the time I am alive. When I am sick, or when the flow of money is not at my way, I feel very old, though.

If you are obsessed by chronological age, you will feel old, your body will then deteriorate, so to if you were overly obsessed by time. There is a whether person on TV called Wayne. I admire his work, for he often says happy birthday to human who live 100 years or more. That is really something to celebrate especially when we know that we can live for a time quite a bit longer than 100 years.

I applaud, in the other hand, HBBs in Hollywood who are obsessed with the youth of their body, like Michael Jaskson. for example. Except that they should also pay attention to the cosmetic of their psyche to feel better about themselves, healthy, and young inside out. In other words the body image you have is the self-image you have. A self image with scarce, negative feelings like hatred, anger, a self image with hurts, will always bring back a body with scarce, malformation, a body you do not like, regardless the number of times you surgically correct it.

It would not make sense to say that my fellow humans in Hollywood have so much money, so much fame, so many other persons admiring them, they do not have bad self-image problem. I cannot say their good self image is what brings them the money and the fame in the first place, so that they do not need inner cosmetic to maintain body cosmetic as mentioned above. For they, too, get sick sometimes, they, too, die after around 100 years. Life can always be better for anyone.

> DP63. *Having something else to do, I put down the baby I had in my hands. I would like to watch him and keep him from putting his hands in excrement, but I have to go elsewhere. When I come back and see that he has his hands in it and he is eating it, sour emotions invade me.*

In my case, it is not an enfant as in waking life for I do not have one, never really had one. If the DP is about child in plain physical life, it is then about the future when I will have some children. In other cases, the child could refer to the creation of a new idea or concept. As there is no specific concept, or idea mentioned in my notes taken when I had the DP for the first time, I assume that it is a metaphor related to the researches I started doing more actively since 1989. At the time of the DP I was thinking of going back to the university. It is a comment on those thoughts, but not a very positive one, given that I have sour emotions during the DP.

It reminds me of an episode of Dawson that I have seen on TV. Her professor asks her to read a book before going to class the next day. In the night before that day many of her friends want her to go and do some activity with her. As the last one insists, she explains to him in plain terms why she have to stay home reading by saying "How about having a baby and leaving him alone while doing some other activity. When you come back, you will find that he has peed, shit, etc." or something similar. This sequence of Dawson explains the DP quite well.

Sour emotions is not a good sign in the sense that there is an identification with something different than self when it's happened. In order words I was identifying with the researches I was doing, still doing now, too. The idea of leaving them for a while in order to attain some courses at the university made me unhappy. Identification with something else than self can be a very subtle phenomenon. If you identify with your car, and after realizing it, you want to "misidentify," there is no problem there, for the car is physical object, it is a form with color, shape, volume, etc. If you want to "disidentify" with a research, it can be a little bit complicated, for they are things that are non-substantial, which you cannot see nor touch.

And then, how do you ask a lover not to love, a physician not to treat patients, a student not to study, a professor not think? That is the way they may become identified with their profession. It sounds like almost a non-sense to say that you are not identifying with your profession. Nonetheless it's the way to go, it's better to identify with self.

The trace in my memory about physical and human baby is this: I am invited to a party at Jaqueline's, Anne Marie's sister, Anne Marie is one of my brothers' wife. I went there with my girlfriend at the time, Lorraine. I heard a baby crying. When I looked in the bedroom of the house, I saw him in bed alone, while everyone else, including his mother, is in the living room or outside talking, drinking and dancing. I sat on the bed for a moment trying to make the baby stop crying. After that I went outside to be with Lorraine. Instead of that I see her in a kind of lambada dance with a Haitian guy I do not know. No, I did not punch him on the face; I felt rather humiliated, grab Lorraine arm, left the party right away.

The DP may be, also, about value and priority, excrement being last in the line of value.

Last night, despite the gap of time between the day I had the DP and yesterday, I felt humiliated also. In fact I am in a humiliation period since last week when the Telephone Company disrupted communication in my telephone line for unpaid bill(Soul Exposed). I have a cell phone, but I cannot use my facsimile machine. I can also go to the library to access the Internet if I want. No big deal for me. Amanda, the roommate who were using my line, said she needed my phone for courses she is taking via the internet but cannot have one line by herself for being only 18 years old. And that I had to talk to Barb and/or Todd who rented the whole house in order for Amanda to use their telephone line. It was Barb I talked to. She left me downstairs where the small talk took place, went upstairs, leaving standing there, yield to say she is busy. I felt humiliated by that(the Soul Exposed again)

Then I thought that Amanda loves me, real romantic loves by which two souls merge from which follow a lot of goodies in term of self- realization. After knowing the pitiful state of my present and financial situation, her behavior became different. On Tuesday (January 28, 2003) afternoon she brought a man in the house toward whom she was behaving like a lover. So I felt humiliated by that too(the Soul Exposed again). At that age, 18, we tend to be promiscuous.

Sure we can love romantically and be in a monogamist relationships at 18 too. Do you agree with me?

Also, she is only 18 years old, allowed to make mistake, her character is not even complete yet.

The DP expresses how bad I feel about the present and apparent financial situation, although real love doesn't have something to do with it. In 1971 I received a letter in which it is announced the discontinuation of my position as teacher on call From Delta School Board. Teacher on call is the position I can occupy. It allows me to stay focused on your researches, my goals for not having to be too preoccupied too much with school stuff, correction, preparation, and report card. I go there, teach the classes according to the lesson plan prepared by the permanent teacher, and that's it. The day after I will probably be teaching another class, even at another school. At the beginning I stumbled a bit, at the time I was fired I became VERY GOOD at it. Mr. Laurence, a district principal, used to hide the card with my coordinates in the office, because I was receiving too many calls compare to the other teachers. But, since the year I received the wrongful dismissal lettern in 1991 I have never found the same position in other School District. I applied in Vancouver District at least a hundred times unsuccessfully. It is why I feel in shit financially speaking, have the above DP.

The soul has been exposed, however ther is the concept of child rearing and developing a self in the presence of one parent of by spending 30 minutes or so with the child everyday or according to a more convenient schedule, 30 minutes during which the child is the boss, but with your help. See more in Psychokinetic Telepathy.

> DP64. *The couple that I see have a child who makes me think of Duvalier. I hear them talking; it's like they are trying to go to "East Main."*

The Ministry of Health in Victoria has an office located on the East Side of Vancouver (east of Main Street). There is one in the West Side called west main. I used to do voluntary work for that Ministry. April 2000 was not my very best month in terms of peace of mind. I was about to move in this house, worried about the inhabitants. I didn't want to end up in a situation similar to the one I was moving from and having to move out again.

When I was volunteering for the ministry, there was a fundamental "restructuration" of the health department. They were trying to bring the administration close the grassroots. I became chairman of a Community Health Center that was in formation, once. Then I went to an office on Broadway street, met Fay to have background for an agenda. She was so idealistically minded. She thought of all the persons who were coming to that group as if there were saint. She said I had to ask during the meeting if someone else wanted to chair. It was the first time for me as a chairman, although I started that group by gathering their names in the library and inviting them to the meeting.

I was not an expert in chairing a meeting at that time, but I could learn rapidly if I was given the time to do it. I was so stupid by listening to Fay, asked the question during the meeting. Since then, vanished and gone, as Bruce would say, the new chairman cast me aside.

The Democratic Party was in power in Victoria then.

Was the Premier a worried person? Or is the position of President, Prime Minister, Premier is worrisome one? The DP seems to direct our attention toward that angle. It seems to be saying that Duvalier was a worried person, nonetheless, after his regime of terror in waking life, to say that he had a sick ego would be a pleonasm .At his time I was very young, but the fear of macoute (secret police created by him) was real and in me too. When he died he left a country with most of the inhabitants mentally cripple, the DP suggests that this fear contributed to my problems in Canada, in Vancouver. It's nothing compare to the ravages done to the psyche of a whole Haitian nation.

According to what I've heard, a lot Haitians have died because of Francois Duvalier. However, he was the first Haitian president who tried in the wrong way to finish a work started by Toussaint Louverture, pushed forward by Jean Jacques Dessalines. I feel proud of the last two, not so much of the first one, although he is not the only one who committed mass destruction in history. But still he was the first who tried to liberate the Haitians, the real Haitians! The bigger group of them who have not been liberated financially speacking yet. Duvalier gave political power to the mass of Haitians . Armed with that power, they killed rich Haitian persons, took what they have. Did he give them the instruction to do that? I don't know.

Arnold, my eldest entire brother, with whom I had a long telephonic conversation the same week than the DP, said to me that one of our brothers has a son who looks like Duvalier's son. I find this comparison puzzling, but it certainly was one of the triggers of the above DP.

DP.65 when I go back home, I find a great number of human beings there. I think it's not going to be easy to pass through them, but I open

the door, go forward, and attend my business.

Where I was living in Manitoba Street was at five minutes walk distance to Langara College, ten minutes walk distance to Oakridge Mall. I went to the mall almost everyday either to buy groceries or to the branch of the Vancouver public library that is in the mall. There are a lot of HBBs there during opening hours, partly why I see a lot of persons at my place in the DP. I go to the library that often to celebrate the goals that I was working at, the goals I am still working at presently. In the celebration (or reinforcement) of goals, there is a part when I imagine that a lot of customers in the front yard of place buying books. It is another part of the meaning of the DP.

The mentality in the library is somewhat strange. I have just been out of work, having not a cent in account. I had a bunch of unused business cards. I left them at the library bulletin board, after writing with a pen on them that I am looking for HBBs to tutor. In front of the bulletin board there are all sorts of newspapers, posters, you name it. Two days later I received a call from them saying that I had to go and pick them from the librarian desk, for business announcements are not allowed in the library. I pleaded for them to make an exception in vain. I was not very happy with them for that rule, thinking that it was mean to do that to me in this moment scarcity.

Later I thought that it was because they did not know my situation, or because they did not read the part of the cards written with a pen, and that to make an exception for me would be for them to create a precedent against their own rule, something which would not happen in a life time.

Then I remember it was not the first time they did the

same thing to me, asked myself if they found business as honorable as literature, for example, otherwise they would not have bias attitude against it. Or they might think business HBBs are able to place an ad in TV, newspaper. Or, the business cards may make them think of big corporations with tremendous amount of money power. There might have been even envied in their character, which brings to mind Mark Twain" few of us can stand prosperity. Another man's I mean."

Then there was a Karen who is a writer living in Toronto. She placed an ad at the library, announcing her workshop on how to publish a book. I did go to it. There was money involved in it. I had to pay to get in. I started by wondering where are the justice, concluding that, her announcement was acceptable for the library administrators because it was about books, even when there was money involved. It was my business cards that might put them off. They would not come to think that books are more important than students are, in a process of absurd identification.

Inside of the Oakridge mall near the main toilet, they let HBBs place their ads on the wall closed by. I started doing that. I received a lot calls one or two days after having placed the advertisement, the way I found the parents living on Cambie and 43rd (Our story is described a few DPs above). Shortly afterwards, they remove all the ads from the wall. I thought it was because of me, that they might have seen me there too many times, not liked my face, the color of my skin. After one success I was trying to consolidate, to find more students to tutor without paying for the ad. The administrators of the mall are business oriented. So they are not bias against business per se. The citation of Mark Twain may apply to them too. Anyway, I get the impression that almost everyone in Vancouver hate me, want me ro go and live on the street as others.

When I just move in this house on 16 the Avenue. One day I came back from the library, there were a big number of human beings having a party. There were so many of them that I had to bump in many in order to be able to reach my room. It's only later; I thought consciously that the party might have been to welcome me at the house. But, as I was not invited, as I was not told that, I went straight to my bedroom. I never asked Barbara about it. Yes, it is possible that it was a surprise party. Anyway, the men were coming to me with a disgusting homosexual attitude.

When I arrived here would not someone let me know that the party was because of me? That is so bizarre! Yes I am mind reader in the sense that I was dreaming of it a month before as described in the DP, but consciously, I didn't have a clue. In the note I wrote down after having the DP in April, there is no indication of a party for me. At that time I didn't know what the DP was about. As usual, when it's about future events, I know what I was dreaming about, after the events have occurred. Only rarely, I can predict what is going to happen, although I am not focusing on prediction now. I think that part of psychology is too light, should be delegated to lesser persons! Like psychics! No laugh, no fun, no beauty, no psychology, and no soul to expose.

CHAPTER XI

Friday April 21, 2000

DP66. I am involved in a lot of activities that I do not remember after the DP. It's like I am outside and worried about a $ 200 that I have left in the house. Where I am, a child appears with a glass of milk in his hands that he is holding so loosely that it's like it will fall. You say to him:

" Be careful! The glass is going to fall!".

Then he arranges himself to keep the glass straight and keep the milk in it. After that, I see a little girl in night gown, with something attached to her ears as music listeners, Then, I notice that someone was sitting attached to my back all the time *during the DP scene and try to find out who she is exactly.*

I would not leave money in the house on Manitoba Street; I had a coffee table that disappeared the day after. I do not remember if it was inside the living room or outside with other belongings, nothing worth mentioning, of value to me. I could not understand that someone could steal something so insignificant, although I had a similar experience last March. After renting a truck, you pick up the belonging from the storage store. Otherwise, it would cost too much to leave them there and get them later. Before going to the house, I asked the driver to pass to thrift store thinking that you could sell some the belongings I didn't need. There they said they do not buy them but they get them for free from owners who do not have space for them themselves. I had 8 feet of 2 chairs bought from an Ikea (Swedish) store. I let them on the sidewalk; they disappeared a few minutes later. I still have the sitting part of the chairs, but no feet.Said above)

In the past my behavior with friends was a bit strange. When I moved in Vancouver, I cut all links with the friends I had in Manitoba, all links with the ones I left in Montreal. I was traumatized by what I had to do for some of them. I could have got myself in big trouble because of that. The solution for me was to forget them all. I was going out often, did meet other souls all the time, among which to make other friends. It did not appear to me, then, the importance of keeping the good friends as it is now. Before leaving Montreal, I borrowed $200 from Bertrang, $ 200 from a professor, and $200 from Serge. That was years ago. I just hope they all still leaving. It would not be that easy for me to get in touch with them again and pay them back.

At that time, when I borrowed money from a friend or

some other sources, it was like in the deep down of my being I did not have the intention to pay them back. Nowadays, it is the opposite attitude that is true. I apply the principle " Do to others what you would like them to do to you" to every aspect of my life, including borrowing. In other words, I have the firm intention to pay back. I am not going to declare bankruptcy, although that is going to disturb me a bit on the financial side.

In the exercises of celebration my goals, the debts are included. So I think of them every day as well as my goals.

It may be one of the meanings of the $200 in the DP.

The dandling glass reminds me of a rule in psychology. When you see a child about to put his hand in fire, you do not reason with him. You just grab him and bring him away from the danger. You reason with him when the danger is not imminent. Otherwise he would have time to hurt himself. A little burn is ok, is in fact a lesson, but one that can destroy his body and self is not.

I have an MP3(may make unaware of our surrounding, at least distract us and causing an accident, the main reason why I do not use it) that was given to me while buying this computerm MP3 that I do not use, never having the time yet to read the instruction to make it work. Then, I have a stereo with surround sound. I like it very much. It was not very expensive, but it is the best I got for myself up to now. It is branched to TV, CD player, and video player.

The DP brings back to my conscience the bionic woman on TV in the eighties, and Graham Bell who, apparently wanting a real model of receiver to create the earring part of the telephone, asked his friend who was a doctor for a human ear taken from a corpse. He had it and the telephone was created.

I do not really know if I snore loudly while sleeping. Only once, in 3339 west 42nd Avenue, a certain Liza said she was about to come to my bedroom, gave it up when she heard me snoring. She was living in the adjacent bedroom. Debbie I slept with for the longest period of time was not in a position to let me know that even if I were snoring, for she was a big "snorer" herself. I had sleep disorder at that time, I had to see a sleep specialist to regain the night sleep. May be some girl I was sleeping with in the past did not tell me that I was a "snorer" but none of them wore earring device or sound blocker.

One of the person attached to my back is the family doctor I have been visiting since I was living at 3339 west 42nd Avenue, a while ago before I had the DP. When I was going to her clinic I was not aware of her liking, although when I went there she always made me walk to her office in front of her. I realized it recently, after I discovered her jealous of Heather, the roommate, or of younger woman in general. When Heather was about to come back to Vancouver for her studies at the end of August Beth was pressing subtly for me to become closer to her by calling the office of a specialist herself for me instead of leaving it to one of the secretaries, by being more kind toward me then. In September her attitude toward I had changed to doctor and patient relationships, She was kind of gave up for not materializing her plan on time, before the competition with Heather or other young ladies I could meet at the university or may be she was only interested in winning the competition by seducing me before Heather arrives in Vancouver. America is a society of winners as you might say.

Another time she says "you are not young. What are you waiting for?". At the end of December she could not look at me in your eyes to ask me to keep in touch after wishing her to have nice holidays. I figured out that it was because of her feelings for me and because she was going to be busy with family. As I just mentioned, it might be a play, a distancing play this time. For I felt sad before I went to the appointment, and after it, and she did not look to me in my eyes while talking to me.

What would she find attractive in the back of man, of me? I have no idea, except that actress Jennifer L. is admired also for her prominent back bottom; hence it is a sexy future in the western culture. Because Beth is a doctor, I can not ask her freely about her feelings for me without stomping her high professional standard code of conduct . So I am only guessing. I know she has a child by seeing her picture on the wall of her office. I started by thinking she was married. That was a put off on my part. I tend to go toward rather romantic relationships, which are exclusive. After she asked me the question above, I started again to think that she may be a single mother, divorced or whatever, but did not have a man during those days.............

She is the girl attached to my back in the DP for one meaning, later who knows who it will be?

DP67. The picture of a man with a broken arm...........

I am washing a pair of pant in a very small pot, forcing it all to go inside of the pot, after turning the legs inside out.

The pants are blue jeans the most popular clothe in North America. I started wearing it in Haiti, very young. It was unusual, for this kind of clothing is worn only by the so called peasant class, HBBs living in the back country, most of the time analphabet in Haiti. I was student with intelligence a little bit sophisticated, living in Port-au-Prince, the capital, or Dieurond a few kilometers from it, I was living at both places, days of the week in the capital, weekend at Laplaine. So I was not in their category as such, but did have the feeling that HBBs cannot be categorized that way, that we are basically the same with roughly the same shape the same intelligence and worn the jean anyway. When I came to America, and saw that almost everyone is wearing it, it was not a surprise for me.

America is not communist, but there is certainly a tendency of social harmony revealed by the generalization of blue jean wearing. After I left university, started working in the real world, I wanted to shake the sour taste of all doctrines off my mind, especially the communist doctrine. But I am still struggling to succeed this undertaking. I had many DPs on it, still having some more. I already wrote that the deepest idea in the communist theory is to see that abundance for all is possible and to seek its implementation. I do not know if it is clear for everybody but everybody has a sense of that, even in the capitalist America.

The first part of DP 67 recalls my desire to have bigger muscles in my arms, wider wrist in the forearm, something that could be done easily with steroid, however buying it is not quite a legal activity, the practice is not without controversy health wise either. I notice that persons in wheel chair, especially men most of time, have big arms. So steady lifting of barbell will do the job too, what I will try as soon as I have the opportunity to do it. Now, I just have a pair dumbbell of 45 kg each, no time to go to exercise in a community center where there are all the physical exercise tools. In my goals for physical excise there is sport equipment. So I will have everything I need for that purpose in the basement of my house too.

When I just started to live in Vancouver, I met a man at the English Bay in a wheel chair. He was amazing. He encouraged me to go forward, approached the nice ladies who are always there in summer, sun bathing. He had big arms always wearing white shirt and white pant. Each time,

I meet him with a new woman. Sometimes, they are the one who are pushing his wheel chair,

something extraordinary that love does, although his love for these women stood on a shaky ground, otherwise he wouldn't need so many.

Strangely enough, yesterday, Amanda said to me that she was not going to sleep in her bedroom for a few days from last night. I think that it may be because of this DP I started to process yesterday with the picture of someone with a broken arm that may cause some fear of me in her. I know that she is reading my mind, the reason why one girl was wearing a device in her ear in DP 66, suggesting that she has distant hearing ability- even if the information she is getting is not clear. She said once she is afraid of me. I never yell at her, mad at her. Why is she afraid of me? I have the project of taking her hands and put them on my body while saying to her that I am human, like her, not an extraterrestrial being.

I understand better now Amanda and Heather's behavior related to me. When I try getting closer to them emotionally speaking, they both rush into another relationships. I was puzzled by the behavior for a long period of time, for years in regard to other women. I find out it is because getting closer to them is perceived by them as threat to their autonomy. Their rushing into another relationships is an act of self-assertion, related to separateness. When men are pushed by this impulse of independence they start a quarrel. My better understanding of her now should be reflected in my own behavior in relation to her. We have been interacting for six months. The fear should be vanished by now. It was a surprised for me yesterday when I noticed it might be still in her.

The broken arm refers to many issues. Besides what is discussed above, there is also the fact that when I first started to write in infancy, I used my left hand. Later in elementary school I was forced to use the right hand, it is like my body does not forgive the mistake, and that there is always a fight between the two hands. Is there an inner political conflict expressing itself through my hands? Not easy to say. I am definitely apolitical, even though I have some political ideas. The only aspect of it, which is not totally resolved yet, is that I know that not doing active politics, not placing myself in the left or the right or the middle in the politicai continuum, not belonging to a political party, is an avoidance behavior, totally unproductive. Being like that is deciding in advance to take what comes at that level. That is what I do not quite accept yet. I do participate actively in the cause of everything that happens to me .You do not want to make a choice to take what comes politically speaking, the reason for the potential inner conflict.

Recently I try to resolve a conflict between two nations United States and Iraq about to go to war against each other by sending a fax to one leader Saddam Hussein. May be I should try to resolve other conflicts when they appear in the future and so become specialized in resolving this kind of conflict. By doing this, the political role I would play will be enough to resolve the potential inner conflict in me. In Vancouver I had always occupied (will probably always do the same even if I am living somewhere else) a function during Election Day either of Canada, either of British Columbia. That too serves to help resolve the potential political inner conflict. If I take what comes in politics, my mind will have a tendency to give me what comes in other life domains instead what I desire. Instead of my goals, for example, i would have to take what comes. The calculation is based on my values; one of them would be to take what comes in politics, if you did not do any political activity.

DP68. She asks me to get her some

water in a wineglass. I go outside to get her the water, find out that the whether is very tumultuous. Not wanting to be pushed in the water by the wind. I turn back walking toward the house. Then I see a woman wearing a blue dress leaving. I am surprised, asking myself if it's the one who was inside.

In my notes, it was after I gave Barbara the security deposit for the rent of this bedroom I had the DP. After receiving it her attitude was positively very different toward me. I thought at that time, still thinking that way roughly 3 years later, I could have made love with her if I was very awake to the experience. It is because there was a deep connection between her and me that I did not know then. The connection is related to an experiment I am doing that I cannot reveal yet. She said she was about to go on vacation on her own, something she hasn't done since a while. She invited me upstairs where she lives with her family, while she is writing the receipt for the deposit. I did not go inside, afraid to be with her alone while under the grip of a big sexual desire. It was hot she was wearing green short and a top.

The DP prompts to my mind Paulette, a Haitian woman I lived with for about one year. It was my first days in Canada after a long period of sexual abstinence in San Maartin. So I had with Paulette a very active sexual life. making love with her felt so good sometimes; it is like I was never going to be able to finish a session. When she finished, she always asked me to go and get her a glass of water It was romantic love with all its attributes. we were living with a group of other Haitians at first; we left that house, rented an apartment near by on Saint Hubert Street to be able to be alone with each other. She was the one who welcome us to Canada: Laurent her cousin, Michel, a friend I met in elementary school and with whom I cane to Canada from San Maarten, and me.

It was a day I will not forget not only because the door of a bright future was just open in front of me, but also for what happened to me at the immigration. In San Maarten, I was working with Cedric in the in the kitchen of Mullet Bay Beach Hotel. Before I left for Canada, he gave me a big needle, and asked me to buy a new one for him. At that time (and now, too, more or less) the only drug I knew was cigarettes, alcohol, the usual pharmaceutical drug like aspirin. I have never heard, then, of the other drugs. The immigration found the needle in your luggage, detained me for about 4 hours, made body search, long questioning. I only know now that it was a big deal. I still do not know if Cedric whom I thought was a friend was malicious with me by trying to sabotage my move to Canada or not or if he was simply a drug addict.

I started to work the same week I came to Canada in a factory of cloth on Chabanel Street in Montreal. I worked later in another factory of cloth where I bought a bunch of clothes for my nieces living in Queens, New York. I worked later in Restaurant 600 and in a Cheese factory at Brossard a suburb of Montreal. There are one pleasant and one unpleasant experience still vivid in my memory from the cheese factory. Which one do you want me to tell you first? Ok! Let's go for the first one. I was working from midnight to 8 AM. I used to cross a girl coming to work day shift in the same place. She walked at one side of the street to come in the factory; I walked the other side of the street to go home. One morning I crossed the street said hi to her, as she smiled, I proceeded to have a little talk with her and got her telephone number.

There was a factory friend waiting for me when it happened, now I am thinking it might have been because I wanted to impress him I went to meet Yvonne like that, to show him the skills I had at that time with women. Or may be it was because of hard work, adrenaline rush from the factory work. As written elsewhere in this work, it was my first days in Canada, I was wild. The big number of opportunities to make money to live raised my emotional volume to an unusual level. In San Maartin and in Canada life conditions are somewhat similar. Living conditions was better in Saint Martin than they are in Haiti.

The unpleasant incident remembered from the cheese factory was about a certain Norman who was working in the same place. One morning, he saw me talking to Yvonne I met while I was going home, she is going to work, he spit a racist injure, something like dirty Niger. I have been going out with Yvonne for about three months already. So the incident should not be the only cause of the later demise of the relationships, but it was one fallen brick off that wall though.

Before I met Yvonne, I was having some difficulty in the relationships with Paulette. When her mother came to live with her from Haiti, Paulettte's attitude toward me changed drastically. Plus her mother couldn't not accept me living with her without being married. They have a strong religious background. I did not want to get married with Paulette, newly living in Canada, I did not have definite goals yet, was just searching. From the cheese factory one night I called Paulette to let her know that I was not going to her place. That was it with that relationships, vanished and gone as Bruce would say. Then, I met Yvonne, after about three months it ended. I did love Yvonne, despite short period of time I spent with her; she was the first white woman I went out with.

CHAPTER XII

Sunday April 23, 2000

DP69. The image of a leg with many traces

I used to go from Dieurond to LaBoule many times, something like average twice a day, when I was infant and adolescent. The first village is where my father and mother are born as altrady said. The second one is where my past away father had two houses. The first one was build when your mother and father got married. The second house was build years later. After my mother past away, my father built it to live with Mercida. There are many traces or trails to take to go from Dieurond to LaBoule. One of them I used often brings to an intersection. Just before it, there is a house in which lived Frappe(hit), the nickname of a man who had a sick leg from which he past away. He was Arnold's godfather, the brother living in New York. I am not sure if it is because of Arnold I was obsessed with Frappe since the first year of my psychic integrating activity, psycho synthesizing, since the first year I started to really pay attention to my dreams by recording and analyzing them everyday for reinforcement, that was 1989, or if my obsession was due to that I passed in front of his house so many times from Laboule to Deurond and vice versa, or to the graveyard in the nearby or if the obsession was indicating poltergeist that I diecovered later.

It may be also that I was trying to awake myself to the poltergeist , that psychological phenomenon observed in Germany in which there are noises, telephone ringing, radio playing loud in an office without apparent cause, and where it was discovered that most of the time a girl of twenty years old about was having a severe trauma, then was Psychokinetically causing the trouble in the vicinity without being aware of it, without physical means, just by her trouble feelings.

Trace is equivalent to trail, also to mark, memory. May be in the past human beings used to think that memory resides in the body, especially in the legs. Researches have demonstrated that memory is in the psyche, the mind, and they all are non-substantial, need no physical container, have no physical content. But one can imagine the psyche as a person with arms and legs, etc, the mind as a person with arms and legs etc, and say that memory is in one leg of the mind.

It reminds us of "Without a Trace", the television series, in which plays Poppy Montgomerry and others.

> *DP70. The woman I am with has very sensitive melons. I am passing my hands on them lightly, touching, and caressing them. It feels good, like touching velvet. She reacts with some exciting sighs. At the end, she gets up, saying she is going to prepare herself some food.*

It is a desire to get closer to a woman, a desire to touch

someone else9Or was the woman pregnant?), things I did plenty but years before the occurrence of this DP. Or it may be only a way of practicing the sense of touch in DP. For in order to keep all your senses alive I make a point of incubating them and having them in my DPs as often as possible.

I cannot help thinking of Shirley, a roommate the first time I started to live in share accommodation. She is of Irish ancestor. She had small breasts, but you bet they were very sensitive. Obviously I did not have a sexual encounter with her. I know about her sensitivity by her reaction when one of her fingers was inadvertently pricked while watering a plant in the house. I was close by she came to show it to me, so I touched her finger, she sighed as if she was having an orgasm. Maxim the chronological 75 years old landlord was momentarily hospitalized after a sickness. Maxim was the best landlord I had. At Christmas Eve, she always had a big party in her house with lot of guesses and human beings who lived in the house before and who just dropped by. She was a very good cook and a very good host, skills she developed when her husband was alive.

In regard to her sexual behavior, she was very strange. Shelly, her adopted daughter, said to me once that she was sleeping with her adopted son, and that she came on to her once which made Shelly furious. One day, I saw a rat in my suite, I ran upstairs to ask for rat poison. You found her lying down on a coach nude while Shirley was sewing. Imagine! Had they just made love together? One was about 25 years old chronologically speaking, the other 75, two women. They were exposed.

She used to drop her panties at the escalator close to my bedroom initialing sexual encounter between her and me? May be.

Nonetheless, she was a nice lady, at that age all women

are nice ladies anyway. I have mown her lawn; fixed her fence for free all the time while I was living in her house 4 years.

Was the woman in the DP Poppy?

> DP71. *There are many human beings around me. I draw a circle, left top and right disjoint. I show it to them and say" you see it is necessary to finish it, otherwise you can bring the rest of the world with you in your fall.*

At first, I represented myself by a rectangle with a sun inside. Then, I did not like it anymore, replaced it by an octagon with a sun in the middle. Then again, I found the picture too complicated, not easy to make rapidly by hand. I changed it for the simpler figure with six angles, and then again , I kind of get disinterested in the representation of myself, after being reminded by a reading that all we can have of our selves is an opinion, that it's a being not easy to comprehend.

Now I represent myself by a a square directed out by arrows. Inside of the square there are a sun with a few rays, a bird standing on one ray, a heart on another ray. the bird representing the spirit; the heart representing the soul, the sun representing the body.

In the above DP is the symbolization of myself, also the symbolization the universal Self. I did not pay any particular attention to it, when I had the DP that was not going to be processed right away anyway. It was not the first time I had the compulsion to draw acircle. Inside of the first circle I draw there were some diagonal line that crosses one another in the middle of the circle, forming the consciousness in that area with the conscious self in the very middle like a dot, and a few v shaped parts representing different parts of the psyche, with the unconscious self represented by a dot in the perimeter of the circle.

At the beginning of my psychic integration or self-specification, I was not sure of anything; I was running around a bit, inadvertently casting aside important concept.

I still do not have a grant to be able to do the research with some peace of mind. I imagine that if some of my experimentations were complete, the results published, that would allow me to find a grant from private foundation, even from the two governments. It is not the case yet. Nobody knows what I am up to. They might even be thinking that I sleep most of my time, that there are no goals I am trying to create. So, I am barely surviving financially speaking. Even then, I still have to make some difficult choices, bugs of defeat place themselves in my way, that would prevent me from continuing if I do not do something about them. If I had enough time to take some courses at UBC, I would have better time living on student loan from British Columbia and Canada government. Then very little time would be left for the research. It is not like I am chronologically 12 years old, with plenty of time left to play around with, not like the eternity pills is created yet.

The DP is saying if the society does not allow me to continue the research, to create some goals I could take them(HBBs) with me in my fal(bird falling from the sky)

DP72. Demosthene will go buying some stamps or something similar.

One day, in a bus on 41st Avenue going to Oakridge Mall, I met a woman. She boarded the bus at Kerrisdale downtown, came and sat beside me. After a little chat with her, she lets me know were she was working. Guest what?

It was a household stationery store. I was so shy, clumsy, I felt so awkward when I went there and saw her working at her boot or manufacture table. Yes there was a lot of human beings circulating around, other workers and customers. But I could have gone there prepared with a business card to slip on her table while living. I didn't do that, talk to her a bit and left.

The first time I you came in contact a Demosthene was in grade school. He was in it at the same time than his less younger brother Arnold. I am reminded of them in the DP probably because I also have brother with the same name Arnold. But that is not the point. When I was in that class my father had to move around a bit from one city to the other for work purposes. I had to redo the same class one more years. I think it was a mistake to make me go to the same class twice. The mind as you know it, it doesn't require an arithmetic progression to develop intellectual and other skills. With proper preparation I could have even start to go to school in grade 5 or 6 without any problem. Anyway, I finished that class with the highest mark compare to the other pupils, and kept it that way for many classes to come.

Demosthene reminds me also of another incident that was a puzzle for me in the past, but that is not now. Clermont is one of my cousins. I was tutoring him geometry in grade 8 once in the presence of his friend with first name Demosthene as in the beginning of this paragraph. Demosthene found that I was doing such a good job with Clermont, asked me to tutor him geometry also. During the first tutoring session with him I had a mental block to such a point that I had to stop tutoring the next time. I was asking myself why was I so brilliant with Clermont, not with Demosthene. I thought that it was because Clermont were my cousin, Demosthene a stranger. I still cannot really explain it, although it is clear for me now that emotion plays a great role in learning and all intellectual and mental activities. Demosthene had a big scarce on his head near one ear. At that time I was thinking also that his hard head could not make the logical connection easily. It is clear for me now that his head almost has nothing to do with his mind, that there is no such thing as a bony head as related to the mind, psyche, mind being non- substantial, non physical.

Of course, there is the Greek author, Demosthene, the DP may be about his philosophy and that philosophy can be the ubutuator of metaphysics and the headache concepts which ca bring the world to an end.

> DP72. There is a caterpillar and a car parked in the garage of the house. It's like I am doing something in order for them to move by themselves, to park themselves in the garage. Then I move in front of them, look at them; realize the enormous wheel of the caterpillar. The thought of it moving by itself frightens me. I give up the idea of machine having a will to move. on thei own.

In a science magazine, I read once that when the computer science is developed enough some robots will almost have will and then they will replace human beings by killing them, for being stronger, more intelligent than them. Of course we are in science fiction. It is the trigger of the DP. It will not happen that way even in million years. For the number of brain cells is 10 billion, the number of bits of information possible in a lifetime is 15 billion. Computers processes information with sixteen bits at a time, like in a credit card. The number of bits can be more than that by more combinations, but wouldn't be practical, printing machine would have to be wider, and paper size would have to be different etc, on one hand. On the other computer, no matter how sophisticated it is, cannot work as a psyche, unsubstantial, then with capacity of processing information with an infinite number of bits, wider than the universe. Nonetheless, yes, if we are not careful enough, there is a possibility for the psyche to be relegated to a back room compare to the nice machines we can have, which will do everything for us. The machine will do everything you ask it to do by pushing a button. Your psyche will not function like that. It would tell you everything you desire to know, do everything you want him to do, except that you would forget all that in a very short while. Then the psyche will take over, in other word the psyche will do things for you even when you are not fully aware of it. The psyche cannot be compare with a machine really, psyche as defined in the Unknown Reality written by Jane Roberts: "disposition of organic energy; the self maintaining and reproducing pattern of struetures of an organism conceived as power is called psyche"

Or only one self can do the specification of oneself. As soon as someone else is helping to do it, it is not self-specification anymore. May be that what the DP with Demosthene in it was alluding to, that democratic good intention and action has its limits.

I am for science all the way, although most of the time nowadays science is taking care of the superficial thing. I do not think you human should shy away from creating a new concept, when all the requirements are already in existence. The purpose of living according to me is to seek the betterment of living conditions all the time. It is a task to carry out relentlessly. Cloning human being may not be something to do for it is bound to or it could bring more diseases than anything else does. So where is the amelioration of living conditions in that? But working with stem cell looks hopeful. The cells of some of the body's organs such as the heart, the nerves, don't renew themselves. Implanting stem cells in these organs will be useful, will allow the treatment of back damage for example.

Computer replacing the psyche, unlikely, HBBs living like a machine, a sure thing.

And then there is the idea of biological movement, meaning intrinsic accomplishment. You just wait it is going to be done by itself. It is why we do not actualize ourselves sometimes waiting for it to happen instead of pushing for the actualization, waiting for it to be accomplished instinctively. The DP above allude to that no such a thing exists.

> *DP73. Somebody who is going to school and who is 16 years old, a few more human beings that would like to have the same age.*

I don ot really want to be 16 years old, For I did not really like that period of my life. I do want to have a body of 25 years old all the time, because there is no rational explanation for it to be different. If 7 or 9 years old can grow old very quickly; the chronological age is not really a factor in getting old.

Monday April 24, 2000

> *DP74. There is a kind of war between two groups of human beings in which I am involved. They keep me in one of these two groups because I speak French. I leave it, rejoin the other group. The fight has taken place. The group in which I am now move to another place far from the*

opposite group. I am at the end of the group; I see a vehicle moving at a vertiginous speed toward me. I am asked to pass the news until it reaches those in the front line.

the time was to moving from the house on Manitoba Street to the one on 16th Avenue, it was like I was in a war, figuratively speaking, moving from one group of fighters to another. In waking life, I wanted to move out to have more space, I paid $360 for the bedroom on Manitoba Street, and I am paying $375 for the one on 16thAvenue although I am responsible for $ 375 more, but I get that from the person living in the bedroom next to mine. In my bedroom I fit everything I do not need in the closet under the rack of cloths. In the house on Manitoba Street, part of my belongings stayed outside, part in the living room, part in the hall. That accommodation was physically too small.

Then, there was, also, the question of homosexuality. The other 3 men on the same floor were bisexual. When I first move to this house on 16th Avenue in May 2000, my closest roommate was Tamara. I am still thinking of her as if she is a goddess, the most attractive woman in existence. But was it difficult for me with a man who was visiting her from New Zeeland, He was harassing me sexually literally. It was also difficult for me for the same reason with the male roommate I had after Tamara left for England. Jonathan was also harassing me sexually. It is still difficult for me these days for the same reason with Todd, Barbara's husband. He too started to harass me sexually since the day I moved in this house. I still have a note written on the wall in which I write some of the details of his harassment.

I would like to say that the sexual harassment in the house on Manitoba Street was not the determining factor in the moving out that house, for the same is happening in this house. I am still living in it in 2003. But I ca not say that really. Todd is living upstairs with Barbara, his wife and their two kids. His sexual harassments were weak. In the house on Manitoba, I was living in the same floor than 3 other men who were not in any family relationships like Todd.

During the war in the DP I felt weak unable to gather my thoughts. I bet I would not feel quite like that in a real war. I would be rather over the consequence of the minimal financial situation in which I was and I still am. This situation may have been why I felt weak during the DP. Or in the FP I should be gighting some HBBs for one reason or another, it why I got weak.

In Quebec, I was in front of this group of human beings in a way. My major occupation was studying at colleges and universities. In the west part of Canada the picture in that sense is mixed. I monitored French in two School Districts, studied at two universities, and taught in schools. Many times like when I was moving out the house on Manitoba Street, and now, I find myself in minimal financial situation. I started to speak English really in Manitoba. So, language plaid a part in my financial demise in the West part of Canada. The time it took me to get a certain command of the Shakespeare's language, I was, financially speaking, already done with.

Unless everybody has to be the same, has to contribute the same thing to the society in which he\she lives, I too, despite moments scarcity in which I find myself, do contribute something to my society, by open a door for someone, wishing everyone well, etc. In this house I am responsible for the hole floor in which I live, meaning that I have to make sure there is somebody in the other bedroom in order to pay the $750 every month. Presently I am focusing in my "scientific investigation and research" as

Ackroid would say, but before I was involved in many useful undertakings to this society, and afterward I will be useful to many societies by other endeavors and by my writings.

Of course I move from one group to the other. I do not identify with a group, a person or a thing, but identify with myself, the center of consciousness: will, awareness and inner power, etc.. I <u>identify with infinite supply and eternally perfect substance, meaninc the Creator</u>

Although not belonging to a political group in Canada seems to be the reason why I am not always doing well economically speaking, I will continue to be so, I will continue not to do partisan politics.

> *DP76. Some human beings come to my place for some reason. I see vaguely that they are men and women of a certain chronological age. I keep saying "The skunk stinks" for no reason.*

At 3339 west 42 and Avenue, one law student rented a bedroom from me once. He was married, but for some reason they had to live separately for a while. I even sold him an extra mattress I had for $43. He was a bisexual who approached men by talking to them about skunk. How do I know all this of him? That will be for you the reader to find it out.

CHAPTER XIII

Tuesday April 25, 2000

DP75. In my hands there are a lot of things, including a few cooked corn on the cubs. There are some children around, I give them some of the food and felt somewhat satisfied.

At that time I had a lot of belongings I did not really need, I gave some to a thrift store at the corner of Granville street, some to Brian who was a roommate in the house I was about to depart from the house Manitoba Street. I was satisfied in giving those things to Brian after asking him if he wants them. He used to bring a glass full of brandy or some other expensive liquor to me in my bedroom. After drinking so much hard alcohol at once I felt good and slept well. I know that Brian was expecting something from me(he is bi, I am heter) . That partly why I was content to give him those belongings in compensation. for the alcohol.

Corn is a cereal very much used by the mass in Haiti. It is cultivated a lot, but is not exported, is used rather for local consumption. Dry, grinded, and cooked, with beans, you have a popular food in that country and may be in Santo Domingo also where there were as many slaves as in Haiti at the beginning of the colonization of the island. As far as I am concerned, I never liked it very much; I preferred rice. Some of the half brothers of mine believed that it gave them strength. The mostly exported food in Haiti are sugar, coffee, bananas, and cocoa. The culture of rice is also significant there, may be a small quantity of it is used for exportation.

I was distributing the corn on the cub to the children as I used to distribute homework in the classroom. So in this DP the teaching aspect of me was like an underdog. Corn reminds us of horn. It's like teaching the children how to be mean, is what really happening in the schools of the world presently. For the information they receive there is based on conscious knowledge, the ego. Most of the time it is the sick aspect of the ego which is developed, instead of nner harmony, inner strength to go with the external power.

Before they used to beat the student for motivation purposes(practically child abuse). That was a bizarre motivational tool. Yes emotion is good for learning, but it is more like positive emotion or mild negative emotion. Beating the kids to make them perform, what I used to do myself when I did not know better, years ago, is too hot an emotion, bound to cause him more damage than good, bound to make of him a violent adult, even a violent criminal. No wonder, violence and war are still the preferred tools used on the planet to solve problem.

However, there are so many ways to motivate the learner, to get him involved. In the learning domain before it used to be only the baton. Now it is the baton and the carrot with a tendency to favor the baton. The perfect attitude is to use only the carrot, may be impossible in dynamic life, nonetheless we must keep it in perspective as far as learning is concerned, especially with children emotionally still weak, given that adults are not always able to control their emotions, let alone children.

The beating to motivate was a lazy idea and coward also. Why do not we go and beat someone who can punch us back in the face? Heraldo the TV man made me realize this, although it was in context of violence toward woman. Violence against women and children is the manifestation of the most cowardice act; repulsive act that should never be. You arere beating the kids for performance, but they are in a learning environment, which essentially means to stumble, make mistake.

The School Superintendent give me some liquor the first time I met him at about mid night my first moments in Manitoba, touched me were he was not supposed to. That too was violence against me. I was dismissed from my position at Delta School Board (Survivor), without an explanation. That too was violence against me. A professor tried to get me in a love relationships with her, knowing that I was in a no win situation in a relationships with a professor I don't like that way, I tried to find some help from her superior. Instead, the dean said to me that I must look for counseling, insinuating that it was dementia. That too was violence. So violence is everywhere in the school environment. Ne myself I find the forcefull homosexuality and other sexual acts that is going the universities, a sickness.

DP76. There is a lot of water on the park. It's like a boat had just passed in the street. There is a child who clings to one of my legs and who is hungry. It is, also, like I erase myself from the scene in order to detach him from my leg?

Child for creation I am after, it describes the situation in which I find myself right now. The DP may be about sexuality so about love. It may also about flooding with water everywhere in such a way that we need boat to move around, It nay be about all natural devastating events that create famine and hunger in Haiti Africa, anywhere in the world. The hunger can be seen also as sexual craving .

> DP77. *Working at something, somebody appears behind me and disappears. At that moment, I am standing, thinking how to repair a mistake I have made. Then I go back and forth trying to repair the mistake.*

It is to give a path to your wild imagination. during DP beings can appear and disappear at any moment. In that level of reality (incomplere level of reality) we can have an accident, making love and being the viewers of those acts at the same time. Not easy to comprehend for everything is happening at faster than light speed.

> DP78. *Someone is advised to be a candidate to become the president of the United State s and violate the laws of that country.*

I do not know what it means, cannot link it to any event of my life,either of the world.

Wednesday April 26, 2000

> DP79. *There is a dispute between some human beings. One of these beings thinks that nobody likes him, for that what he was told when they came to pick him up. The pickup in*

which he is picked up is covered with some kind of (Bush) leaves.

I think it's about the war that is about to happen between the United States and Iraq. Last year, November or December 2002, I had a DP on Arsenio and some light. As he used to close his first TV show by saying "Peace", I interpreted the DP as if that war was not going to be. When I heard at Entertainment Tonight that Arsenio was going to host a new show, I realized, then, the DP might have not meant peace, but rather that the comedian was going to host a new show. Before knowing that I was up beat about the possibility of peace. Today I am not, although we can never be hundred percent sure about what is going to happen in the future. What will Saddam do next?

Yesterday, in the news on TV, I heard that the Canadian government sponsored a new initiative for peace. I think the intention is right, but the move itself is wrong. September 11 did not happen in Canada nor in the other allied countries in disagreement with the United States on this war. So they do not have the right perspective. The Americans have suffered, they know that we cannot opt for peace at any price, that sometimes to have peace, we have to fight. Because the disagreed countries like Russia, France, China, have big gas contract with Iraq to protect, that there is political divergence between the present government of Canada for being liberal, and the present government of the United States for being conservative, there are many reasons to disagree with the United States.

They forget that democracy, market economy, despite their pitfall, are the best economic concepts we have now, consequently, must be promoted side by side with peace. They forget that only democracy and peace in Iraq will be able to bring a better life for the great majority of humans beings in Iraq, the middle East, and the oriental countries, hence, appease the mind of the rest of the world in regard to terrorism. Everyone is speculating on the intention of the Americans, thinking that that they want to fight to have fuel market monopoly. May be, but they are they the only one capable of liberating the human beings in Iraq off the grip of powerful dictatorial government.

How about that?

There is the treat of being ambushed in the DP too.

> *DP80. At work, I am sitting on chair facing another worker. There is a wooden stick that I throw at him that he catches and throws back at me. After a certain time I think about work, decide to stop.*

Two men playing with a stick in a DP, it's look like homosexuality to me. Or was it one-man one woman? Or do I become homophobic? Or was it a fight? Or, is it simply there to liberate some kind of energy? Or the men be in competion to get the love or the favor of a woman.

> *DP80. It's like three human beings working in the same office: one other man, one woman, and I. The woman is younger than the other man. She needs a new pair of shoes. The other man suggests that I go with her to a shoe store to buy it for her. My answers that "It's not necessary".*

Alice came from South Africa. We took the same Sky train at Main Station. We both got off at Grandville Station and went to The Bay store there. As I saw her looking a bit lost, I approach her and asked her if she needed some information. That way we became boyfriend and girlfriend little time after. We went out for about 2 years.

She found work at Sterling where they sell women's shoes in the Pacific Mall. Then the relationships between her and me got bad. May be I was too much cut up from the world by the research and she wanted to do as much experiences as she can at her 25 years old. Then again her South African background were slightly different than the North American one. Then again, I was not working for a salary at that particular period of time. I suffered a bit and the relationships with her had to go.

Shoe may be an allusion to soul as well

The DP reminds me of her and one of my most cherish desires to hear them talking about The United States of Africa or the African Federation or whatever the political shape they would want to give it.

> DP81. There are many HBBs in the party. It is like everybody is lying down, including me. There are Anglophones, francophones, Haitians, and some beings of the animal species. As if somebody pushes a dish of food in front of me for the first time, and that I push it back. The same moves are repeated a couple of times. At the end I say if it's happened again, I'm going to throw it out through the window. Then, a black woman appears; I feel satisfied, take her hands, and pull her toward me.

The dish makes me think of the lottery game in the sense that the money gathered at each game is to many like foo given to many fronm a dish. If it is the case, then I nisbehave in the DP, meaning I did not take the dish, I did not take the money for being to oblivious to the situation, to myself, to the extraordinary thing I can do by discovering mysrlf and being it.

The black woman could represent my mother, one of my entire sisters or half sisters.

Thursday April 27, 2000

> *DP82. A group of musicians is playing a musical piece. There is a man of short height who plays the violin, who is obliged to stand beside the group in order to be able to do both play and see the director at the same time. The director is standing at the back of the group.*

Last night (February 23, 2003) I watched the Grammy Award on TV. I did not even remember the content of this DP I had in April 2000; last Friday I had only the time to write the date in the computer. I did not remember if there was going to be a Grammy, nor if I was going to be able to watch it, being able to take only two TV channels: Global Television and the channel 3 or Radio Canada. I was ironing cloth, the TV was on mute and closed captioning, and I was listening to classical music at the same time. It was after the ironing at about 8:30 PM I noticed what was going on. The DP, world events, and me were in perfect synchronization without even consciously knowing it.

I saw him and listened to Bruce Springteen Street music! Ed Bradley, Ashanty, Sheryl Crowe, the famous Avril who bows, and Norah Joanes who swept the floor by taking home 5 awards. It was the first time I saw her; heard later on the Fox radio station in Vancouver, that she sold a lot of albums through word of mouth publicity. One presenter of the Grammies said that he would like the war atmosphere to vanish as soon as possible to be able to come back to peacetime. All in all, it was a pleasant evening in the company of the Americans crème de la crème on TV. It was the celebration of excellence, not just in the crème de la crème, but, also, in every human being, whether it is exploited or not. I wish there would be days like that more often.

We can compare a HBB's psyche to an orchestra. Psyche with different parts, such as body, the soul and the spirit and the I working in harmony when we are not alien to ourselves. "In Love and the World" Robert Sardelo gives a description of the I: "fixed, has more to do with the future, creative, encompasses both the individual and the world".

The I in comparison with the ego: 'result of the past, accumulation of experiences, empirical sense of ourselves, which ends up to be identified with the body"

The I is what we have when our individual soul meets the Soul of the World. In other words we have a sense of I in the context of the world, in the presence of other individuals.

In waking life Bruce was the person I met at the Ministry of Economic Development and Housing. Apparently he became recently the manager of a whole section in the ministry. That may be connected, with me, in other words, I was may be the creator of his promotion, as well as the fact that Norah Joanes won 5 Grammies, although I am not able to give more details of her connection with me for the moment. But the connection with Bruce is clear. When I was in secondary classes, Mercida of a a darker skin color than me had a son, Ironce, who is of very light skin color . She was living with my past away father now equally of a very dark color of skin. Together they had 8 children, excluding Ironce for comprehension sake Anyway, human

159

beings around were speculating that Ironce was not the son of my father, that he was rather of Bruce's son, Bruce is of the same color of skin than Ironce, was the Maire of Croix-des-Bouquets the suburb of Port-au-Prince, where was the administration of all the surrounding smaller villages including LaBoule where Mercida and my father were living together.

It was nothing of my concern; I could not have done anything about it, about Mercida sleeping around. My father was always away for weeks or for months. When he was away for long time, working at place far from LaBoule, he usually had a woman where he was working. So, Mercida was not unjust to him in a way. Nonetheless I felt so bad about it, that it is still governing my life a bit years after the event.

When my father was away, I spent the best part of the time with my grand mother living at Dieurond, a village next to LaBoule. I felt better in her environment than in Mericida's, not only because she was not my mother, but also because she was mad and was vociferating her venomous feelings quite often. It is to suppose that she was not happy with her living arrangement with my father away quite often. When Soys (pronounce Swais), my father came back home a couple of times, he came to look for me at my grand mother's place, asked me to kneel down and beat me without any apparent reason. That puzzled me for years. I was asking myself what was wrong without being able to find the answer. It's only after I started the analysis of my life I began to think that he might have wanted me to stay where Mercida was, like a kind of watch dog, to prevent her from misbehaving sexually. There were her own children she had with my father, one of them, Anglade who was living with Mercida at that time, is only a year older than me. But they were her own children, would not necessarily report something suspicious about their mother with another man to my father. The beating may have been because I didn't play the role of spy on behalf of my father around Mercida. The whole thing let me with a vivid emotional scarce.

Which is healing now, considering the promotion Bruce in the Ministry of Housing and economic Development just had. It is the indication that there is forgiveness, that I am at peace with myself in regard to person named Bruce who was involved in the formation of the scarce.

The promotion is the real reason why I wrote previously in this work that everyone is useful to society in one way or another, willingly or not. I only met him in an office. He knows nothing about my past consciously. I know nothing about him consciously, yet I have been an agent in his promotion.

The DP reminds me of a woman in my head all the time, a musician. Her first name starts with a B. She was kind of my soul mate.

DP83. The picture of a car with a flat and long nose. The total image is very bizarre.

Can I be a car, I mean can a human being represents a car and vice versa? Most African descent persons have flat nose.

The DP reminds me of Jaguar, Lamborghini and other sophisticated cars.

Friday April 28, 2000

DP84 There is no light in the living room where I appear. I climb a chair to screw a new bulb. As soon as finish with the bulb, the chair falls down as if it is intelligent, I walk away

> *and appear again near a bush fence where I see peaces of a broken glace.*

While living in the house on 3339 west 42nd Avenue, I saw some pieces of broken glace near the fence, once. It is the trigger of this DP. At that time I did not pay any attention to it. In the note I took immediately after the DP in 2000, I wrote that the broken glace looks like a structure which is going to be undone, without writing anything specific about it, not knowing any structure it could be about. Two years later, I called David who was living two houses west of mine, and whom you had met before at a meeting when I was involved in health system "restructuration" in British Columbia. David told me that the house above was totally rebuilt by the new owner. It's only to day in 2003 I'm making the connection between this DP and what was going to happened to the house.

There was a selling sign in front of it right when I moved in the year 1995. It was not a new house, something that could be easily seen from the outside, for the old painting was scouring, making some pieces which were falling down under the pressure of too many rainy days in Vancouver. In that condition, the house was never sold. In October 1999, the owner decided to paint it; hired a Greek worker who did an excellent job. The house was sold very soon after the painting. In that context, with that knowledge, it was not easy for me to conclude that the new owner would undo the whole house, consequently not easy neither to interpret the DP in that sense. When I learned from David the fate of the old house, I was working at DPs I made many months after the one above. It was forgotten, vanished and gone in my mind. In other words I understand this DP only today.

The DP makes me think, also, something about the

possible war in Iraq between Mr. Bush and Mr. Hussein, United States and Iraq. I do not quite get it yet. I would like to understand right now, though, before the war really happens, in order to prevent it if I can. Peace is something I am for, although it is not worth having it at any price. If I am the slave of someone who wants to make peace with me while I still stay a slave, it obvious that that peace is no good. I become a little more prudent about it since my own nephew was ambushed and killed about the same time than September 11, 2001. That is why I understand the Americans a little more than anyone else. They too had September 11, when two towers was flattened by two planes killing everybody on board and almost everybody in the towers in New York.

> *DP85. Sitting at this table to eat, I notice that there is only a piece of bred and a kind of powder. I eat them, but some of it falls everywhere on me. Then I appear outside, sitting where I hear two persons talking to each other. One of them asks the other to go and make an apology to me, what the other does. Then the blue and white colored pen with which I am writing becomes very short suddenly, and it is like some animals are pulling me back by my shirt.*

DP reminds me, between other things, a song of Billy Joel in which there are these words:

"I hear the secret that you keep,
While walking in the street"

In my individual soul there are humans, animals and

plants, meaning in my soul they are all my friends, and are in my dreams.

On TV at night in the Gerry's show before the DP I saw a dwarf married a woman of normal height. That would explain the shorter pen in the dream. Why blue and white colors? In what is it related to me other than that I expect to get married some day and have zillion kids? It's true that I have a lot to say about kids, but I have to skip the analysis of this DP to pass to another day, for there are 365 days in total with many DPs each day to analyze.

CHAPTER XIV

Saturday April 29, 2000

DP86. Standing in the back of the vehicle in which I am traveling, I am about to go and ask the woman standing close to me if she would accept to make love with me. At the same time we find ourselves both in front of the vehicle. Again I move to tell it to her, the vehicle stops suddenly in the middle of the river. It is as if everyone gets out and washes themselves.

I recall one of the conditions of human life which is always traveling, wanting it or not, and that with a vertiginous speed two ways at the same time. The other day, in a DP I saw the earth turning around the sun. It was an unusual DP.

Not very far there was musical sounds coming from a house symbolizing the sun where there are so many gases moving making noises like an orchestra.

I recal, also, of the Titanic broken by a bloc of ice in the middle of the Atlantic sea, killing many human beings. It was like the universal intelligence was telling the English and European HBBs that America had already enough inhabitants, that no more was needed by this accident.

In this DP sexuality is associated with something dirty, for everyone gets out of the vehicle which must be a boat and wash themselves, be cause I was about to ask a woman to make love with me. Or is it that way because there was no love between the woman and me, because I had just just seen her? We fell dirty inside because we are at war with ourselves. If there is peace inside, no matter what kind of sexuality we practice we will not feel dirty about it.

> DP87. HBBs are sitting on it. One person has his hand on the key to start the John Deer that I see and which is a little bit open. Instead of running, it makes a huge noise at the first trial to start the engine. At the second trial, it starts but stops right after a few seconds.

This engine was choke or its life was about to be ended. I thought I could buy my own commercial house while living in 3339 West 42 Avenue or, at least, before moving out. It was not the case. I still want to buy the first commercial house to rent as a shared accommodation. I figure out it will happen very soon after one of these "stops and starts again". The DP brings that to the surface of your memory. After all these stops and starts again are the expression myself development which is not very progressive. In other words I am still in total darkness as to what I can do. I am thinking of buying a house while I could think of buying a 1000. We are not out of the wood yet.

DP88. I am driving this vehicle while I am sitting face in the opposite sense, and singing: "Je reviendrai my love, Ne pleure pas surtout. le ciel n'est bleu my love que dans tes yueux si doux."

Does this vehicle have computerized driving device. It is a possibility in the whatness of creation, but not quite in waking life yet. So I was dreaming of it. The dreaming in the dream!. "I hear the secret that you think, while walking in the street" These few words are part of a Billy Joel's song. The ones in the DP are of Dalida, or Sylvie Vartan, I do not really remember. It's one of the songs I like in adolescence. "I will come back my love. Above all, do not cry. The sky is blue only in your sweet eyes." That would be a rough translation of it. Debbie has blue eyes. I adore blue eyes women, may be because I am accustomed more with dark, brown, dark brown colored eyes. Blue eyes are an excitement to me. However, in the depth of things, color doesn't matter much to me as far as girlfriends or wife are concerned. In a scale of 1 to 100, you'll add 2 points more for blue eyes, 2 points for natural blond hair.

I remark that in the musical atmosphere, love is sung often. I always wonder what kind of love is singing. In the one in the DP, the lyric appears to be romantic love. I am not sure of that for not remembering the whole song. In the modern world, or in the developed countries like France, there is not enough space/ time for romantic love, despite the reputation of these European countries for having more human beings in love romantically than other countries. Being passionate about someone of the opposite sex does fit well in an era and a country where attention is grabbed by so many distractions like work, entertainment, where men are defined by work and actions.

Although what I am driving in the DP is a boat, it reminds rather of some good times I had in Manitoba. The village where I stayed while being a French monitor in the School District Pelly Trail was small. There weren't very much for me to do in Russell during the weekends. Many times I went to spend them in Winnipeg. I went to Winnipeg with someone who is driving, with Joseph Poitras, another teacher who had a brand new station wagon when he went to Winnipeg for business purposes, or I rented a car. I had many friends in Russell and some other villages around, but they were all teachers, busy during the week. After being oppressed by work for 5 days of the week, I was like a loose canon, in a car going to Winnipeg for the weekend. I was so happy, passing by fields and fields of grass, of wheat, canola and so on. It was being free.

One Saturday morning I was making one those trips in a bran new car I rented. Radio was open totally. It was a very nice day. So I was going very much faster than the speed limit. A traffic controller stopped me. I told him that I was going back to Montreal gave him an address in Montreal. So I never heard of the incident afterward, as I was not going to Montreal. At that time the Sting's song " The Police " was amongst the songs which were played in the radio very often. I met many women in Winnipeg. My life was almost a paradise on earth.

I wish I could have a house close to the sea sometimes. When I was a child my family used to travel from Liancourt to Port-au- Prince to Croix-des Bouquets to LaBoule, during holidays such as Christmas, Easter. The first city on the trip after Liancourt going toward Port-au-Prince is called St Marc, close to the sea. When I reached that city I was invaded by a rêverie (rêve=dream) that no word can express, triggered by the view of the sea. Was it because of the color of the sea, or the vastness and the mass of the leveled water?

I am not quite sure why, but it made like the view of the sea, want to have a house close to the sea.

Iave two more things to ad to what is said above, one is that the DP are really the development of the firsts DPs that is there are link between that you can find by an accute look. The second is that the driving is not just the driving of a car but rather the driving of myself. There is problem in the previous DP. The one above is an sexplantion as to why I am having trouble, for driving face away. In other words in the DPs there are the solution of all the problems' I have, I pretend not seeing them, because they not in conjuction with my belief. We do that all the time I am still doing it. It is a lack of self confidence as you say.

DP89. Andre Meralus

His name Andre Murat, was rather my less younger brother's friend, the brother who is living in New York. I only remember that Andre Murat bought himself a small truck (like a pickup with two long seats in the back which is covered on top) once and had some difficulty to drive it the first time.

Or is the DP about the moralistic part of me? Is it moralistic to be heterosexual? Meralus sounds like moral. So this DP is saying that my problems are caused a moralistic consideration, my moral sense is the culprit, although I am not ware of that. This DF still focuses on the problem, religious moral label, social moral label, you name it.

Sunday April 30, 2000

DP90. Sitting on the porch of a house in the middle of two women to eat, a third woman appears with a jewelry on which is written something. I try to read what is written on it but do not *succeed, the letters being too small for me to see, but the ladies who were already with me understands, being able to read it Then I appear on the yard of a big building. A woman, her father and husband appear in a car. They offer to take me home. I find the woman attractive, am thinking of obtaining her good grace when I am alone with her. But her husband went to get his car. It is with him I am going to go home. Then I appear again carrying a wooden structure with two women in front carrying it too. I pass through many doors in places not very nice to see. I want to walk as fast as the ones who are helping me, but I am afraid I'll hurt my legs while climbing the stairs by doing so.*

It is about a psychological experimentation you are doing, although you do not clearly understand the message yet. The jewelry makes suppose Jewel the singer; I would not have any other explanation for her presence except that I like her songs have many of her CDs. I like her very much too. It would be almost impossible to meet her, not having too much to do with the music industry. The lyric of her song "My Hand" makes me speculate that there might have been channeling between us, but that is not the point. The fact of the matter is that I cannot give to much information on this particular experimentation without jeopardizing the validity of the results I am still waiting for.

Then you did sleep with a married woman with the aware agreement of her husband who was my friend too,

Alourde. In another case I did go out with a married woman once, Tam. Her husband was living half of the planet away from North America. In both cases the women were the lovers.

In other words, I do not like very much being mixed with women already in relationships, despite what the DP suggests.

DP91. *While walking in the street, I find a briefcase that I have inadvertently lost.*

In the briefcase I lost in the pacific center, there was some books borrowed from the library that you had to pay for, the important letter received from Delta School board, important in case I want to sue them, something you would have already done if I had money to pay a lawyer, Which make me remember it may be them who paid somebody to steal the briefcase. There was also the e-mail address, some pictures of Lisa Dergan, and some counter samples of the experimentation. These items are really important for me, given that they are irreplaceable.

There is the concept "guide" in parapsychology. You I am not very comfortable writing about it, for not being able to see its importance in this field of study, psychology, parapsychology. According to some psychic there are many sorts of guides: the Runners, Helpers; the Teachers, Masters; and the Joy guide. The televised series Angel something exploit the notion deeply. There is a heavy religious connotation(Talk Like An Angel, Live Like an Angel) attached to psychological guide, probably another reason for someone to be uncomfortable about it. But the fact that I find the briefcase in the DP reminds me of the Runners, in the sense that it was him who found the briefcase you have lost in waking life.

That said about guide does not mean at all that it is necessarily a useless concept. I felt uncomfortable, also, with symbol, in particular with the extensive way the concept is used in psychology and especially in parapsychology without being able to see the need of it. Besides, it was also used in almost all-primitive religions. Sometimes I think it is the principal handicap in the mental and physical development of certain groups of human beings and certain countries. You have in mind Haiti and the most popular religion in this country, the voodoo. In it the symbolism is very well set and developed in itself. But most of the humans practicing it are not doing well financially and intellectually speaking. Nowadays, I reconcile somewhat with the concept, in a special psychological way. The proof is that I have self-symbol . Would it allow me to have better understanding of temperature, energy, etc. in the long run? My will symbol is bull. Would that allow me t o get a better understanding of wild animal in the lung run? So symbol can be a plus in our lives, if used in a practical way.

All the above paragraph to say that if you reconcile with the concept symbol, you may reconcile later with some other concepts that are useless according to you now.

The thing is one cannot loose an inner ability. We can become rusty after a while without using it. In that sense having non-material things is more of a possession than having material things that can be lost or stolen. I agree with some religions teaching that. But when they try to make me believe that the spiritual is more important than the material, I disagree with them as well as when they behave with the universal intelligence, the Creator as if it is a person, when thy pulls it down to the level of a person, when they behave with it as if it could be in favor of some human beings, against some others, U am totally lost.

The most important reason for having symbol id that

with the symbol you can see the unseable, my will is not visible, my self is not visible. Now I can see them in direct perception, communication or exprience because they become an image.

second point is that, I suspect that asgel is the name that human behing in the past was trying timidly to give to the Creator (small religions choke by the big ones. The concept angel actually is in religious belief. By fear of for reason I ignore is not attributable to the Creator. Still only the Creator has the qualities of angel such as purety, liking everyone, etc, although the creator let us free to be, even killing ourselves.

> DP92. *Sitting in the front porch of my house, I hear a man calling his wife "Cherie" and telling her that if she doesn't feel well she should go to the drugstore. Then, a tall man appears near me. He his telling me how I can extend the house, make it bigger. Then again, I go inside with him to show him the outside bush fence through a very narrow window. While looking outside I see a few corns on the cub on the grass already eaten partially. The bush fence is of a very nice green color, I am very happy to see it.*

Although I will not really analyze this DP, it indicates the important issue that the drugstore tends to replace the psyche in terms of health. I said before that too much attachment to drugstore, doctors, and other health agencies and institution is attachment to sickness and death. Moreover that attitude is very expansive. In Canada presently a lot more money is about to be delegated to health institutions. I think it a waste of money and energy, that the money would provide better services if it was spent to help us educating ourselves on the functions of our body and our psyche and on how to take care of them, especially by a proper use of our dream body. I am not in a position to influence a crow now. You figure they would spit in my face if I go and tell them that. They would think I am too poor, morally bankrupt to have good ideas.

Hospital and doctors and drugs are for when we are sick and suffering harshly. Must of the time we are like that because we do not take care of our soul.

> *DP93. Some of Prashire's friends are in his room. They say to me that he is in jail. My answer to them is that I already know.*

Prashire is a person living in the same house than you on Manitoba Street. He is of African Ancestor like me. I remember that he was the one who suggested to all the other tenants to move out. When I went back to get my security deposit, all the other tenants moved out, I was told. Yes the owner of the house came on me too strongly before finding out my sexual practice, and consequently he was too harsh about belongings I had in the house and outside of the house, because of his sexual disappointment. He was making a lot of noise about the belongings. The other tenants observed that, figured out that he was unfair toward me. But I would never suggest to the other tenants to move out because of that. For one reason, they too were harassing me sexually, other reason is that I would not want to put his business in jeopardy.

That week, that time while trying to comprehend that DP in this house, I was in a tense situation. Barbara wanted me to tell Amanda to remove her bed frame from the room in front of her bedroom because they are in Barbara's way. I thought that room belongs to Amanda more than her although she always makes it look like a garbage room. There is a storage room in the floor I was responsible fpr, it's already fool of her things. She talks to me as if I had had to talk to Amanda about it. I didn't. Yesterday, not seeing the frame, I asked Amanda, she said that Barbara asked her to remove it from there, that she put it in her closet. I thought it was abusing her, and, it reminded me of Carla Homolka and Bernado's murder of young women. May be I am exagerating , but we will see. I thought that Barbara was jealous of her.

Monday May 1st, 200

> *DP94. There is a party. I am having a chat with a tall woman wearing a white dress and who has big racks that I am caressing. She mutters some words. She says something like "Would you buy me a drink?". Then, I go outside with her and stop on a hill to look at HBBs agitating afar and down. It's like there are some soldiers who are fighting. There is a young person who walked toward me and tries to hit me with his foot. I grab him by that foot and send him in the air. He falls down on iron wire with pins.*

In the notes I wrote down on that day after having the DP, I said that it was imagination, that I would wait to understand that the woman looks like Barbara.

In complete life, I do not consciously have the wish of a sexual relationships with her, although some life observer think that all human relationships are basically sexual. The fundamental reason for that is she is married. If she were not I would try to have sex with her, not having any sexual outlet nowadays. She is a sexy woman, although she has two kids. It is with Amanda I wish to have romantic relationships. My present living condition does not allow it that much. I am not making any money, still am very busy. It is the reason in the DP, it says "Could you buy me a drink." Alluding to that I need to at least be able to buy a woman a drink to be in a romantic or other kind of relationships with her. Most women do not care for that in a developed country, I guest it might be a question of honor as far as I am concerned.

The white dress brings to mind another DP where I was in a romantic embrace with Britney the star. I met her in a gallery in the DP; she was wearing a white dress. Yes in waking life I find her very attractive, but would not form the conception to be in a romantic relationships with her, because she is way beyond me in terms of social status. For the moment I do not even have money to take a bus to go downtown meet a woman. How would I do to go and meet her wherever she is living now at least for the first time? I can have million of dollars in one hour later today. At 10:36 AM, the time it is now, it is not the case.

One of the other women I see during DPs is Milla the fashion woman. She has such ravishing eyes. It is not clear to me if she is of Ukrainian or Polish ancestor, but one reason for the connection would be that I lived in the house of Ukrainian family once, the other reason would be I went out with Polish lady once. Milla can be of Russian ancestor too. I think it is not nice to ask someone where they are from, unless in an official context such as immigration, It sounds racial profiling, even though most of the time it is done by curiosity and a need to better understand the other person.

This is why I am not definite on Milla's origin, and will not look up for the information either.

Some women have some knowledge of me with such precision that it is freighting. There is a certain Geri (I find her very attractive, would marry her a thousand times) the Spice Girl who was reported by a journalist as saying "If only I could find a nice Canadian man to fertilize my eggs!" She was talking to me for knowing my intention to have in vitro babies, for knowing about the experiment I am doing that I cannot reveal yet in order not to invalidate the result. I know someone else who knows about the experimentation. Is she queen of England? Many other women artist know about it too. They let me know by doing or saying something in TV, Film, and so on. Her Majesty the queen helped me understand what was really happening. These women wanted to take part in the experiment too. It is the only reason why Her Majesty is in it too. I never met these women in waking life. If they know who I am, perhaps, they would not accept willingly to take part in the experimentation, doubting I could be doing such a thing.

DP95. The picture of woman wearing a black skirt

May be about black women. My sister is the only woman of that color I see in my DPs nowadays. I am not very much involved in the human community physically and presently. I spend the nicest part of my time focusing on the research. The only time I meet a lot of HBBs is when I am looking for a roommate and put an ad in the paper. Only once I had a black woman roommate yet, she stays for a few days. In Vancouver there are not too many.

DP96. I leave the house in which I live to go outside for a walk. When I want to come back, I cannot

find my way to the house. I end up
at place where there are a lot of
animals. I throw a stone at them
softly. It reaches the target. I throw
some more that do not touch their
targets. Among these animals, there
are dugs, cats, pigs, and birds. It is
like they transform themselves there
in front of me. They have a better
physical form, the birds become
bigger. Then I appear again in a
kind of cul-de-sac in a hall. There is
a young woman who blocks my way
back. She is nude, leans against
the wall, and turns her back to me.
The time it takes me to get ready
for action, she is already having an
orgasm. I ask her to wait, but she
cannot hold it. Then she let me go.
I continue my way, thinking that
they canot accuse me of making
love with a minor, given that I did
not touch her. I appear again at
a different place on a structure
in iron. I thought it was a hill,
when I realize the mistake, it starts
running and let me down softly in
the street as a moving escalator. I
continue walking, meet someone
who recognizes me. He appears to
have seen what have just happened to
me, and is laughing at me because
of that. I tell him things in French
that I do not remember, but that
ends by "Tant mieux pour mon être".

I continue walking, climb a wall beside a street, a kind of sidewalk more elevated than the usual one. When the street becomes narrow, I step down from the elevated sidewalk. Then, then I see a luxurious car coming at me rapidly. I am afraid it is going to smash my body.

I will make only a few comments on this DP. It is long enough then let little possibility for misinterpretation. The animals represent animals too in plain in complete life, they also symbolize human beings, well, may be a different kind of humans. It reminds me again of the saying of Darwin that I am going to paraphrase, human beings with animal spirit. Children, crazy people, animals have strong emotion and, they do not hesitate to indulge in it(It is comparing children and women to animal. But I am not the one who made the statement) That is to say they live more by their emotion than by their reason. That the kind of humans the animals symbolize in the DP.

Then, there are the ones I am living close by in shared accommodation. According to the DP, I am transforming them, making them better persons just by living close by me. What is strange in all that is that I do not voluntarily choose the way I'm living now. Not too many human beings would choose to live with almost no money, no car, no house, and no friends no wife, always researching something that is elusive. It is like a fate fallen on me for reasons I thought were mysterious, but which starts to unravel its meaning nownow. Who am I to think that I can make people become better person by living close to them? I would never thought like that consciously. Now I do.

In the elevated sidewalk, I am in transcendence or higher consciousness. When it becomes narrow, I am about to step down to consciousness or waking life or plain physical life, or complete life. incomplete life (but I may be the only one using the expression. Yes, a DP is a dream, but is, also, the highest tool available to human kind.

This DP came to me the first day I moved in and sleep in this house where I am writing right now(16th Avenue). It's Thursday morning, 8:35, I do not quite know what the whether is like. Yesterday, 5-o3-2003, was sunny day. Tamara was my roommate at the time of the DP; it was pleasant living close to her. Plus the excitement of first day in the house, that is why this DP is so long, probably.

DP97. One of the woman living in this house is very well clothed wearing a nice pink dress. Ut seems that she is going to work.

At the time of this DP it was Tamara who was working at Ballad, the company where the fuel cell is being developed in Canada. But she did not wear dress; she wore blue jean pants. So the DP is a wish that she would wear dress, something practical in Haiti, but impractical in Canada where it is cold. In this DP then I am in my infancy or adolescence. Tamara was born in England, is living in Australia where she was brought up. Apparently there is a permanent work exchange program between Australia and the rest of the Common Wealth Countries such as Canada. I lived closed by three Australians in such program at three different spans of time. It is not very clear for me if the program exists between Australia and US.

Amanda is the woman I am living close by presently. She says she wants to be an accountant, it's like also she has talent in music. I think she should pursue this field rather than accounting, but if she prefers accounting that is where she will succeed. It does not really matter in which field she develops herself. What is important is to have a field and work at it a life long. As someone wrote, perfecting your living conditions is a life long occupation. You can never retire from it, despite the fact that retirement becomes an institution in modern and western countries. It is totally wrong. It is a killing industry that way. Service such as pension is good, but you, human beings of all countries, should make it so that you never retire from the process to reach the high destiny which is yours, that as long as you live you are achieving something or, at least trying.

CHAPTER XV

Wednesday May3, 2000

DP98. Many persons and I are together. A man gives me money that they ask him to give me. He speacks of a certain Robert. He tells me the answer of a letter that I have sent to someone else, It is like he gives me two kinds of money, for I put them in my pockets in way not to mix them up before counting them. There is in this DP, also, this woman who reminds me of Siliane. Knowing that I have cooked food in the fridge, she reminds me of that too.

I did receive last week the answer of an e-mail I have sent to Ministry of health about some grant to finish and publish Kickitwell Or Else, a stop smoking, addiction elimination and prevention device. He says there is no grant available for the kind of project, that I may write him back to let him know more about it. It will be a surprise to receive the grant from him. Addiction is a delicate subject in this government, because of the drunk-driving incident in which the Premier of BC was involved recently while visiting a Pacific Ocean Island. The members of the government would probably like to forget totally about the subject.

I will have a lot of money some day, may be, or I will be worth a lot of money. It is one of my dreams. Then I will have a foundation to give some of that money to HBBs in countries where it can be put to good use. I will start by the villages where my parent where born. They need everything in those places. I will help with clean water, electricity, and telephone. Then I will identify countries with the same or similar kind of needs and do the same in these countries too a little bit, as much as one person can do. I know that the Caribbean Islands, Africa, Asia would be qualified for this project. In the developed countries I will adopt a different approach by helping HBBs such as new immigrants and the poor.

If I was born in the right environment I would probably be in the music industry as a singer. By now I would already have all the money I need. In the developed countries, it is like anyone is better off by being an artist in music, movies or in TV, if I want to have a lot of money. In Entertainment Tonight last week it was said Oprah is worth a billion $, earned $150 million last year or in 2002. Leonardo Di Caprio acted for $33 million, Britney Spears sang for$ 35 million. Tom Cruise earned $25 million a film, Roy Romano $800000. These actors, singer and TV show host earned lot money, spent a lot of money too. They will be able to work for as much money if not more next year, but this astronomical amount of money they've earned does not necessarily mean that they are rich. Oprah is rich because she is worth a billion. It deepens obviously on how much money coming in and how much going out

It was a surprise to learn that personalities like Castro worth $335 million, Arafat $1 billion, and Saddam Hussein $2 billion. In the case of Saddam, we know that gas becomes a precious commodity, and that there is plenty of that in Iraq, but how did Arafat and Castro get that much money? They accumulate it over a long period of time. Cuba is a communist country, in such a place money is not used for exchange of goods.

Another surprise in relation to money was related to Capital one and City Financial. These two Canadian lending companies surprised me by the amount of money they are worth. First, I saw in a solicitation letter I received from Capital one that this company is worth $ 90 Billion. I thought it was so big an amount. Then I received the same kind of letter from City Financial in which it says they are worth $ 3 trillion. I thought about it very frequently for a week. Then I remember a meeting I used to go to where they talk about derivatives, estimated amount of money, then I calmed down.

The banks are facing a similar problem, or there is derivative in banks too. Unable to know on a day to day basis the exact amount of money left in the bank by the depositors, impossible to know that quickly how much money has been withdrawn and how munch has been deposited, they create money when the lend money to customer. At that moment, they do not know the amount of money they have in the bank. Go and tell a banker that he is creating money out of the wind?

When we think of money, we do not necessarily means money as in the gold/silver or any metal coin on which the Roman goddess Juno Moneta was represented. We do not mean either money like spade, knife as it was used by the Chinese at the beginning until they discover the concept cash, but we mean all sorts of money.

Myself I am not in good relationships yet with money, so I do not allow myself to accumulate wealth yet. There are certain things about money I need to know first. Just after I started the research I realized that money is a curious concept. Imagine that at the beginning salt was used as symbol for money used to pay for work, and where the concept salary comes from. After barter was abandoned as means of exchange of goods and work, human started to use strange concepts to replace barter such as eggs, coconuts, blankets, liquor, and tea. All in all it was a surprised for me to see how the concept money evolved from barter to these currencies until the diverse and elaborated currencies of the modern world. May be I have to know that before I can accumulate wealth.

Moreover, I've read in a Roman Sonaya book something like "You donot create money, when you bring it into your life, you tape on a flow that was already there. When you create wealth you do not take it from someone else. You become part of a flow of money". I paraphrase, but, essentially, I think that that is what I have read. It is something useful to know, for even after the defeat of the practice of the concept communism in economy, itis still in the back of the intellectual mind that money is the evil, like a human plague. If Karl Marx was aware of the concept flow in relation to money, history may have been different, because in the communism frame of mind, you feel guilty of having money that you take from someone else whom becomes poor by the same process. Now we know money flows from one hand to the other. You do not take it from someone else.

What is strange, also, is that in one hand the communist partisans say "burn the churches". In the other their attitude toward money is clearly borrowed from the churches. They both hated money, at least in theory, They both showed contempt for merchants and moneymakers. The reason why Robert is mentioned in the DP. It is Jane Roberts who wrote" The Unknown Reality" and who made me realize that religion and the communist theory where riding the same path.

> DP99. We are on large terrain. There are a lot of human beings and activities. A tall thin woman wearing a dress passes near me. She looks like someone who is very agitated. I say to her something like "How do you do to be in such a good shape?" Then a man lying beside me and reminding me of Princivil gets up, speaks to the woman, starts to dance with her, brings her to a corner, gets his equipment out ready for action while still dancing with her. You find that he is bizarre to do such a thing in the middle of everybody, but I too start to be ready for action, start to pee.

Princivil iwas a half brother who past away a few years ago. He and I were born the same year. There was a connection a little bit particular between him and me in comparison to the rest of half family. He was very good in sexual relationships according to what he told me. I am not sure if he passes away because of that. No, I myself never tried to make love with a woman in a dance floor? I was not young and foolish. How could I do such a thing, I'm not Tonclin.

The terrain is related to field theory in psychology or to terrain I would like to be able to buy and develop. I have to come back to these concepts later.

DP100. Somebody appears with a big pot. He wants some help from me to put it down, but realizing that he wants to place it where there is already a lot of boxes, you say "These things belong to Siliane. They cannot be touched."

Here is a compulsion not to win big in the ppkg. But at the same time it is also an expression of the energy created by the issue, winning, not winning in the lottery game, as such it is the beginning of the resolution of the problem, in other words the beginning of winning. Each time I make a positive move in life, I win anyway, but that's another issue.

The boxes for Siliane who past away. Obviously Siliane is a metaphor for a woman I love, girlfriend or wife in the future. In my bedroom there is a huge closet with many boxes containing my things. I do not even remember what is in them. U would like to sell them, am too shy to organize a moving sale. In the DP there is allusion that I will give them to this woman.

DP101. Appearing somewhere, I see some human beings sitting around a table playing cards. I am looking for Siliane and asking for her. A woman says that she is not there. Then, I say "Let me help you" or something similar.

Lot can be said about the DP, but there are too many to work with, we are going to work with some of them.

At the end I wrote "Or something similar". Because most of the time most of the details of the DPs are forgotten, blocked by the ego or because we have them in a deep sleep state. Nonetheless, it reminds me of Angelina who was the main character in a film call "Something Similar". At least the title of the film is from the DP. In DP we are in communication and interaction with the whole world. The research that I am doing but cannot talk about yet is the other link with Angelina, although it is not sure who in the film had the idea.

The deck of cards of red color that I bought once is still here somewhere. I use to do intuitive exercise with it by guessing which card I pick face down. Does it inspire a big TV show called "Deal Or No Deal" with certain variation such as the cards are less and become briefcases? Like I said while analyzing one of the first DPs, the effects of The Soul Exposed are pervasive and worldly.

The third comment on the DP is related to individuality. In telling the woman "Let me help you", is there the respect of her individuality? It seems that I should have said "How can I help you?" to respect her individuality.

We have to come back to it later.

DP103. I meet Sejourne in the darkness. I never spoke to him before. I have fear of him. He speaks about Arnold.

One Sejourné I new was very tall (6 feet plus) and thin. He is of the chronological age of my brother Arnold. There might have been some fight between them about women. Another Sejourné I knew has a brother, Gagne who is equally tall and thin. His presence in this DP would be justified only by my desire to earn or to win i (I win means je gagne in French) money.

In other words, the fear of winning is what prevents me from winning. It sounds odd, but there is such a thing as the fear of winning for many reasons: The fear of retaliation, the fear of the responsibility the winning will bring with it, the fear of notoriety, of being overwhelmed by too many HBBs, and things etc.

And there is also the fear of not winning. We may come back to it later.

Friday May 5, 2000

> *DP104. Seradieu needs something; he asks it to Chantal who says no to his request. Then, I am sitting beside Marguerita; he walks up to us and asks her the same question again. I am not happy with him and say something like "if you harm her; I am going to harm you too".*

Seradieu's parents' house was separated from Chantal and Magerita's house by a cactus fence. The two girls are my godmother's daughters. Seradieu is the one who hit me with a stone while I was a child, leaving an indelible trace in your right eye. It is not really clear to me if it is why I am near sighted. That was a long time ago, there is no reason now not to be happy with Seradieu. He became a soccer player.

My godmother almost replaced my mother practically after she past away. Etiennette, my godmother's first name, was very good to me from infancy to adulthood. She was (I do not even know if she is still living, a very hard worker. Her husband and her went to work every day as long as I have known them. In their area the main culture is rice. The last time I saw Marguerita, it was in Montréal. It is not clear to me if Chantal is in Haiti or in another country. My godmother and her husband Job had also a couple of twin Marcel and Marco. I do not know what they become, something which is bordering me very much so. I figured out I had to do something for my godmother who was so good to me for such a long time, and if she is not alive, to do it for her children who are a bit younger than me.

In Montreal I was rather wild, always busy with getting pleasure of all kinds. I did not have the time to think of the past, to think of helping my godmother, while I was making money. In Manitoba I was in a similar situation and as wild as ever. In Vancouver, I started little by little to become a different person, forced by the new circumstances. I was totally incapable to adapt (still now too) with life in this province and in this city, although I decided to stay here after a voluntary choice. I do not accept not being able to make a lot of money, I do not accept not being able to make money at all. I am most of the time in a bad mood. I cannot help my godmother and or her children, even though I think of it. When my father became bit and pieces a few years ago, I could not even go to Haiti to participate in his funeral.

Chantal reminds me of another Chantal. Arnold's wife, Anne Marie, Antoine, Anne Marie's brother where living in Chantal's brother's house. Antoine and me rented a bedroom and were living in it as roommate It was a nice house. There was roses' tree beside our window. At night I used to have pleasure looking at the projection of shadow and light of the roses' tree branches dancing in my bedroom, shaken by the breeze outside. It was a big house with a lot of bedrooms. One day about 7 PM there was a blackout. Somehow Chantal, a very young and nice looking mulatto , and me were in the same room at that exact moment, and somehow we started kissing deeply. Chantal was probably under age. It was a surprise for me; I did not talk to her before about it, or about something else. I was an adult, I thought she wanted to go all the way. When I made a move in that sense, she said no, or made me understand what was her intention. So we only kissed . She was the initiator. It is an unforgettable moment passed during a blackout, strange, isn't it? Did I make the blackout unconsciously?

DP105. I am preparing the food I am going to cook. I think "we have won".

Since Amanda moved in the house on 16th Avenue there was a kind of jealousy against her from Barbara and Tood. Barara is in love with me. Todd used to harass me when there were nobofy around They think that I neglected them and paid attention to Amanda alone. They make it difficult for Amanda to stay. Last Monday Amanda said she is going to move out in May 2003 or June. The DP may express how Barbara and Todd felt when it was analyzed. They have won.

The DP may be saying, also, that <u>it is a good idea to think of winning while about to eat in the sense that the behavior may increase the probability of winning in PPK game or predication psychokinetic game or lottery</u>. I play once in a while and think that one day I'm going to win big. In the mid time it seems that I have to reconciliate with myself and bring to the surface of my psyche the knowledge that I have buried by fear and misidentification. Then I will be able to control your mind and make it make me win big. I have won a few thousands $ in small portions and over a stretched period of time.

I call the game PPK after noticing that each time someone wins big in it; it is because this person has done a spontaneous psychokinetic act. Of course everyone has the ability in his mind. I keep the concept prediction with it because it is not really a problem but the whole thing look more like "psychogenesis, a kind of poltergeist" to me.

I had problem with the concept of soul that I assimilated with religion. In other words a big part of myself was not functioning properly for not being recognized and promoted. I was forced to write The Soul Exposed to cross the religious barrier between me and my individual soul and the Soul of the World. In religion they call the two souls demon.

> DP106. *Something like "it is open for me to cash at nine o'clock this year".*

I probably meant to write "at nine o'clock today". And the DP is probably ironical in the sense that it meant to say rather itis not open for me to cash, if we consider that in my in my complete life presently I do not have any money, and any concrete hope of having some in the near future. I may have million of $ one hour later today, but that kind of hope is subjective.

At that time I was hoping to go back to university. 9 o'clock may be a reference to that. Anyway, 9 o'clock AM is the time we usually start to work in America. The DP is saying something in that sense too, because I start to work immediately after cohffee usually around 8 o'clock.

> DP107. *I see Gramond's brother, Lamartine, going out of Siliane's house. I get big stone in my hands and say "if I hit someone on his head with this stone". Then, I walk toward Siliane's house and look back to see him running away as fast as he can.*

Gramond and Lamartine are two brothers. Lamartine was living next to my parent's place. What can not we imagine in an attempt to protect a sister when one is only a child?

> DP107. *This little dog climbs and clings to my feet, as if it feels bad,*

but it falls down to the floor while saying it feels good.

At that time I was sick in my knees and feet and shoulder quite regularly. I went to emergency in many hospitals for it. They call the sickness gout, and suggested that it is long chronological age related. Nowadays, I notice that my sicknesses are disappearing. I had a cyst on my face for about 3 years; recently I woke one day with a ball (one-inch diameter) in my face where the cyst used to be. I became very emotional about it, seized by the fear that they would have to cut it leaving a scarce on my face the reason I did not do surgery for it in the first place. I called the family physician; she booked an appointment for me with the specialist. Before that date, the ball and the cyst disappeared like by enchantment. Cellular knowledge, according to Jane Roberts, will cure our sicknesses, and help in maintaining a body young for a long period of time, <u>the psyche not being affected by time</u>.

The conclusion is that some sicknesses are in the order of the growing pain idea.

Is the DP indicating pleasure and pain principle, in the sense that they are not independent of each other, true to a large extent. However, one can have pleasure by pleasurable input too, what humans do all the time when the buy a drink, go dancing, to movies etc. In life in general we rather have a tendency to think that pleasure is absolutely linked to pain. But that is not true. In the Freudian psychology they think like that I guess, and Freudian psychology was an intellectual paradigm for a long period of time, if not even now.

CHAPTER XVI

Saturday May 6, 2000

> *DP108. This woman is talking to a man in her bedroom. After a couple of times, I put four fingers around his neck and say "this neck is it big?"*

This one brings my mind back to the period of my life when I was excessively jealous and egotistical. I had different ways to manifest the jealousy. When I was in early 20s I hit Jeanine, the first woman I ever loved, with my fist once, I will never forget that moment as long as I live. It was such cowardice, stupid act to do. I love someone deeply, a bundle of positive emotive package. Then I hurt the person. Now I know the saying in psychology that <u>rage and similar emotions are right underneath of love.</u> At the time when I did that to Jeanine, I did not have a clue. I was focusing on the beloved; that was a good thing but not the right way. Unselfish jealousy is guardian of love anyway.

Rage is egotistical while madness is not necessarily.

After sometime, I said to myself that it did not make any sense to be hitting woman I loved, that it was may be because of the fear of attacking the other men that was, also, at the cause of the jealousy. When I heard Heraldo expressed similar idea in one of his TV shows by saying that men who beat women are coward, I was convinced of my idea to focus on the men, the other aspect of the jealous feeling. That was, also, the wrong attitude. Love is something between two human beings, a lover and a beloved. When beloved is not responding, yes, it is to give it up, with in mind that love cannot be forced is mutual given. So, we are very far away from the physical punishment, which myself had tendency to use in the past.

I went to Debbie's place to be with her as usual after 6 years of a relationships with her. Instead of that that I found her with another man. I did force my way into the house, chased the man out. But I did not touch Debbie, although I have never seen her again.

All that to say that the violent attitude toward women I love is thing of the past.

> *DP109. She is walking beside me. I ask if I have already seen her. She answers no, that she was never in this city before. "Then I ask again "where do you come from?" "Hastings Street" is her answer.*

When I was teaching in Abbotsford, I was still leaving in Vancouver. So I had to commute to there everyday in the Colt the name of the car I had. Most of the time I took Hastings Street up to Canada Way up to Abbotsford. Some other time I was teacher on call in the North Vancouver School District. Most of the time I passed by Hastings Street to go the schools there.

Another time there was 5 students who were failing their French course in the same class. I tutored them during a whole summer. The school is located on Hastings Street or nearby.

It is a worrisome place for me; I go there only when it is absolutely necessary. But I met Alice the girl I was going with once and she said she was living on Hastings Street.

> DP110. *Looking at the mountain afar, I notice the white perimeter of an empty terrain. I look in front of my house, I see a man working in a banana field. I talk to him a bit saying that I have just noticed him working in the field in front of the house. Then he asks me to tell him why. I say it is because of the lianas and all that greenery in front. Then he comes close to me and tells about a tobacco garden that he had in another part of Canada. After that I cannot understand what he is saying.*

The last sentence is probably to mark that he is a stranger to me. I have his picture in the book I call "Kickitwell Or Else", which can help to quit smoking. I did a little bit of research before writing the book. That is how I came to know him. The topic is that growing tobacco is very tempting, and when started it is difficult to quit. They have more money for it than growing tomato for example. Yes I had a small banana garden once. At that time, Siliane my sister who past away built a house right where I had the garden.

> DP111. *In the market place at Croix-des-bouquets, someone I do not know keeps standing at my back.*

In the end I push him, he falls on the ground, hits his head against a rock. Afterward, he gets up and goes with a trace near his eyebrow. After a while I see a group of very small children, armed with a baseball bat each running after me. I do not know what to do, given that they are very small children, I would not want to fight them. I am thinking. At that moment a group of very small children appear at my side too, each equally armed with a baseball bat. They attack the other group; that allows me to walk away from it all. Then, I meet a man who reminds me of Yanick. I am afraid of him.

That market occupies a notorious place in my psyche for many reasons. It is located at about 2 kilometers from the elementary school called Charlotin Macadieux where I did the first part of my schooling. And my grand mother Sylvira was in that market five days a week buying and selling. At noon you used to go to the market to find her and to have something to eat from her.

I have already mentioned that when I was 6 or 7 years old Seradieu hit me with a stone that left a trace near your left eyebrow. It is in the DP at the same time than the feeling Yanick created in me because he had his hair in very small balls. At grade one we were in the same class and I found his hair frightening. But the DP is suggesting that there is a link between the incident with Seradieu and the fear of Yanick's hair.

DP112. In this group of HBBs in which I am, as a joke I ask one person

> *if she wants some opium. Another man asks everybody to leave, comes nearme and to tell me that mother gave me a beating once when I was a child, because she did not understand what he told her.*

This man should be my father Soys or sawais and the woman my mother Eucaris. They both past away, my mother since I was about 6 years old, my father a few years ago.

It is not clear to me why there is opium in the DP, I never tasted it, I only know about it a bit in books.

The beating was because I was eating mangos fallen from the tree with reddish color as if they were ripe, still they were not ripe. I remember she was pregnant. It is the only image of her I have in memory. If there were not this incident I would not remember her at all.

> *DP113. From the neighbor's house opposite to my house, I see some military persons in the yard of my house. I am afraid, asking myself what is happening there. They stay there for a while. Dieudonne and some children cross the street and join me. They explain to me that the "macoutes" are there to arrest someone who made an obscene phone call to a child.*

In the house where I am living presently the DP was made. I do not know the persons living at the other side of the street, never been in contact with them, never even seen them, would not know what they look like if I met them in the street. 16th Avenue is 6 lanes big Street leading to University of British Columbia. So, I find that it is a stretch to think of the HBBs living across the street as neighbors. In 3339 West 42nd Avenue, it was an all-different matter. This part of Vancouver West Side is more like a residential area. Most of the cars using these streets belong to persons living around. As soon as I moved there, I noticed the family that was living across the street. They had a jeep Cherokee parked in front of their house. Each morning I saw the father taking the kids to school in the jeep before going to work.

Fran is the name of the mother. She came and introduced herself to me a few months later after I moved in. When I moved out I was not in the perfect mood with her, police came to my house a couple of times. She and the other neighbors did not like that, told it to me, for one thing. For the other, she was probably expecting something from me that was not very easy for me to give her.

It brings us back to Haiti, at your mother's house. There, there was a Dieudonne living with Adam across the street. Adam was a very good friend of my father, probably why I sent this fax to Mr. Saddam Hussein last month, asking him to step down to spare his life, his family's life and his wealth. This morning March 17, 2003 I do not know if there is anything new in the news. Yesterday, 5 head of states met in the Azores Island after which there was talk of last opportunity in terms of time to avoid the war. I hope Mr. Hussein would follow my advice even at the last minutes. War is bad for every living soul. It is only effect is destruction. But, still it is no good to have peace at any price.

Last Saturday something unusual happened to me at the Vancouver Public Library in the branch in this area, Dunbar. Last week I dreamt of blond person. Someone talked about her to someone else by saying that it was the nicest blond he had never met. I did not pay too much attention to the DP, by Saturday I forgot completely about it. At 4 in the afternoon, there she was. She directed her look left and right in the library as if looking for somebody she knew. I smiled at her; she went to counter, come back again taking a sexy posture while passing by me. I smiled at her again. What is strange in it all is that she looks like someone between 14 and 17 chronological years old? I was asking myself if she was with her parents at the library. She looks like someone I could marry. If she were 17, waiting one year until she is 18 to start going out with her would not be a big deal to me. I am not sure if I could wait for her any longer. Then, I will definitely not be in relationships with under 18-year-old girl. I do not want to get involved in illegal activities. So it is a may be.

I do not meet women as easily as I would like to. There are many reasons for that. The DP is suggesting that one of the reasons is the deep fear of "macoute", Duvalier's secrete police acquired when I was living there.

What the DP is saying also, I guess, is that to have anything to do with that girl would be obscene.

DP114. *The person from whom I ask to borrow things. He\she lends me a big key.*

The souls to whom I wrote to ask money for the earthquake detector project do not answer my letters yet, except one out of 17. In her answer to me J.K. Rowling only says that she received plenty of requests like mine and that she gives to charity when she can get involved in the project. Is involvement the key of her successes? What is sure is this psychological belief that when you are involved in a project, that feeds you interest for the project, vice versa I supposed. In other words involvement and interest are in a causal and circular relation. Strangely enough, it's not the same for satisfaction and interest, nor satisfaction and involvement.

The person gives me a big key instead of what I asked for. By doing so, he allows me to create more of what I asked for. The same idea is promoted in psychology too: <u>it is more important to know how to create money and things than having a lot of money, lot things.</u>

> DP115. *She is wearing an open top dress. You ask her if she is cold. I tell her too that I understand when someone is working in the entertainment industry she must wear this kind of dress often. She answers to me that she is satisfied, I understand.*

Is it Britney? I would not quite be able to say. It is clear, though, that she is working in the entertainment industry under the title of singer. Apparently she would not only wear open top dress, but work without a dress at all like a wild animal, or more or less as the Hooters' girl. I know psychically many girls and ladies working in the entertainment industry. But when we met for the first time in psyche, we did not embrace, as it was the case with Britney.

Not having met her complete life, I have not get a clue what she really is, what she is really thinking and doing. That is also because I am not very familiar yet with psychic relationships.

Unfortunately, I can't really say the name of the person the DP might have referred to for the same research purpose. That would destroy the research totally. I can only say that this person is the cause of some malfunction in me.

> DP116. *She is in a missionary task in foreign countries. It is not finished, yet they change her schedule..*

Sometimes she has two different things to do the same day. She is out doing mission activities. During that time somebody enters into her bedroom. So she file a complaint about violation of her private life. They explain to her that nobody else has done before what she has done the reason why they came in her room while she was away.

It is probably about the body of a person and his consciousness. Apparently the consciousness leaves the body and comes back frequently while the person is sleeping. It may be also about the will that is to be given one task at a time, to increase its power. For example, I myself have a weak will. For in the same Saturday May 6, 2003 I had 11 DPs. Too many to make a will powerful enough to create my goals. No wander I don't earn any money to live on yet. My will is too distracted(One task one time still sound too metaphysical for me).

It would be very bizarre to refer to myself as a she, although I used refer to myself by you for fear of being too egotistical. I live my bedroom always open after I go away. One reason is in order to let some fresh air in. Another reason is there aren't too many HBBs living in the house, there can't be stealing. The last reason would be the door of my bedroom stays open, the door to go outside is locked.

Yes sometimes I see the trace of somebody who has been in the house during my absence.

Violating privacy refers also to the experiment I am doing and cannnot elaborate on yet. Still, I can tell you this: the subjects of the experimrnt are choses without their consent, because one purpose of the study is to prove that we can communicate before we meet in the complete life level of reality.

I do many things that are never done before including communicate with the subjects and having experience with them, I make love that way with other women, not the subjects and I have psychic acess to almost all HBBs on earth, it is why the question of privacy is raised in the DP. Those have never been done before.

> *DP117. Somebody gives me something like $30 with green and red bills and says to me that he will come back to get them tomorrow.*

There is no green bill in Canadian money or maybe the color of a 10 dollars is considered green; I do not know a country where there is such a thing. I think the expression "green back" refers to money. May be originated from Ireland. Apparently, yesterday May 17th, 2003 was an Irish day. I notice that green, the color of the planet is also the color Irish HBBs "identified" with, as the Russian souls are "identified" with red.

There could be a puzzle in the DP, for there are red bills in it, and one Canadian red bill only is fifty dollars. I wrote 30 dollars as the total. Nonetheless, in the DP itself I am not sure of the amount, why I wrote "something like". Or the total is more, or it is not Canadian money.

In any momey game , especially in the Casinos we can win a lot of money and loose as fast. TDP is suggesting why I do not win a lot of money at the game yet. Learning, learning how ro behave with money.

> *DP118. He appears near me while I am doing something. When I see him he has a little piece of paper*

in hands that reads: "The debts are dropped according to a law".

Refers to bankruptcy laws, which say that after a debt has been filed at the credit bureau for 6 years, it is dropped. I am not totally in agreement with this law anymore, because I think when I borrow something from someone I have to give it back to the person no matter how long it takes me. In complete life I do not have money yet, so it maybe because of not having it I think that way about it, and that when I have actual money I will have the urge not to live according to my thinking, the urge not to pay my debts, especially after they have been dropped at the credit bureau. We will see.

Monday May 8, 2000

DP119. From one house to the other I come and go many times. I do not see Aronce, I am worried. Yanyan says to me that he went to sleep at his mother's. I see Germaine, she is wearing a nice dress, and I am admiring her. I appear afterward with a lot of things in my hands. I want to go inside of this house by the left door; I am prevented from doing so the first time. I direct myself toward the right door; I am banned to enter into the house by there too. Then, I come back to the left door to find it wide open. I go inside the building. There I see a lot of dry leaves. I say to myself that I'll have a lot to do. I see Yanyan's husband who seems to be preoccupied by something on the ceiling of the house.

Aronce is one of my nephews whom I tutor for some time before I left Haiti. Once, brother Italien, his father, said to me that Aronce had the highest marks at his schools for a long period of time. So, I am proud of myself a bit when I think of him too. Yanyan is the nickname of Italien's wife. But Aronce is not her child, So, in DP, sometimes the principal actor is my brother living in Queens, New York, some times it is me. Germaine is Yanyan sister. She was pregnant of my child. At that period of my life I was not ready to have a child, I did not even know if I wanted to be a father or not. That decision was made long time afterward.

As everyone else, when I was at secondary school and at university, I was more or less a leftist politically speaking. I did not have to make the choice. It was what was unconsciously promoted in the intellectual milieu, even more so at the University of Quebec in Montreal among the universities I attended. I discovered later that it was not the way I was going to go, that I was not going to be active in politics at all, <u>although in psychology it is to believe that there is no such a thing as no choice, that when you do not make a choice it is because you made an unconscious choice to take what comes.</u> At the basis of my political belief is the theory that abundance is for everybody who wants it. If I was an active politician, I still would not be a leftist or a rightist, although this idea is an assumption of leftist political belief that nobody is talking about, what everyone is doing in practice.

I applaud the Czech and the Slovak souls for splitting the previous Czechoslovakia in two without a fuss, without bloodshed, peacefully. Those two new countries are not the richest country in the world, but there, is created an example which is exceptional, an example I would willingly try to emulate if I was active in politics. War does not just happened. It has to be wanted by two groups of HBBs for it to occur. That's the way it has been all the time, which makes the example of the Checks and the Slovaks even more significant. I wish it would be done the same way all the time: dispute between individuals and countries solve peacefully.

From one house to the other is the story of my life. I did it between Laboule and Dieurond, as already said, I Port-au-Prince it was between the places where Italien and Arnold live and some friend's places and my ant place where I lived. In New York it is again between Italien and Arnold's place. I did monitoring and teacher on call jobs, almost always a new school everyday. That sense of freedom came to me very young.

> *DP120. A group of 7 or 8 men are passing by in the street. They are making a big noise. It's like Prince Charles is among them.*

In Montreal, once, I was working at the post office, and was going to college the same year, very happy to find a job for the summer. I was not aware of any strike between the postal employees and their boss. Suddenly a group of men arrived at floor where I was and made such a noise. I thought they were going to attack me. It was my first years in Canada, was not very familiar with what really happened in similar situation. I did not even realize that the men were hungry at me because I was undermining their strike result by working for the post while they were on strike.

I am not against strike. There are so many holes in the capitalist economy that when there is a balancing force in its internal structure it is a blessing. So the possibility to strike is welcome in my mind which does not mean I would agree with any strike at any time. Despite the right to strike, many human beings are coping badly in a capitalist market. These are among the one who do not have capital; the ones who do not have any money at all and most of these strikes are not there to help them.

The only connection I would have with Prince Charles is in my family name, which is Prince also(psychic experiences with the Queen, another matter). In my father's family there are Charles too. They are the fighters in the family. They are Cameau Charles Abou Charles, Lamartine Charles, Yapoon (nickname) or Anibal Charles, and their father, Charleus Charles. They had a reputation for being very hot tempered, in fight very often. In my generation there is Gesner Charles. We are about the same chrono age, went to the same elementary school together, were very good friends. As 80% of the Haitian population are illiterate, there was no incentive for Gesner to continue his schooling. He became a farmer as most of his family members.

Those are the reasons why I would be dreaming of Prince Charles, and of the royal family. I sent a letter to his mother asking if she can help me with the project of earthquake detector. I do not have answer from her majesty. But the letter has been to its destination, it was not return to me, unsolicited letter, probably went to the garbage can. Or may be she is afraid I would be claiming some heritage for being born in the same family than her majesty? As far as I am concerned, it would be only a psychic heritage, " mine but not mine" as Jane Roberts would say. But, I would still send one to Prince Charles too. May be this letter would have a better reception.

I am in psychic communication with the Queen. That when I discover what a kind and humane person Prince Philip is. I could have a friend like him certainly.

Reminds me of what used to be G7 Meeting, what is now G8 Meeting, after the inclusion of Russia. As It used to cause leftist groups gathering and making big noise, intervention of police and violence, I asked myself why then the place of these meetings is not kept secret, or publish at the last minute? It appears to me that the most powerful economic system in the world needs the leftist groups as well as the leftist groups need them.

CHAPTER XVII

Tuesday May10, 2000

DP121. Some HBBs are going to get married. Other human beings are talking about the future husband and wife. I do not know them, do not recognize their names. Then, a man appears coming from a room in my house where I find a tall white woman to whom I ask to tell me what he and she were doing in my house. Understanding that I am not happy, she pulls the man toward her, and caress his body a little. Then, I say to him "Ok, I am going to live you alone". But he seems to want a fight and speaks to me with a finger pointed toward me. I bite his finger and say again "Otherwise you would have been strangled". "Autrement ou tap being strangled"

is the original sentence, French, Creole, and English.

Of course all the DPs are about life or everyone including you, and things. This one is alluding, also, to the famous research mentioned many times in this work, but of which I cannot give too many details yet in order not to invalidate the results and a kind of psychic jealousy. In a DP our desires, our thoughts are manifested right in front of our eyes, therefore, what we have above is, also, a projection of a personal desire to get married to a tall woman?. So, in it a step is taken into the future. With the soul it is mostly about the future.

I doubt I would still marry a woman who is having an affair as suggested in the DP for many reasons. The main one is having an affair with someone else says that I am not in romantic relationships with her(and that she is not either in love with me), and I would not marry a woman with whom I am not romantic relationships.

When someone points a finger at me, he is trying to create a fear by reminding me that he has or may have a gun. It is a sign of being really mad as Saddam from which name we are able to form the two adjectives sad and mad. At 10:30 this morning I do not know yet the state of affairs as related to the war started Wednesday March 2003 in the afternoon between the United States of America and Iraq. At four o'clock this morning I open the radio but there was no talk about the war. I fell back to sleep. After I got up at 6:15 I decided to follow my schedule as usual, so I will not have time to watch TV before this afternoon. Yesterday, according to the news, there was a lull in the fight, for, since the first rain of missiles in some strategic points in Bagdad, there seems to be no real sign of command from the Iraqis. In the United States government, there was a desire to wait and evaluate the situation to find out if the war is still on. Yesterday there was no concrete decisive sign that it was the case.

The war as should be expected is worrisome. It is not clear if the first missiles have killed some of the Iraqis government members. But 12 English men and 4 Americans are already dead by a helicopter accident. I rationalized last night by saying to myself that many more human beings have been killed in night club in Singapore, in a airport in Philippine, in two towers and two planes on September 11, 2001, where it was not supposed to happen, and that the war relatively is not the biggest evil. Then I thought that one of the unconscious reasons for war is probably boredom, in that case we need more big international parties like Christmas, Olympic games in order to discourage war at the same time prevent HBBs from being bored. If I had to institute that big international party, I would not choose any theme related to religion, another cause for war or reason of war.

> DP122. I start by taking some small fruits from a tree, give them to a child. Then, Siliamène appears. She comes from a course she is excited about, taught by a policeman about helping others. She talks, also, about working in a vacuum. I was going to say a bad word to show how I felt, something like "Fork them", but do not finish the sentence. I say, instead "the same person who's teaching that is going to play dirty tricks afterward". The talk is taking place in front of an empty land. After I finish talking to her, it's like the land is all planted of potatoes.

The potatoes plant leaves have been taken away what made the land looks empty as before. Then I see piles of brown potatoes all over. All the changes happen right in front of my eyes.

Siliamène was the cousin I used to fight with when I was about sseven, eight years chrono age without an explanation for the fight. She was my real and sure cousin, the daughter of my mother's sister, Joisila, from the same mother Sylvira my grand mother. So there is no possibility for a hiatus in the link as it would be if we were cousin by masculine branches. This DP is then about heritage. In it there is tree then suggestion of branches, fruit given to a child, suggestion of passage of wealth. Siliamene's father, Philogène, was relatively wealthy, When he died his wealth probably went to Siliamène his only child.

This group of HBBs Have the particular habit of walking all the time bare foot. In that country 17 to 20 degrees Celsius are found only on top of high mountains. The minimum temperature at night is around 25degree Celsius through the whole year. So, the weather doesn't discourage this kind of practice. Bare footing HBBs existed in all countries in the past, of course. It was a surprise for me, though, last August 2002 when a woman came to look for a place to stay bare foot in Canada. I was looking for a roommate, she said she was living in an island around the greater Vancouver, where she read my ad in the newspaper. She said also that she cultivates all the food for her needs to live.

August is the hottest month around here, she reminded of my go bare foot family and parents.

The DP is trying to reveal one of my projects: gather some wealth first than have children to pass it to. I do not think my children would have a high probability of survival, let alone having a good life otherwise. I may be making a mistake by thinking that way, but my own life is forcing me to think that way. If I created them and become bits and pieces soon after, I think the might not have a good life either, because I would not be there to raise them, to make them realize the immense power of the psyche. But I feel better about creating them anyway if I can leave them and their mother some wealth. I know that 80% of HBBs are "normal" like me, do not indulge in criminal activities, do not have exaggerated psychosis. Still, after a good look at my own life, decide not to have children before being sure I can leave them some wealth.

There are some inconsistencies in the DP. She is excited about the course given by the policeman, yet she feels that there is a vacuum in her life, reason to be unhappy. By that the DP might point to contradiction in me related to your project of children(or would it be an allusion to the overpowering ego).

"Working in vacuum" I think "Axworthy" after writing the beginning of this line, meaning, the ex-Minister of Finance in Canada, and may be next new Prime Minister. I really think that he is showing too much zeal to be a Prime Minister and that can impair his ability to govern a country, impair his excellent skills in finance: "When you become too intent to maintain reality, you loose it, for you deny reality the creativity on which it rests" Jane Roberts. But it was not what I was was imagining when you started the paragraph. I was at feeling empty and love, for that when we are forced to look for someone else "appraisal and bestowal of value"is lacking.

There are also suggestion of issues on racism, and creativity, but it is time to go to another day

Thursday May 1, 2000

> *DP123. The bus in which I am is full of HBBs. So much that I ca not see my own hands. While going off the bus, I have the impression that one of my hands is in someone else's b ody. I see a woman right in front of me moving hers forward in other to get off the bus also. I follow her thinking that my hand is in her hand. When I am out of the bus I find that my hand was in another man's.*

Each time there was going to be a terrorist who were going to detonate a bomb in Israel, I used to dream of it a few days before it really happened. The Palestinians are the one who are living close to the Jews; they know why they want their own separate country. Killing civilian is something no one going to like excepts the fabricators of terrorism themselves. *It's a gibberish act that does not reflect courage either. Anyway, the image "yI cannot see my hands in the bus" in the DP brings up in my mind amother one of my projects: the earthquake detector, for one of the side creation will be a big accident "preventor". If, after I had those dreams, I called Israel and told them that there going to be a terrorist in such bus with such number of HBBs. They would pee on that letter and throw it in the garbage can. Nonetheless, I know that those things can be prevented and that, the " big accident preventor" will be the best tool against terrorism, even if nobody is paying attention to me about it yet.*

Who said that the unconscious self is too serious a subject to make a joke about it? After I got off the bus, I found that my hand was in another man's hands. What else could it be? But figuratively it is also a wish of harmony in a group of HBBs.

In the human race, in other words, a wish of the end of war in general, and the on going one in Iraq today. If I you read about psychology, the first thing you will notice is that we are all connected with each other at the cellular level, in other words, we are all connected psychically(and spiritually too). That is why I can be hand in hand with another man in a DP, why nowadays I feel so bad each time I am about to watch TV. I come to the point where I associate it with something bad, something to avoid, because of the report on front line of war in Iraq.

DP124. When I get out of the house, I see a few persons outside as if there is going to be a fight. I say "what is happening here?".

After they left, I see two thin guys fighting. I pull them apart from each other by placing myself between them and push them apart with my two hands, and say to them that I am going to call the police if they don't leave it alone.

Reminds me of what I did once. Coming from a party at two in the morning, at the corner of Burrard and Davie Streets in Vancouver BC, I saw two young men fighting against each other while waiting for a connecting bus. I went in between them, push them apart, said "give it up". One of them responded "I am bleeding, what about that?" I said again "it's ok to give it up". They left, I went back to the bus top, took it and went home. In the morning there was blood all over on my jacket as if I have been in a fight myself. I was, only helping.

In October 2002, I received a call from a researcher. She said it was for global Television Company. During the interview. to answer one of her questions I said I agreed with the war in Iraq but for my own reason which is to help the Iraqis have a new government so everyone of them can freely participate in the amelioration of life conditions in their country, to keep their society going, to prevent it from dying from lack of individual input, the part I did not tell her. I was thinking of Haiti, of what it is to live in a country where there is a dictatorial government for a long period of time, all the miseries, the inhibitions it creates, etc. Recently this idea becomes more or less Mr. Bush rhetoric, makes me think that it was questions for a political research I answered to in October, these ideas are mine, that they do not look like what would be found in conservative political platform. If it is so, I am happy to have helped, especially when Canadians do not really agree with the war, do not officially participate in the war(Then the democrat opponent candidate in US defeated at that time was making threat toward me, toward Canadians by saying that he would ban Canadians from going to the United Stated).

A woman, Iraqi in opposition to Mr. Hussein government, talked about the war. At the end she said she loved Bush. I would not go that far, but I have faith in him, does not wish the death of Saddam Hussein and his family the reason why he asked him to leave the country before the first cruise missile fell on Bagdad. We all are human beings, make mistakes, have fear of the unknown etc. The composition of Mr. Bush's government reveals his sense of pluralism and inclusion, that he is not thinking he is from a superior race. Then, with or without him, I have an anchored good faith in American society. History shows that some of the Americans are excellent human beings and thinkers like Abraham Lincoln, Benjamin Franklin etc. A small percentage of them are criminals like in any other society. But all in all I do not worry about them going to war in Iraq. Some HBBs in country like Canada, France, Germany, Russia would not agree with me. That is their prerogative.

DP125. Somewhere in a street, I see a student I know. I am happy to see him, say hi to him.

The trigger of the DP is certainly the fright I had while talking to a tape to leave a message for Jacques Bertrang animating a successful radio emission in French Canada. I was very nervous, could barely talk. I was asking him to send me a CD promised during the show. May be I was not comfortable with the asking. Or may be because that Jacques brought to the surface of memory Jean Jacques Dessalines who gave independence to Haiti. I will not say that I dislike the concept of independence but I certainly think that it is not always to desire. Presently I am thinking that Haiti should be annexed to Canada and or United States of America, and or France if Haitian population, American population, Canadian population, French population agree, of course. I think it would be for the higher goods of the four parties and for humanity in general, in the sense: more voluntary individual input, better society.

This DP activates in my memory, also, boulevard Jean Jacques Dessalines in Port-Au-Prince where a cousin André Éli has a property that my sister, Monise, is managing. The DP is saying that the "cat has bitten my tongue" while talking to the tape that day because Jacques Bertrand is not my comrade, my school body. That made me nervous.

There are three persons wearing the name Bertrang who can be the cause of the nervousness. One Bertrang I knew when I was a child. He was responsible for the very large sugar cane farm part of Dieurond. He was a thinker living the real sophisticated life, very rich, had plenty of mistresses. One of his other women, Pierroline, was living four doors down my parent's house at LaBoule. He tried to give inhabitant of these primitive villages a taste of sophisticated life by organizing through Pierroline disco dances.

The other Bertrang is man I met in Trois Rivieres, Québec. He was a teacher too. I met him through Michel Muir, a friend I met at the University of Québec in Montréal. So Michel , the school comrade the DP is alluding to something similar in the future. As we said soul is mostly about the future.

Bertrang Trois Rivières was also a psychologist, had certainly a great influence on me.

The last Bertrang triggering the nervousness while talking to the tape was someone I've never met, and think the Creator. He had a reputation of a mean person in the government of Duvalier father. One day he just went in front of Pierre Novembre's place yelled for him to come out and killed him. That happened close by Chantal's brother' house where Arnold, my elder brother, rented an apartment. One of the bullets of the shooting left a whole in Arnold's apartment door, enough reasons to be that nervous while leaving the message for Jacques Bertrang in Montréal.

Friday May 13, 2000

> DP126. It's December 31 night. I think of bringing something to a woman. I find a brown dress on a hanger and think it will be what I will give her. After a while on the street I do not see the dress I had in my hands, turn back 180- degree;

meet a person who says she saw the dress in the street. I continue, find it, turn back 180 degree again.

Debbie used to give me a few gifts on December 26 for 6 years. Then, I noticed there was often a predisposition for quarrel in her for the rest of the week. The DP makes me realize that I did not give her any gift during the holidays. I gave her a gift in November for her birthday, and other time for other reasons, but not during the Christmas week. Probably, she was not happy with me because that, because I did not reciprocate in the gifts area at Cgristmas time . Most HBBs are upset this period of time of the year anyway. It takes many years to discover this mistake.

She, Devin her son and me used to spend December 31st at a party at Barbara and Don's. They are her friends, a married couple with one kid, Bruce.

About 20 persons were participating in the party at the beginning of the night, at the end about 10 HBBs. Debbie and me used to leave at around three AM. There was no dancing in those parties as such. I talked and drank; the kids plaid together. Once, at the beginning of the night I opened a bottle of Champaign that was already agitated. The cork and campaign flew away while a woman was hanging her glass waiting for some Champaign. Someone took the picture of that action. I still have it with me and in my documents. Is it Freud or one of his followers who said relationships between HBBs are always sexual? Not Freud, he would talk like that only about sexual fantasies. Even when Debbie and I did not succeed in merging our souls, but we had a lot of good moments together. Those parties witnessed some of them.

The DP is practically saying that I should give her cloth at Christmas time.

> DP127. December 31st, in bed with this woman, I am caressing her body. She becomes very excited, starts talking unintelligibly, then it is clear that she wants me to go and look for her ring somewhere in the house and bring it to her in the bed.

Another one saying I should propose to her. Still, let us continue.

When I met Debbie at Pellican Bay, the nightclub we were both in at the same time, she was already married, already had Devin. I did not cause the rupture of her relationships with her husband; it was already broken or about to be. I was the last circumstance that allowed it to effectively happen. Everybody is talking about the excitement of first days in love relationships. It is like some HBBs are even addicted to it, so they are always looking for the next relationships to be able to enjoy the excitements of first days in relationships. No one is talking about romantic love, a love that can grow, that can sustain itself ad infinitum. Still, it has been happening all the time. That is why there are about 50% of married couple in their old chrono age.

Yes, I still would like to marry the woman I love after we are sure we can live together.

> DP128. On an enemy camp, there are many structures. I go near one of these structures; a bullet is shot at my feet from another structure.

They said yesterday (27-03-03) that it was not easy to know exactly what is happening in the war in Iraq, to have an exact count of dead and prisoners in both camps, and that there were 5000 Iraqis surrendered, or made prisoners in battles. The day before Mr. Bush asked congress to vote and sign a bill for 75 billion $ for war expenses and 6 months of occupation.

CHAPTER XVIII

Saturday May 13, 2000

DP129. I appear entering into my house. There are a lot of activities near the entrance but outside. It's like someone is moving out, or the woman I was with is leaving me. I see things outside, I am asking myself if they are mine or not, if she had just tossed the belongings out while I was away. One woman in the neighborhood is ironing clothes. The iron looks like a cup in 5 dimensions in which there is only syrup. I want to help her with her ironing task but it is difficult for me to move the iron on the clothes. When I go up in my apartment, I do not see her. There are a few things in the rooms, but it becomes vague in my mind,

"translucide" in front of my eyes, I do not recognize what I see.

Cup in five branches may refer to this: "neither space nor experience can contain the psyche, because of that it creates the dimension in which it operates, has its experiences"

Cup in 5 dimensions is also a reminder of the Pentagon, the office of the Head Office of the US Army. It is the link that proves what I say elsewhere in this work that some of my ideas where used by the top officers in this army to make the war against Iraq more palatable. I was questioned by the supposed market researcher for global television company, she mentioned a number of reasons according to which there should be a war in Iraq, and asked my opinion on these reasons, I declined to elaborate on them, but told her that the war should be done to help the Iraqis liberate themselves of a too long dictatorial government. I told the researcher, also, that having lived in Haiti, I know how bad it feels to live in such an oppressive atmosphere. The ideas were repeated many times during the first days of the war. I was not surprised by her questions, as if they were coming from someone with whom I was intimate relationships. I thought it might have been Heather, who might want to have precise information on me such as my sexual activity.

Such detailed information about me is written only in this work, The SOUL EXPOSED. The Pentagon might have known about it through computer piracy. Another way for them to know about me is through their spoke person Miss or Mrs. Clark? Miss Clark herself would know me through the experiment I'm doing in telepathy.

Furthermore, the DP reminds me of what is happening to me nowadays with Amanda. I would like to merge in love relationships with her. It has been a long time since I have done such a thing. I am very rusty in the domain.

In other words I am not or I have not succeeded in my desire of merging my soul with hers. I do not have physical sexual dysfunction. Mentally it is a different matter. I do not function effectively. As you know, 90% of the failure to merge are from me. Nobody is perfect, as you say, so Amanda must share 10% of the blame. The most difficult thing for me to interpret from her side is that she has a couple of male friends, I do not know if she is going out with them or not. I do not want to ask her. I hope at least to be able to make love with her. If I ask the question, she will think I am "objectivising" her (making an object of her) and shot her heart out from me.

She is moving out next month, meaning May first. She was mistreated by the couple upstairs, by jealousy, may be. I am friend with Jake their son of 4 years old. Jake did not like Heather, so I assume he might not like Amanda either, understandable, he is only 4 years old. But, it is not easy for me to figure out the attitude of his parents, except that it looks like jealousy. Anyway, Amanda will leave.

So, she is moving out, I tried to make love with her before the moving day. I kept repeating the same mistake: get busy at something else when she is ready or completely misunderstood her advances on the spot. She said someone gave her flower at her birthday, but she still looking at me in a long languorous fashion. I said to myself, if I cannot sleep with a woman available in the same house, I cannot sleep with any woman at all. The DP may be saying, though, that the connection, the romantic love with her is impossible, that I left the house, found my belongings outside when I came back (jealousy of the HBBs living upstairs), that I should forget the project of making love with her all at once. It may be saying, also, that if I become involved with her, I will be so preoccupied by this intensive romantic love, that I will not see clear enough to be able to continue the research. But, as you understand it, the preoccupation **by the romantic love is largely compensated by the goodies resulting from this kind of love such as I become more creative, my sexual traumas gone and vanished, organizer of all of the lover's desires, agent of change etc.** So in no way I will exchange a romantic love for other kind of love or something else.

But there is also the philia love.

They say that we are a bit conscious while dreaming. The above DP expresses that too. The DP may be also about other couple. the cup with 5 branches, and the moving a metaphorical prediction of The black general in the US Army being demoted, for cocky reason probably.

> DP130. I am in my room. A man throws a piece of paper in front of my door. I ask him to take it off from there and tell him that I will not myself move it from my door to the next door. Then I appear elsewhere in the same building, trying to stabilize a piece of red hot iron balancing in the air, using a long spoon with a sort of cup in one end to do it. As I do not succeed in stabilizing the floating iron, I pass the spoon to another person.

The first thing I thought after writing this DP in the computer was not being able to do something for good, to bring a project to its last step, we have a tendency to pass it to other person. In other words it is about the fear of responsibility. I was like that when I was younger, certainly, why I am still trying to have children, when other HBBs may be preparing themselves to die. Of course, it was an unconscious(or other level of consciousness) fear that no one will have consciously. The unconscious power will use, sometimes, someone else for the misdeed. I was chairperson of Health Reform Council of the West Side Vancouver. Faye, employee of the ministry suggested I passed it to someone else. I was unconsciously using her to do that. Or other individual has penetrated my space of the psyche. by likeness or other kind of connections.

The piece of red-hot iron in the air is pointing to momentum and consolidation(Is it an allusion to sexuality?). It is saying that the iron can be shaped at will when it's hot. Also a metaphor for my libido in this state now because of 5 years of total sexual deprivation (Desperate Housewifes). I will have to come back to the subject.

Can 5 represent 5 hundred millions dollars?

> *DP131. Many HBBs are eating. I am sitting beside one of them. He is looking beside himself while eating. I explain to the one facing me that the one beside me is like that, looks always beside himself while eating. Then, the one facing me starts to cry.*

It's a bizarre one, makes me think of HBBs in general who are always looking at what the other has or has not instead of looking at themselves to see or find out what they have or do not have. Then, this kind of attitude is conducive to war? Beside, according to the way I see life right now, I agree with the saying **"All the important solutions reside in self"**. So this DP sends us to the behavior of the American society in general, externally oriented compare to the European society, again, in general, "innerly" oriented.

It refers also to digital operation, language, or whatever this adjective is. I got the idea, a bunch of little batons or bites standing up and connected by an electrical impulse that are used to count or to write according to the computer program. When I just arrived in Canada I wanted to study the computer. I was not disciplined enough to pursue that goal. At that time Microsoft did not exist. Now, its president is worth 60 billion US dollars. It is that I would ever want to have so much money for any reason. Although the expertise in the computer science would allow me not to go in teaching field and, so, spare me so many headaches.

It is the occasion to recall Vincent Van Gogh's painting that is to say The Potato Eaters, also Edison and artificial light.

A DP taken from an infinite context often points to an infinity of meanings. We live in a waking life with a finite number of things we can do in one day. What I am trying to say, again, is that <u>I will leave it up to the reader to find meaning in his own life corresponding to this DP in particular, all of them in general.</u>

Before I leave this one I am going to indicate two more meanings to it. The figure who is always looking beside himself while eating may refers to someone not facing reality for one reason or another, someone who sees things the wrong way or not seeing them at all. This is no good for creation, for **to create you have to be able to see reality accurately all the time as it is and when it changes. The** one crying is emotion, the one looking to the right, rationality, and the one in the middle representing intuition. That is my last interpretation of this DP.

DP132. Someone appears; he looks like an English man. I ask:

"Do you come to see the woman in the house?".

"Sometimes I go to a store and ask myself-- What the hell am I here for?" That is his answer.

"Something that happens to everyone once" I add. Then I go out for a walk together, he met another man, tells him the same story.

It is probably about something Robert Sadello reports in his book Love and the World, that is the crowd in the mall composed mostly of HBBs without a purpose. They are in the mall but what they really want to do is to find the escaping door. In order words these HBBs are not in direct contact with their soul and their spirit. They don't have goals.

The observation is neither capitalism nor about market economy. It is about a rich society without soul.

The DP suggest that the English HBBs are like that. With my consciousness I would think it is a problem pervasive in all occidental countries and the rest of the world, not just the Anglophones.

I already said in this work that I believe that most criminals are so by default. They were forced as a young person to follow a path, which is not the path of their soul for one reason or another. They are living outside the boundaries of their destiny, of themselves.

Someone was discouraging me in order not to buy lottery ticket in the DP.

DP133. He brings me a paper; it's hot as a wrapper of a hot pizza. But it is a scientific text with lot of equations. I place it somewhere in the house. Someone appears in the house, I show it to him and ask him to touch

*it to feel the heat coming from it.
Subsequently, I start working. Later
I notice he is writing on the paper,
I make it clear to him not to write
on it.*

The DP is not difficult to understand by anyone, still we can say that the hot paper in refers to the Soul Exposed. It is hot may be because it is new, it is hot because in it there are Intuition, the data coming from the psyche and the understanding of them, the DP and the understanding of it. In that sense we can alsotalk talk about a scientific book referring to the Soul Exposed. It structure is very simple but it stand on its ground The person writing on it may be a critic. Here is what Arno Gruen in his book named the Betrayal of the Self about this kind of work:

The fact that there is any psychic health left in our world speaks for the strength and the pervasoiveness the ability to have a direct experiences that are rooted in needs and goals.

*DP134. I am with this woman and
going to leave. I want to leave with
her, but do not have a clue on how
I am going to do to find money to
pay the transportation.*

In the DP I probably thought that I was in Haiti where there would be problem of transportation and woman. In Canada the only time I have problem with transportation is when there is a strike by the employees of the transport services. I live in the backcountry for 6 months, Comox British Columbia. I had a car almost the whole time. Yes, in the North American countries also, we can have problem of transportation if we do not have a car and living in back country place like Courtney BC We can have transportation problem also if there is a natural disaster such as a snowstorm or an earthquake.

Who is the woman I wanted to leave with in the direct perception? May be Amanda.

I lived also in other backcountry, Russell Manitoba. I was working there, had a lot of friends there. It was easy to use a friend's car or to rent one.

DP may be about things that will happen in the future

DP135. The friend I meet in the street says to me that he had presented the pants, I will have to fix it myself, he was told.

I don't have too many friends in Vancouver. When I was teaching I had the opportunity to make many friends, but I had only two goods friends Ed and Tony? As I replaced them a lot in their classes, when we met it was a satisfying moment.

From 1993, I lived in shared accommodation, there would be the opportunity to make a lot friends that way too. Nonetheless sexual motivation that I do not approve prevented that from happening. All the men are bisexual and they do not care about who I am or my sexual practice, or my heterosexuality. If they do they would ask me about my sexual orientation when they move in the house NAfter that I would feel the accept me to have a different sexual orientation and that I accept theirs too. Instead, they just bombard you with subliminal messages for homosexuality. Then, starting the relationship that way, friendship is eliminated.

Sunday May 14 2000

DP136. There is a big machine in this classroom with automation and buttons to make it move, and to move also its superior parts. As it is the first time I am sitting on it, I feel a little bit strange. The students are standing and are everywhere in the classroom. I ask them to sit down and to be quiet. One of them starts to laugh; I slap him in the face, ask him to go and sit outside.

I haven't and would never do to a student tin complete life. So thid part of the DP is a catharsis . Yes in Haiti corporal punishment was the kind of motivation that was used to make learning happened especially in the lower grades. So I started by using this teaching technique myelf too. But at university in Canada, I discovered quickly that it was not the way to go, that it was better to use the carrot instead of the baton at any stage of the personal development, **that the ultimate motivation tool in teaching is involvement, because of it is in a causal and circular relation with interest.**

Nonetheless, we could still think that the use of baton as teaching tool in school is one of the causes of war, may be. But Darwin theory of evolution misinterpreted can be among the most important causes of war too, the survival uf the the fittest in the theory may be seen as if it is a good thing to kill the weak HBBs. As well as the theory of biblical creation, as well as that human beings are too outwardly oriented in comparison to inwardly oriented (alienation), as well as misunderstanding of the nature of consciousness.

Who says "War is individual conflicts magnified in a million". It is to assume that who ever said it was thinking as above. The conflicts drag the individuals away from themselves. They are oblivious to their own inner resources physical or mental and so from the outer resources too, for inner and outer forces are indisolubly linked. They look for their personal gratification in the society in other individuals only, instead of giving and taking pleasure. But as they are living an eternal internal conflict, they see the other individuals as their enemy, A whole society ends up seeing another whole society as an giant enemy to submit by any means in order to solve their own internal conflicts.

Some HBBs are still thinking that some of them are weak and that the weak ones should be eliminated. Where this warrior attitude comes from? Of course at university too where evolutionism is the paradigm, because it teaches the theory of the jungle according to which only the strong animals survive (Does it remind you of these words of song 'The strong will survive") The small ones have been eaten by the big ones.

How many declared religious war the world had known? Of course, reality is big, impossible to be contained and to be completely understood. One theory can describe only a version of it. Even then, another theory may have a different explanation of the same part without being wrong like two identical cakes differently sliced.

Some of us think that war creates jobs, stimulate invention. Imagine creating jobs for HBBs. by killing other HBBs, creating jobs for them by killing them. Jane Roberts in The Unknown Reality puts this false belief in perspective by these words "Because **consciousness creates form in joy;** there is no murder that you have projected that is not out of misunderstanding and ignorance of the nature of consciousness"

Yesterday (April 2, 2003) I've learned that the American

Army is advancing toward Baghdad. I count that it is at the cost of 60 Americans lives, Iraqis multiply by hundreds. I've learned, also, that the stock market was up because of feeling of an imminent end to the war, the Americans and the English dominating the air also dominating the fight. I've learned also that Mr. Powell(the black general iduring the comprehension of a previous DP) and Mr. Romspheld two war secretaries of Mr. Bush government are in disagreement as to how to reconstruct Iraq. By the Americans and the English men or by the United Nations the position of Mr. Powell? I would say He is not wrong on that. However, fairness for fairness, the Americans and the Englishmen have the last words. If the leave the task to the United Nations it is their prerogative, but they have the right to it. Itis costing them lives.

Just before the war started I sent a letter to Saddam promoting the United Nations solution.

There should be a diplomatic school in Prague and Slovenia where Americans, Iraqis and all this planet inhabitants could go to learn diplomacy and how to live with each other around. The Czechs and the Slovaks have demonstrated by example what they know about human being, about living together in peace, solving problems peacefully. They split one country in two without a fuss, without a blink of an eye. I applaud them, make me proud of being human like them and hope they will always serve as an example to follow, as character to emulate. It is not quite clear to me the process by which they have arrived at their peaceful solution. I know that they are human with imperfection and worries. Nonetheless, I admire the way they choose to settle their differences.

In Haiti, I was trying to do the same thing, using civilized means to settle differences when I was teaching in school and did not get my pay cheque. I asked the students to stay in their seats quietly and wait for the principal-owner of the school. He ran toward me like a bull instead. There is allusion to that in this DP too.

Al in all the ddirect perception is about the the teaching og automation in school, there is no teaching at all of idividiality. All the scholar instrument in society and in the schools are geared toward acceptation and compliance, aceptation of errors and lies .

Nice cars , nice women or men, imagination can go wild with this DP.

> *DP137. In this classroom as student, and as I was away for some time, I pass an arm around the neck of another student, he explained to me what has been done during my absence. At this moment I see some very tall women who are moving around and who are smoking. I say to Horcel to be careful about women.*

Horcel is someone I met in the equivalent of grade 8 at Lycée Toussaint Louverture at Port-au-Prince. I was very good friend with him and Michel. Him and Michel were always together. Michel is living in the US, Horcel in Montréal.

If I did not have that last sentance in the direct perception I would not really know its meaning. For it's about Toussaint Louverture himself who started the political liberation of the whole island, which was Haiti(only part of it is Haiti) . He was brave very determined, and almost invincible politically at his time (year 1750 +). But the famous Toussaint had a weakness for woman and pleasure. The French new that and took advantage of it by inviting him in party where they ambushed, arrested, and sent him to Fort Jura a jail in France to spent the rest of his life.

I hope I do not have an unconscious fear of joy, and fear of punishment. I think it is the religious HBBs who frown upon pleasure, consequently when we are having pleasurable moment we fell we are going to get punish for it, unconsciously of course.

> DP139. Somebody finishes his work. He eats some small bread that I have placed on the table, gives some to another person.
>
> (Yvette)

Yvette was the name of the teacher who used to share her lunches with me in grade 2. I used to bring no lunch myself, because I was on my own and too young to think of that.

> DP140. I am at a counter in a store where there is a pile of caramel in small cubes. I say to the person behind the counter "How much a caramel?" As she doesn't answer my question, someone beside me says "they cost 10 cents each" then a child start to cry bitterly and loudly. Apparently, another child has hit one of his fingers. At this time I have my hands in my pockets looking for change to pay for caramel I bought. It's like I give the retailer 25 cents which is bizarre, given that 25 is not a multiple of 10.

Reminds me of what happened at Choices, a small supermarket on 16th Avenue when I was living at 3339 west 42nd Avenue. (So 2,3 years before I came to live here on 16th Ave, I knew I was going to live on 16th Avenue somehow). Anyway, that time I used to take Friday off and called it Psychic Friday, day when you dress up, went out in the city without any neither clear destination nor thing to do. I bought a bunch of caramels at that store that were given to me in a small bag. I was eating them from the front of the store, saw a mother and her child who looks at the bag and says "I want some"(I was in a similar situation once before at Metrotown Mall, may be there is a pattern there to analyze, may be the mind is saying that it is a child who eats outside as I did). So I gave him some caramels, he had his two small hands full of them. He was so happy, her mother was so happy, I was so happy, one of the greatest moments in my life.

Strangely enough, today (April 4, 2003) there are 25 million Canadian Dollars, for one US dollar, to win in Super 7 or PPK. Therefore May 14, 2000 I was predicting what was going to be in that store in April 4, 2003; the link is the 25 cents and the 25 millions $. Reminds me of Russell Crowe and a Beautiful Mind. The psyche is so nice so precise so magnificent. Just thinking of it makes me feel as if I have been drinking, as if I was in the la land, floating in space, sometimes.

I wish the DP would mean that I am going to win the 25 million today. With it I would create a foundation with 10% 9 the automatic feeling I have to give is false, have to give is not giving anyway)of the amount=$ 2 5000.00. With the rest of the money, I would create some of my goals. It is likely that the pot will be different, for the 10 cents indicate a different total, and may be 30 million. Last time the biggest amount in Canadian lottery history was 36 million won by 4 persons, so 9 million each. This DP makes me think that we may be in for a similar situation next.

The draw of super 7 on Friday April 11, 2003 gave the 30 million to one person in Ontario. The 10 cents in the DP it was to signify $ 10 I won in the preceding draw, that is, when the jackpot was 25 million.

. The game is won by intelligence and intuition, dometimes it may be just intuition, some other it may be just intelligence. In game such as super 7 with 21 million possibilities, HBBs still play the whole set of seven numbers. Their mind and there body mind and soul are capable of the necessary calculation to obtain the wining set of numbers. Universal law or the Creator does not participate at this those sorts of things, otherwise it would be bias. It takes desires, will, individual or specified mind.

That is partly why I detach true psychology, from the study of "God" or religion, although these two studies have a lot in common with psychology where the main preoccupation is the psyche. In religion it appears that "God" could be bias to forgive one person instead of another, to bless one person instead of another. In psychology, I learn, instead, to deal with my goals with fierce determination in order to create them, exactly because Universal Law will not help me at this stage, will stay neutral. I cannot be specific(or individual) by taking order from someone else, even if it is from the religious "God,"even if it is to win 25 millions dollars. Specific means I am the only one to do the work with my powerfull I.

In the soul practice, there is no "God" above us. We are all co-workers. I myself think there many gods and the Creator. The gods and everything else are created by the Creator.

DP141. *Standing in front of something all black, I have an erection. Then, I notice that behind that thing there is a woman.*

Being in the black in the market economy usually means being in the profit. This DP may be referring to this "marketic" phenomenon. It supposed to be rare in this kind of economy. For it can be argued that market economy is not an affluent economy rather a scarcity economy. It is the concept of value that makes things that way. The price of a product is inversely proportional to the quantity of that product in the market. In other words to keep the price stable or high, there is to be an optimum quantity, in other words there is to be a scary of product. Sometimes I tend to think that it is creation of poverty pure and simple

It has been this way until now. Nothing inside the market economic system really requires the scarcity. There could be more money available so that the bigger quantity of a product can be absorbed as quickly as it is produced. There could be an international price different from international price, etc. With a set of mind always looking for better way, creative solution, the scarcity requirement in the market economy would vanish. With the set of mind of abundance for all who want it that way, the mixture of value and scarcity in market economy would disappear for inconsistency and uselessness

Libido and black market do not make sense, libido and an enterprise in the black or with substantial amount of money left, in the account receivable left. Or maybe there is some link I do not perceive yet, not having been in the black yet.

At 2 in the morning, she came at my place I made love with her I only met her once before at a party in my place. At 10 o'clock the same morning I had an interview for a teaching position. It was a success.

Did that lady sensed that I was going to have the position before she came to my place, then tried to position herself in my life in advance? Last week I thought that

Barbara upstairs wanted to make love with me while I came close to winning 15 million dollars at Super 7. Was the same phenomenon described above at work? If I had really made love with her, would I actually win the 15 million? It was possible according to the idea that consciousness creates form with joy. When I was sensing her availability for sex, I knew also I could win the 30 million dollars or part of it. But, I did not make the connection between the two situations. I was having a tremendous amount of tension and terribly frustrated after having won 50 dollars by playing 4 wining numbers when there was $25 million to be won. Instead of letting the tension play its course and correctly interpreted the DP on numbers I had that day, I shot circuited the tension down as quickly as it came. If I had made the connection with the possibilities for love and winning, I would take the advantage of both, it seems.

If I am true to myself I have to admit the connection between love making and winning as it is believed in certain religious groups. Making love creates such a nice feeling. Intimacy is of such a value.

> DP142. I climb a structure; afterward I am afraid that it is going to scroll down on itself under my weight. Because of that fear I decide to let myself slide down of it, but some of it comes down with me by the way.

There is the fear to become too big(bodily wise) after winning a tremendous amount of money. The DP is saying more precisely that I decided to win just a bit of money from the 25 million dollars because of that fear(or the wish for expansion). Why would that be? Having a lot of money does not necessarily translate in becoming big, in having too many pounds in my body. In some cases the opposite is the truth, allow the choices of food. With that much money, i do not have too much stress; I do not have bipolar depression. I am not pushed to eat by neurotic or psychotic compulsion. It is more likely that I will be able to control my weight after winning a lot of money. Not only me , but also many HBBs choose to win small amount of money in the game in order not to gain weight, bizarre behavior.,unconsciously of course.

There is also the fear of being a star, having a very wide span of an audience, and then while on top losing my seed of wit, falling down as a bag of garbage. This fear can prevent me from creating my goals, from realizing my dreams, from winning 25 million dollars.

CHAPTER XIX

Monday May 15, 2000

> *DP143. She is talking to a man who is selling something. He does not seem to understand that she is in a courtship with him. At the end she gets mad, complains of his insensitivity, that he is interested only in what he selling. Agreeing with her I say "There are some Hobbs who only buy what has been shown to them". Right?*

My love life is kind of dead now. Last week I have decided not to pursue a courtship with Amanda. I have tried to get close to her, showing her that I missed her when she is not around. The same day, I went out from my bedroom to the kitchen saw her going in her room with one of the guys I used to see her with. That is what has triggered the decision. Although, i do not know dor sure what kind of relationships she is in with these guys, I said to myself that she does not want really to have anything to do with me as far as relationships is concerned, that it does not make any sense for me to want romantic love with her while she is seeing other men.

To say the truth, I do not know what to think of woman presently. I do not know if I should try to be in a romantic relationships with one of them, if you should just make love with some of them, I am totally lost in regard to that subject. There must be lot of blocks brought forth to consciousness by all sorts of stimuli. The brute and severe break up with Debbie may have created mental scarce that are still active in my psyche.

Last Thursday, Jake, Barbara's boy of 4 or 5 years old closed her out meaning that she was in the basement where my bedroom and Amanda's are, but could not go back upstairs where she lives in the house. She was in the escalator yelling for Jake to open the door. I went to find out what was happening to her. After she explained it to me, I asked her if Todd, her husband was not home (thinking he could open the door for her, but that question seems to have stimulated more emotion in her). She said he was out for a week. She gets my mail, used to leave them in a little basket in the basement. On Friday she left a Todd letter behind mine. I thought it was an invitation to love or rather sex while her husband is away, at the unconscious level, though. I did not take advantage of the situation. I was doing something wrong.

But Todd's letter put me in a bad mood. For 3 years he has been suggesting homosexual relationships with me relentlessly without any consideration for my heterosexuality. His letter triggered violence in me instead of anything else. I would move out from here today, if I knew I was going to a different kind living . If I move to another bedroom in a shared accommodation concept, nothing will change. There will be other bisexual to bug me. Barbara and him have a shed in an island somewhere around Vancouver BC. She suggested once that I should go and spend sometime there with them. I do not know if she knows about Todd bisexuality or not. I found her suggestion repulsive because of that, although, if it was a different love outlet, I would plunge to it without hesitation. The last time I made love with a woman was 1998 in a hotel in Oklahoma, even though heterosexuality is my only sexual practice.

One part of the problem seems to be communication. The women I came in contact with use subliminal messages to talk to me. It does not work for me. Rather than leaving Todd mail with mine if Barbara told me squarely that she would like to be with me , the probability for my acceptance would be 90%. The subliminal message she used not only triggered negative memory of Todd's sexual harassment toward me, but also let me the time to contemplate before deciding yes or no. I had the time to think that making love with married woman is not my favored thing to do that she has small children who could suffer from that action. Also if Todd left her because of me, I would not be able to be with her on a long-term basis, not because she is not attractive enough, but because I have other plan for long term relationships. In that situation, her children would suffer even more.

Most of the time, Amanda used subliminal message to communicate her sexual desire about me, the time it takes me to decipher the meaning it's already to late. Her mood has changed, my mood has changed, and we both become engaged in other daily activities.

One girl who is working at the Dunbar branch of the Vancouver Public Library uses to flirt with me. One day, she was alone between two library shelves. I stretched my hand with a business card to give her in order to establish contact with her. She said she would rather not take it. The following day she came to work well dressed and behave with me as if I should ask her out that day. Recently, she repeated her behavior, come at work well dressed and behave with me to ask her out. When she said she would not take the card, she was not concerned about her employment. She may have thought it was too literal the way I tried to establish a contact with her, that I missed the subliminal part. If this is the way she thinks, it is ok. But how am I going to do to try to establish contact with her again after the first refusal? After it, it became difficult for me to even speak to her again. She could have taken the card without calling me immediately afterward. It is like because I did not use subliminal message it was not lovely enough, it was not sexy enough, appealing enough. Or she was concerned about her job, not knowing if I am a spy or not. Jewl sings a song about it I think the song says that "the game drives to the edge of mental sickness "or something similar.

True, being too literal may cause a psychological disturbance called "stricter", when our mind is plays tricks with us because we have been too literal, have not deveoped the subject enough and so on. It is also true that using subliminal messages all the time to communicate desires for love is a mental disorder itself. That is why I think that these means of communication fit better HBBs practicing bisexuality. They are the ones who do not want to reveal their loving emotions, or who may be in turmoil about revealing their good feelings for one sex while being pulled in the opposite way in their mind by the other sex. In subliminal messages nothing is revealed, very convenient for bisexual. I do not know why the women here in Vancouver insist on using subliminal messages to communicate sexual desires. Lots of good moments that could be spent together are lost that way. So much the worse.

There is also allusion to materialism in the DP when

it says some HBBs buy only what they can see. No time to develop here, it will be done later.

Tuesday May 16, 2000

> *DP144. In the house there is a housemaid. When I wake up, she is already there. I left a bag beside a chest of drawers before I went to bed the night before. As I do not see it when I wake up, I ask her if she had thrown it in the garbage can. She does not answer me directly. She has a sheet in her hands, I thought it was the one that I have, but looking at it closer I see that it is not the one that I have.*

It reminds me of the time during a hot, hot summer in Haiti. I was at one of my brothers' place, near the Presidential Palace. He was working; I was alone with the housemaid. She came to the bedroom a couple of times without underwear, something happened between her and me. I was still in grade 11, or the equivalent. It was such a powerful experience, left its mark in my memory. After a few months she said she was pregnant, had to have an abortion.

I gave a sheet that was given to me by Debbie to the last woman I was in love with, relationships that practically ended in 1998. When she asked me for the sheet, she probably knew that it was going to be finished between us too. I myself did not know, for I expected to keep in touch with her for the rest of her and my life. Previously, after the end of the love relationships I used to cut it from there for good without any further contact. After the end of the relationships with Debbie which ended abruptly as usual,

I said to myself that from there on I was going to keep in touch with all my past relationships. After the end of the last relationships in 1998, I realized that there are two persons in the equation and that the other one may not want to keep in touch. You wanted to keep in touch with her, but she cannot for some reason.

It is almost always like that with me. I wake up in the morning, I do not have a cent, but I still have slept with a bag with million dollars in it in the house. "How can that be?" Don't you think? It is easy; I have it in my imagination. Even when I forget about the whole thing the bag is still there. Anyway, bag is a symbol of money to me after I have made it so, not so much the bag itself, but the content of the bag which can be sugar, coffee, rice(symbol for money) etc. I discovered recently that I could not hide behind symbols in order to hide anything from HBBs really. It is part of their psyche too. They know something is hidden, even if they do not know exactly what it is. When Amanda just move in here, bags and me obsessed her. I stood by counter of the kitchen, she came near me, took a bag under the sink. She bought a bag with fancy color, put it in the fridge, etc. She knew that bag was important for me, but do not know the details of it.

DP145. The mafia

Dangerous subject. I saw a film on TV recently where the main character is a member of the mafia telling his life story. That is how I come up with a rational explanation of President Robert Kennedy death(It was suggested in a show), that is, his father may have been some how mixed with the organization . After his election as president of the US, his brother was determined to clean it up. The mafia, then, arranged the assassination of Robert Kennedy, by a sniper. This explanation is acceptable to me because it sounds good, 90% probable, very unlikely not to be true, still not hundred pour cent true.

When I have money I will buy Lamborghini, the only reason for which I have this DP, for it is originally made in Italia, as the concept mafia may have its origin in the same country. Italia the little point of land in the sea of Europe, one of the greatest country in the world, historically speaking. I do not quite know how I came up with a video entitled "Rome: Power and Glory". I am fascinated by it, play it times and times again. Yes, there are lot of fights in it. Yes. War is not my favored thing. Yet, I am fascinated by the video. It is a version of the beginning of big cities, colonization, democracy, dictatorship, slavery etc.

The person who fascinates me the most in the tape is Pompeii. He was a farmer, but when Italia was in danger of being sized by an army of strangers, he was called to Roma, given full power in Italia government. He became the head of the Italian army, liberated the country by chasing away the armed strangers, and returned back to farming. He is one of the fabulous persons we ever had. Magnanimous, very powerful inside out without abusing his power, used it when the circumstances justified the use of it. It is surprising to know such a person has existed even though human beings are like that basically but rarely show it.

Another greatness in the tape is about the Etruscans; a group of HBBs even more advanced than the Romans at the beginning where the latter have learned the concept of big cities and its needs like water supply and drained. The Etruscans were very developed for their time in engineering and in terms of sexuality. Their sexual acts were displayed in public like that, without a trace of shame as it should be. They were not inhibited in any way about their sexuality. Their ingenuity and their attitude toward sexuality made their greatness. Don't you agree?

DP146. *The image of point on a sheet of paper.*

When I had the DP I was thinking about atom and absolute, especially about the idea that all the universe, everything that exists, could derive from an atom. I have been reading on Field theory in psychology where I get these words "Since by definition the field is a state of all possibilities the inner truth says I am getting to know the absolute by playing here in the relatives". I don't quite remember if they come from a DP or a book. It is not specified in my notes.

Absolute reminds us of the "absolute reason in Hegel, and absolute body in Nietzsche" and that after we attain the absolute stage we cannot go anywhere else. In order that kind of thinking in metaphysics cannot go anywhere. It puts an obstacle to all avenues. It is why when I think of absolute thinking I think of ceramic. However there is no absolute somethig in the DP.

I was thinking about the astronomic number of things that exist in one-person life, that one person has to do everyday, and the necessity of making choices. I was thinking of the sun, the sea, the stars, the mountains, and the valleys, countries with different HBBs speaking different languages. I was thinking that one person will never be able to experience all that exist, that he/she has no choice but to make a choice. I was thinking about the number of choices I already made in my personal life, valued choices, choices without value, and that it does not serve a purpose to ruminate the ones that do not have value, to learn the lesson and go on living.

I was thinking "Time, valued cost of period"

In other words, I was thinking of Sophia, the Soul of the World, the Creator Creator at the source of everything that exist.

In the presence of the infinite the universe may be measured as dot. certainly the nature with gazillion stars and planets.

> *DP147. The person I went to look for to talk on the cellular telephone is Peres Catule. When I am back, I do not find the telephone number I want him to compose. I ask someone else for it. He does not remember the number either. Then I go down to a room to pick up the telephone that was on a desk. While I am looking for it and canot find it, Peres is talking to his brother through it. That upsets me a bit, thinking the time I find the number I want him to compose, he would used up the antenna time left in the prepaid telephone service that I have, in order words he would not be able to talk to the real person I want him to talk to. The room is dark, yet I see a being in it who reminds me of Bi nickname for Princius who used to be my uncle and my godfather when he was alive. He is talking to me in an unfamiliar language.*

Peres Catule's parents have a house a few steps away from my late parents' house in LaBoule. He was supposedly the Don Juan of the primitive area where a primitive kind of life is lived . But Don Juan in the depth of thing, as the say, was rather someone who could not succeed in love. So there is no glory to be a Don Juan of an Area. He may believed it was something especial to be a Don Juan in an area, not so much because he is illiterate, but also it is the belief of a big portion of HBBs. in the world, intellectual(without intuition), educated or not.

This subject is developed extensively in Relation Amoureuse,.

My brother Italien was living with Raymonde with whom he was supposed to have made a few children. He was away at work all the time. Raymonde was not sexually satisfied may be or simply was a slot. One day he, living in Queens in New York presently, surprised Peres in a sexual act with Raymonde. The way this brother Italien was at that time, if he caught Peres he would have killed him. Thank the Creator, Peres had the time to run away. If not he would be in bits and pieces today. Italien left Raymonde and married Fernande with whom he is living and have four children Marie Geo, Philip, Regine, and Doris. He was supposed to make this bizarre route before he settled down in a relationships.

I was very upset and sad when he found out what was happening to him with Raymonde. I was a teenager at the time, unable to process the event correctly. Add to that the belief that there was value in being a Don Juan. At that time I did not know that Don Juan was a big failure in love. I probably unconsciously compare Peres and Italien and concluded that Peres was better than him in love. In *reality, Peres did him a favor by showing him that he was in the wrong relationships. It is only now I can see life that way, put things in the right perspective. That is it for my therapy.*

Peres has a sister who married Edward, was some how mixed with Haitian mafia it is like, for he was going to be killed by them one night if he did not yield while being transported in car at night. He was liberated, became a shark, moneylender lending a 100% or more, level not being fixed by any law in Haiti. Edward became VERY RICH quickly, after he fails to die. As if this kind of tension were needed for his self to come out of its cocoon.

Princius Prince, my late godfather was a bit like Peres. Since I have known him he went from one relationships to the other, a little bit like Don Juan. He, too, probably thought there was value to be like that. It seems to me now that all involuntary single persons are victims of this belief in the human psyche. There is a reason why what happened to Don Juan made history, crossed the fence of space and time. It has a big negative impact in the human psyche. He was mistakenly taken for a success while in truth he was a failure, as you say. Persons in romantic relationships only are succeeding in love; not HBBs who deal with love like a grasshopper or a stallion. And, there are only successful actresses and actors in Hollywood who understand this phenomenon. They marry and remarry again and again looking for romantic love. Isn't it?

Bi, late godfather, would be a good occasion for me to remind myself of the big salary I want to have compare to the pitiful ones I used to have, stopped to have until 19991, had more or less from 1995 to 1999, stopped to have again since year 2000. In other words, I am still waiting for the big one. Joseph, one of half brothers was working for this rich farmer Claude. He had one office in Châteaublond where I used to go and pick up Joseph's salary for him each 2 weeks all year long. Chateaublond is at about one hour walking distance from Laboule. Something happened between Claude and Joseph who quit or got fired. Bi, my uncle, was Joseph helper sort of, Bi replaced Joseph. Then, I (was in adolescence) continue to go and pick up this salary at Chateaublond, but this time, for a different member of the family.

The reason I, instead another brother or half brother, were the one to pick up this salary was because the late father was teaching me a lesson in earning a salary. He was the one who got Joseph, his son, the job at the first place and asked Bi his brother to be Joseph helper. My father was always working as a heavy-duty mechanician, and working with bulldozer for big farming companies. When other company needs workers, they asked him. He helped my half brother and uncle to get the job, asked them at them at the same time to send me to get their salary when I was adolescent. Nobody explained it to me. I figured it out myself. Enough therapy, right?

Then my late father was abusing me physically, partly because I did not show any interest in what he was doing. That may explain, again partly, why today I am still having trouble in earning a salary.

And that is why we say that when the calling of the child is not respected, we may end up with a socialist, a rebel, and a criminal.

"Bi he is speaking to you in another language" is probably referring to that I can barely speak Creole nowadays for having left Haiti for so long, and having so little contact with Haitians in Canada, especially in Montreal where there should be by now more than 50000, United States, especially in New York where are living lot more Haitians.

Or may be Bi is just a metaphor for strangers, other individual living in other places in the world. He was not a bisexual to my knowledge, although the nick suggests it.

Peres may be a metaphor for fear(peur), in which case the DP is telling me that I am not called by the subjects because they have great fright vis-à-vis the telepathic phenomenon.

CHAPTER XX

Wednesday May 17, 2000

DP148. The fruit, which is given to you, is of a brown color and is in container of rectangular shape.

The lady I met in 1996 with whom you had a 2 years relationships was of brown color. This DP is saying that I am still not cured in regard to relationships with women since the break up with Debbie. When I surprised her with the other man in her apartment, I had to break her window to get in once inside the other man flew the coup, if I may use this image. Days after that I regretted it, thinking she had a 9 year old son (beside, him and I were in excellent harmony) sleeping in the house. It was something I did in the heat of the moment. The unknown rival was married, called me anonymously 3 days before, asking me to leave Debbie alone, and go back to my country, Haiti that is, as if Canada was not mine too. That did not help to calm me down when I surprised him in Debbie's house. I was already irritated by his arrogant attitude.

I reacted violently because I did not understand yet that it was the love relaticnships between Debbie and me that did not work, because there was a problem between her and me, but not between a third person and me I did not even know. I reacted like that, also, because I loved her very much at that time.

It happened in 1991. The same year you received a letter from the School District of Delta in which it is said that my services for the School Board was no longer needed. The school never gave an explanation as to why exactly they felt I was to be cast away(Survivor). There was a few incidents before the dismissal. I was a teacher on call in Delta School board. One principal, Mr. Laurent, was hiding the card with my name on it in other for me not to receive too many calls. I got mad, called him and said to him that if he did not stop doing that I was going to there and get him with a kalashnikov. If Debbie reported what happened to her with me to the School Board, and if they put the two together, they might have judged that I was no fit to teach.

Then, it would still be unfair to me. I do not have any serious criminal record. I was in good standing in all the schools where I taught in the district and all other districts. If they listened to Debbie, dismissed me from the teaching position in those circumstances, they would be showing that they are very unfair toward their employees.

The man Debbie was having an affair with was married. or whatever it was between them.

I started to believe that is what they did . They never said to anyone why I was dismissed. Then I was having serious difficulty connecting with white woman since then. What happened to me with Debbie happens every day to million of HBBs around the world It is not significant enough to cause that kind of mental block. Debbie must have done something afterward, reporting me, causing me to loose my position, to be unable to support myself financially, causing me to be starving must of the time, for it to be that important in my psyche. Thatis what the DP above indicates to me that I am not cured yet with white women, must go with other colored women as far as love and sexual relationships are concerned.

Is it about sugarcane the biggest product of exportation in Haiti?

At 3339 west 42 Avenue I had once a roommate with last name Braun. She lived in that house with me as a roommate for about 3 months. She was going out with a man less younger than her chronologically that is. She was working for a key company (making key), had many friends male and female. I did not sleep with her. She said to me once she was going to my bedroom, changed her mind went back to hers after she heard I was snoring. It might have happened as she said or it could be a way for her to tell me that sexual relation between her hand me was possible. This last interpretation comes to my mind now, not when she said what is above.

She moved out in October. In November, I received a letter from Lisa, a woman's picture I have seen in Playboy, to whom I have sent a letter asking to meet her. The one that was living at my place and who just left before I received the letter was also of first name Lisa. The correlation would not be easy to explain, but the fact is there. It was like the first Lisa that have lived in the same house than me some how motivated the playboy Lisa to answer my letter, for she might have received a 1000 requests like mine. <u>Would there be a psychological theory, concept and function to develop here. You the reader will figure it out.</u>

Amanda who is about to move out from this house has

a body of a flat shape or rectangular shape. The DP may be telling me; also, something about her character type by reminding me of the roommate named Braun. In order words, the DP is saying that they are of a similar character in terms of sexual and love relationships in order for me to understand Amanda. When Lisa Brown was making love, everyone in the house knew. She made a big "scruitchy" noise. The Soul Exposed.

I personally associate fruit with woman sexual apparatus.

> *DP149. The adolescent moves toward me. He wants me to recite the verses of a poem that I started to read to him once when we were having a meal together.*

Devin, Debbie's son, is about 19 chronological years old now. When he was a baby, an infant, I used to baby sit him. I went to Vancouver Public Aquarium with him once. May be it is him this DP is referring to.

I was a poet when I was adolescent. I left many boxes of books and documents at Lise's in Montreal. The poems I wrote while adolescent might be in those boxes. I was friend with Lucarne who past away. He was a poet and adolescent too. We did not recite our poems. I wrote one for Roland, one of best friends living in New York presently. I was reminded of Verlaine, Bodelaire Etc. Les Fleurs du Mal", French poets, Emile Neligan, "Poet Québecois" who past away in his twenties, Van Gogh and his friend Paul Gaugin.

And a kind of syndrome I call Van Gogh Syndrome, or artist's syndrome. It is as if dealing so much with a different kind of reality, the ibncomplete one; they become unable to deal with the plain physical reality or the conplete reality.

Nowadays, things are different, in the time of Van Gogh (1853- 1890), artists used to practically die of hunger, because of their inability to deal with complete reality, or because of <u>Van Gogh syndrome</u>. Picasso apparently used to paint for a cup of coffee. Van Gogh himself was unable to meet a woman, establish a relationships for a while, according to history. I suspect I, too, is suffering of the syndrome (Plus a similar psychological phenomenon you will call Japanese or Shakespeare or Romeo and Juliet's syndrome: the belief that romantic love cannot be obtained while living. Romeo and Juliet die.

So the DP is a trip in my adolescent memory, in the past may be. For DP is rather about the future, a kind of borderline phenomenon, something about the past something about the future and something about the present. Always triggered by something in present life ot moment to moment life it seems. For the futuristic part I did send a poem to a celebrity in 2003, although O did not remember this DP then, there are so many.

DP149. The person I see is Abou. He is nude. The hair on his body catches my eyes.

. Recently there was report that Abu Abbas who was involved in big crime was arrested. The nudity in the DP may be a metaphor for that he has been arrested, meaning that his game is revealed he cannot hide anything anymore. There was a picture of him on TV, etc.

Yesterday, April 20, 2003, more of the Saddam Hussein top lieutenants were arrested. Itis as if the Americans still fear this group of HBBs. I see no reason for that, except, fear is not rational, it is a feeling, cannot be really rationalized. Otherwise the insistence on the part of the Americans to arrest the ex- president Hussein's group would not be explainable by itself. It is very unlikely they would be able to organize a coup, retake the power. They are rather running away in the hope that they can save their skin, by fear of being caught by the Americans.

It would be stupid for the Americans to attack Syria or any other state in the region unless they have been attacked first which would be a case of legitimate defense. They are born from parents who have demonstrated exceptional frame of mind, a superb structure of thought. They should live up to that legacy and show real leaderships to the rest of the world by not using their air superiority in war to attack smaller countries. It is probably a warrior's rumor that they would go for Syria next. They should be careful not to fall into the trap. If I see an adult abusing a child in the street I would be repulse, revolted, want to kill him.

Yesterday, I've heard that 850 millions dollars in Americans bills were found in a house in Iraq. It is like the country is filthy rich as you say. They were talking about of billion and billion of $ to be collected to reconstruct the post war Iraq, and asking the question as to which one of the two bodies should be in charge of the collection, the American or the United Nations, although the latter is divided and weak.

I wish I would be an Iraqi citizen right now. I would have my eyes fixed on the ground looking for kerosene, made gazillion dollars, and be happy ever after, although having a lot of money mostly only accentuate feelings, does not really create them.

There is an Abou in y father's family. Sure when I was a child, there is a canal like a little creek group of HBBs there use to take a bath : adults and children together. Abou used to join us sometimes. As said earlier he is one of the fighters in that part of the family branch.

Do Arabic HBBs' bodies have more hair than the rest of us? Should we ask such a question? I do not know the answer to that question. I like having a lot of hair on my head, the doen not necessarily means that I like GBBs with a lot of hair in their body, but it is not a criteria to pick a spouse. I definitely do like seeing hair on man's body. It is too much information for me.

> DP150. This boy asks me to give him 46 of something. I consult the person with me to know if it is really something I want to do. Then I go upstairs in order to find him these things. I find them but leave them alone for a while. At this moment someone else appears upstairs and asks me to find him a pencil sharpener. During the time I am looking for the pencil sharpener, the adolescent I left downstairs comes up, wants to have the 46 things that he asked me. I tell him that they are there but I have been busy since, have had no time to take care of his request yet.

In the DP where I had a set numbers and play them at super 7. Four of them won 40 dollars. In the set of numbers there was also 46 which was not among the winning numbers.

After the following draw one person won 30 million dollars.

The DP is surely about what happened between Barbara and me . As Amanda was moving out, I had to look for another tenant to replace her, and as I do not have a cent in my name, with no regular telephone, only a prepaid cell phone. Barbara offered to help me with the finding the tenant, mostly because she has something to do with Amanda departure. When she called the newspaper to place the ad, they ask her for a telephone number. She came downstairs to make sure she got my telephone number right. I wrote the ad for her with her home phone number in it. When she came downstairs, she was already mad at me for writing her number in the ad. I told her that my cellular phone could not take that many calls, thinking that it would use all prepaid antenna time after a few calls, and I would not have money to buy more antenna time before the end of the month, when it would be too late to look for a tenant. She said in her telephone she would become my secretary, something she would hate to be, and that she was going to wait for her husband to ask his advice, and that she was tempted to cancel the whole thing. She went back upstairs furious.

I was very upset for a while not knowing what was going to happen to me in terms of place to live, for at the end of this month (April, 2003) if I did not find a new tenant, I would have to give her one month notice of move out. It is not that I did not want to move out of this house. It is not mine, I know that thing can be in such a way that I have to vacate very quickly anytime. I didn't like very much the perspective of having to focus on moving instead of the research. After a few weeks of advertisement at UBC and at Dunbar community, I give the bedroom to Mike, the first person who asked for it. Actually, Mike was the second person who asked for it. The first one was a psychotherapist. But I was very slow in understanding him to make the closure with him. That what the pencil sharpener would refer to in the DP. I was rusty in my skill to rent.

What is interesting here is that I had the DP on

Wednesday May 2000, and it described what was going to happen in April 2003. Are you convinced now that when we have a dream, we are in infinite time and space wise?

It is still not clear who the adolescent really was and why he was asking for 46 what?

Upstairs and downstairs may be metaphor the gods level of existence or the Creator. The adolescent asking for 46 things bring to the surface of our minds a Christmas wish. So Santa Claus is the name given to the Creator. There are many names like that such as angel, guardian angel, immaculate conception in most of the religions. Those epithets apply only to the creator, although it is not a male neither a female being, It is not really involved in free enterprises, It is not born, meaning It has always been.

DP150a. From the table of this classroom on which

I am sitting; I see four persons arriving, one examiner, and 3 examinees. The three sit down and start the exam right away. Their faces look familiar to me. I say to myself that these three are always passing an exam. New and younger students appear then in the classroom. One of them starts to whisper in my ear, but finishes the sentence very loudly without paying any attention to those who are passing the exam. A few minutes later they decide to go I feel relief, still sitting at the table. Somebody make a noise similar to a coq at 4-o clock in the morning. Then, he says something I decipher as being "6 I am born". Later I find

out that it really was "I am bored".
That surprises me.

Barbara(has the same descent, ancestors as one of the subjects in the experiment) and her husband are together I am not sure for how many years, but it is clear for me that they are bored with each other in their relationships, as it is usually for middle chrono age couple. The excitement of the first few months of the relationships has long gone and made place for routine. Especially when the glue in most relationships is excitement. The cultivation and the growing part of the love in the relationships are often left alone, if love was there at the first place. It is the recipe of boredom in relationships in later years. I have the impression that she wants to have sex with me(her husband told me she loves me, another time he told me he does not mind if I make love with her). Her husband is certainly in a campaign for homosexual relationships with me. I have been here for 3 years, never gave him any reason to believe it is something I could do with a man.

6 refer to the play of set of 6 numbers at the prediction psychokinetic game or lottery may be. I have been playing it for a numbers of years; never plaid a set of 6 winning numbers yet. So it is a challenge I am determined to take on. Not only a set of six, but also a set of seven, a set of 8, a set of nine, and a set 10. Knowing that my self can do even better than that, one of my goals is to take up on that kind of challenge. Another one of the goals of mine is to show what I can do with my psyche (body, spirit and soul) in order for the world not to neglect it, what is a temptation given that machines makes life look so easy for us. It is possible that we care only for machine or very much more for it than for our psyche. Then there would be the danger of nuclear war

and, of course, the disappearance of our planet with us in it or life on it.

Strangely enough, when there was 25 million dollars to be won at super 7 recently, April 6, 2003, to be exact, I plaid only four of the winning numbers. That day nobody won the jackpot that became 30 million for the draw that was won by a person from Ontario. Barbara who makes me very mad nowadays is from Ontario. I would have a tendency to conclude that some how she annoyed me in order to prevent me(or for winning it) from winning the 25 million dollars to leave the amount for the person in Ontario to win the next draw. Her parents are living in Ontario presently. What I cannot explain is how would she have such a power on me? Even if there was an explanation, that would never take the responsibility for loosing that day from me. She would never be responsible for what happen to me. I am the only one responsible for that. I was directing myself wrongly.

The table at which I am sitting reminds me of the Mendeleheff chemical table of elements. Then, there would be the story of naive persons who thought there would be a chemical formula to transform all metal in gold(Midas complex: there is only we are all going to eat gold). In order words it is about wishful thinking, in my memory not necessarily from me personally, but from HBBs around me, in the world.

Coq usually wakes up at 4 in the morning. Coqs are very masculine type of bird always fighting with each other. A similar feature would explain the fact that I did not win the 25 million that day in my personality to be corrected before I could win as much money, assimilating the game with coq fighting, with war. I am not sure of that analysis of what happened that day.

I already plaid a set of 5 numbers in that game, I am expecting to play at least a set of 6 numbers, although I would win only one to $60000 for that in Super 7, around 100000 or more at 6/49 although the natural technique I am using does not guaranty an arithmetic progression, neither a geometrical progression, neither a progression by leap, but any one of them, any time.

The person who started to whisper in my ear, stopped and spoke loudly may be Britney. Whisper in each other ears is what we do frequently in any given day, telling ourselves that we love each other and other things. Then, she started to speak loudly because she is a star, may be.

Whisper in each other ears, what everyone who is in good relationships with his body, soul and spirit does with friends and whomever. Despite of my attempt of explanation of the reason why I did not win big that day, still do not know it. You do not want to write so much about human defeat in this work in order not to bore the reader. The DP made an allusion to that too.

After all, the real meaning of the DP I think is about the passage from the incomplete life to the complete life, symbolized by the coq which wake up us at around 4 AM in the past. the sense passing an exam to reach to consciousness does not ring a bell to me. It sounds rather biblical. To be born an infant does not have to pass any exam. The whispering on the ears, is not the mark of consciousness for me either. Otherwise I have so many nice looking, intelligent ladies whispering to my ears often, the state of affairs would already come to consciousness and then I would have one with me almost everynight. There already is an impposibility in that statement.

CHAPTER XXI

Thursday May 18, 2000

DP151Appearing at Artibonite, it's like I have taken the metro to get there. It is also like I am in a school where the principal is busy at something, says something like "I saw you at some place before". As I have never been to the place he names, I answer him that it may have been at another place he saw me. Then I tell him that I was born in that place opposite to the school. Then he moves to go to do something else. I go, then, to Clementia's place, beside the house where I was born. I see my godmother's children, talk to them a bit saying that I am going to come back to see them again, but at my godmother's house that time. Then, I appear in the street looking for my godmother's house. By inadvertence, I enter into a family's house. The children there ask me many questions. One of them asks "what does it mean" "I want to impress you with something?" My answer to him is that he wants to become my friend. Another one speaks to me about death, I say "Everybody dies sometimes". At that moment, I want to leave that house to go to my godmother's place, but I cannot find my glasses. While looking for them a woman says that she has called at my godmother's, and that everybody is waiting for me there. I ask the children, then, to look for my glasses everywhere, in the toilet, in the living room in order for me to be able to leave.

It's so long compare to the other ones; it speaks for itself. You, the readerm still need to know a few key points to understand it. Artibonite the name of a river originated in the Dominican Republic and falls in the sea near Saint Marc, one of the relatively big Haitian cities. So the portion of land the river crosses from its source to its end is called Artibonite too. I was born in that area, north east of Port-au-Prince, where your father was working and living with my mother and their children. They themselves were born at Dieurond, close to LaBoule and Laferonay, around 200 kilometers east of Port-au- Prince, where they have a house and got married.

The house facing the one where I was born belonged to Beji a small business lady, Lelio's godmother. He is one of my 4 brothers living in US presently. The DP may be saying that my taste for business started at Beji's place. There was a small private school at the other side of a tall bush fence north of the house where I was born. The owner of that property and the school was Mr. Class.

Clementia was the mother of was godmother Etiennette who married Job. She plaid a big role in upbringing, for my mother gave up on living when I was about 6 years in a chronological calendar. In the DP I avoid to go to my godmother's house for a reason I do not know, something that happened before I was born, or just after. Seradieu, the adolescent who hit me with a stone near your right eye was living in his parent's house separated by a fence next to my godmother's house. I do not think the avoidance of my godmother's house is related to any incident that is known to me.

There was one telephone line used by Brignac, an American farmer, connecting his office to the rest of a huge farm he owned around at the time when I was born. I do not even know if that line was connected to Saint Marc a few kilometers away, let alone Port-au- Prince quite a bit further. There were the slow train, cars and trucks from the capital to Artibonite. Life there now should be similar to what it was when you was born. I doubt there would be telephone line for everybody, and metro, although I have not been there for years. When I go back there if can help, it will be in that sense, although, I have already too many projects.

I am going to have some kids. May be that was where I entered by inadvertence. So the DP is setting something that will happened in the future of course. It even seems that I was in death bed with the kids, so even further in the future at the end of my life. I hope to live 140 year or even more.

That class near at the other side of the fence whre I was

born may have had an influence on me becoming a teacher later.

> *DP152. In that school where I appear at the last workinh day of the week, one person says to me that I should sit on a cart to protest something. A young woman forgets to bring cotex from downtown, has to go back there in order to get it. There is a draw at a ppk game. Someone wins one million dollars. The principal is going away, makes it clear to everybody to wait until he is back before they do anything extraordinary. Another person says to somebody sitting beside me that he is the one who wins the million dollars.*

In the note I wrote after having this DP there is no mention of the specific trigger of the DP. I wrote that it would be nice to win one million dollars now, would make things a lot easier for me, that I did not know why there would be in it a woman who would have her period, that the fact that they have their period has nothing to do with school or ppk game, that I resented that I still do not win in the game to create my goals yet, that I know the solution is almost in my consciousness and do not know why I do not pick it up during DP time, that the DP was unfocused.

These notes were written immediately after the DP. Today is April 29, 2003. I feel more or less the same way about this DP. I probably know a little bit more now to put the DP in better perspective. But it is true that the DP was unfocused, a mix of references of experiences I lived in Haiti and in Canada. The person who asked me to protest what was done to me when Max Emeran, a good friend I had in

Haiti. I met him at Lycee Toussaint Louverture equivalent of s secondary school in North America. When the director did not pay me that month of teaching in his school, Ecole Frere Polycarpe, Max suggested to me to protest the situation. One afternoon, I asked the kids to stay quietly at their seats until I am back, stood up by the door. The principal was making his round of visit, when at my class, he attacked me. I fought with him; two months later I left Haiti.

No specific recollection as to why the woman is in the DP. That part reminds me vaguely of the periodic table, that a the beginning of the research I had to decide between creating a formula to play the game, or to play and win after attaining the required spiritual growth, and that I decided to go for attaining the spiritual growth instead of the formula. Is he one who sits beside me is another part of myself, the part which is is very active even when we are sleeping. Or the woman I am going to marry. ?

Who wins the million dollars? It didn't happen to me in the past. Of course it does not now, may be in the future.

I always have the impression that I know the set of winning numbers of the power ball games of all times and all places, meaning any place and time in the world(then I don't win yer for expension of horizon purposes, may be). But, because I am not wining as I wish yet, I don't feel allowed to write about it. The solutions of our problems are in our consciousness. We get them when we are focused enough. Focusing is the same as concentration, one thing at a time. The day I had this DP I definitely was not focused, for not only there are 9 DPs, also each one is composed of various contents. They are not ground for focusing.

Probably, because the prediction game is supposed to be a lucky game, so, an irrational game. The fact that I do not think that way does not mean that it is not in my mind actively influencing the rest of my life, until I do something to counteract the irrational inner prompt.

The school in the DP may symbolize a school in incomplete life, a school in complete life or both. There is sin equa non (without which none) conditional link between the two levels of life anyway. No I do not think it can go from the complete to the incomplete as far as original event is concerned.

The Soul Exposed is a school too, in a way. It will help you to develop your self by puting in contact with your body, soul and spirit. It is a kind of hands on practice.

> *DP153. From where I appear, I hear a noise from a gate. When I go and see somebody who reminds me of Anglade speaking to a woman. It's like this woman has two children.*

It may be about the couple upstairs, Todd and Barbara they have 2 children. In other words, the DP may be saying to think of them as half brother and sister. I do not see them like that. I see them like strangers, although I know that we are all connected psychically. I do not have sexual relation with either of them, will never have that kind of relation with a man anyway, but always ready for that kind of relationships with the other sex nowadays. Thinking of other HBBs as brothers/sisters or half brothers/sisters would be a deterrent in that sense. If I see someone as my sister, I do not want to have sex with her.

The DP may not be about them at all, may be about a woman with whom I was in love and whose going to have two children with another man(don't we know it all already?).

And one of my half brothers Anglade lives in Haiti, taking care of my cousin and father's properties. He quit school early, liking rather working in the farming fields. He did not like pleasurable activities like I did. The noise at the gate indicate that there is a dance inside. The DP may be putting in perspective our two different characters, our two different personalities.

Or it may not be about Anglade half-brother at all. It can be just about an Anglophone with whom the woman I was in love will have two children.

> *DP154. A person brings some yellow pea soup in an old red trunk. As if it is a Swedish woman who does that. There is still some pea soup in the trunk. There is a container with drinking water there. Somebody throws a cup of yellow pea soup in it. As I am looking at him in a surprised fashion, he says he is going to fix it up.*

Three days ago, Sunday, Todd came down here to try to fix the water heater. Tuesday night I had a date with Amanda who will move out Thursday. When she came here and learned about the water heater's condition, that there was no hot water, she went back to her friend house to sleep there so she can take a shower there. The water break down had kind of spoiled it for me and Amanda. I offered to boil some water for her, obviously she did not think it was a good idea, may be thinking that I am some kind of a freak. I do not know if she left because she was shy after that happened between her and me or if it is in her character to be able to function only when everything is perfect(Amanda was may be very upset because we were going to make love for the first time and then broke the water eater by poltergeist, see Psychokinetic, by me).

This morning Todd came again to light the pilot light

near the water heater. I told him it should have been fixed by now. He said that the owner of the house is from Honkong, used to take care of the house at the beginning, is neglecting it now.

You do not know why the Yellow pea soup and the Swedish women yet, except I used to like chick pea of yellow color, for iron,

> DP155. *The store where I appear belongs to a woman. I see Gramont and Lamartine behind the counter. That surprises me. The woman says it sucks. Next time I come back to the store, I enter into it by the back door. On my way in I see a woman sleeping on the raw floor. I lie behind her and sleep too. I wake up in her bed but a real bed. She was already sitting on it in a way that says she is hiding something. Then she reads a telephone number on a paper and is surprised that the telephone number belongs to another country.*

I do not work with the DPs on Saturday and Sunday. Usually on Saturdays I work at the celebration(to reinforce) of other goals for about two hours at the library, Sunday I work at filing DPs I had the preceding week. What is bizarre is that I am analyzing the DP today Friday April 29, 2003, the last working day of the week) On Fridays I used to send mail to rich HBBs(the Rich and the Famous) looking for financial help to create the "detector/deviator/accident preventor". I even tried recently to connect with Mr. Bush to ask for a grant for the same project. I could not connect with him. My e-mail was returned marked unknown sender. In that e-mail I wrote that I have a project of interest to

US. Then, I am living in Canada. The President might have been surprised that I am not living in US the most powerful country in the world now. It was in the heart of the war against Iraq. There might have been some nervousness about my e-mail to the president. I sent it to the White House, not knowing the proper address where to ask for the grant, e-mail in which I ask for such address, besides. Detector/deviator/preventor is also, about preventing earthquake and sending them in places where they can do no harm to HBBs. and their properties, the reason why what I wrote is of interest to US. I was thinking of California where earthquake happened(Is it really happened?).

I did foresee that the last space shuttle would blow up in the sky. I woke up mad, sent a fax to Iraq representative to pass to Mr. Hussein. I was probably thinking that he would use the shuttle incident to say that Russia and US do not have air superiority anymore as their vessels are blowing up in mid air. Yes they do not, but not in comparison to other countries, but in comparison to the psyche by which I can still help the most sophisticated machine, the most advanced science and technology.

Gramont and Lamartine are two brothers in Haiti to whom I never spoke. I do not really know why they are in the DP. Can you say what is the telephone about? Unfortunately I am not able to.May be about an rxperiment, may be about someone I would like to call me, however, who doesn't. May be she knows my telephine number but decide not to call me for that we se not come from the same country.

DP156. In the street I meet two tall men begging. As am accompanied by some other HBBs I think that they are bothering them. Then, I remember having seen the beggars in the same street every time I pass there. So, I tell them not to bother my friends, continue walking and talking with them, telling them how bizarre things were at Christmas time. I feel that I am happy and talking with them so freely.

This week, Larry Campbell, the maire of Vancouver was asked to do something about the beggars who are a nuisance for business downtown according to the news. He said that there could not be legislation against beggars being in the city, that the problem will be solved when an efficient solution is found. I think one solution would be for the government to give them more money to spend even then, some of them might choose to beg. It is ok. Of course in an economy of scarcity for value that solution would not fit. Then, why the scarcity for value? The economy is saying "Starve to give me value, starve, starve and starve".

Reminds us of this saying "Wealth without a big heart is an ugly beggar"

I do not know if there are some days when there are more tourists in the city than others, because in those days they could restrict begging.

In rich countries HBBs choose to beg. They would be able to survive with the money given to them. In most cases they beg to exercise their freedom. It is still better that way, better that they have freedom and can exercise it.

DP157. My friend had just taken her bath. I put an arm around her abdomen in the presence of a white man who does not seem to be happy of my gesture. Then I take a screwdriver that I keep in one hand while caressing her body with the other. The man comes near me, looks at my hands and goes back to where he was before. Then, I appear in an empty house with this woman. I put something that looks like dark hair on fire. It makes a lot of sparks, the woman asks me to carry her out of where I am.

The first time I went out with a white woman, Yvonne, there was a Norman a white man who tried to fail my relationships with that woman (He was probably a homosexual). Actually may be he had succeeded, for after 3 months we broke up. In the book "Motivation" by Robert C. Beck, I have read yesterday that in a list of objects, the ones in the middle of the list will be forgotten earlier than the ones in the top part and bottom part of the list. In other words my first relationships with a white woman will influence all of my further relationships with white women. I do not believe that. it would be so if I give more importance to the present and the future than the past , I am like that, I give more impotance to the present and the future than the past.

DP158. A salesperson I know appears in my house. He is well dressed. There is somebody in the house who is not happy to see him. He leaves. I wanted to talk to him about the Canadian Buyers Association I have just created, but do not have the time to implement.

The trigger of this DP was the reading of a magazine with the name indicated in the DP. It may refer to book I wrote but was unable to publish up to now. Iwas abot to succeed the method to quit smoking. BC tel cut the telephone for unpaid bills. Again once more I mismanage my self.

> *DP159. I am leaving this place where I am living to go somewhere and come back. I see my bicycle among many small bicycles. I take it from them. It's like I am afraid of having done that.*

As said above, it is Amanda who's about to move out from this house. She has a bicycle, I had one too, and it was stolen behind Vancouver Public Library. The DP is probably indicating what her feelings are.

I understood very little of the DP when I had it May 18, 2000. This is what I wrote about it then "IT IS MY STOLEN BICYCLE THAT I TAKE, THEREFORE THERE IS NO REASON FOR FEAR. NONETHELESS I WAS AFRAID DURING THE DP. IT IS WHY I THINK THAT THE DREAMER IN THIS PARTICULAR DP IS NOT MY ADULTS SELF BUT THE ONE THAT WAS FORMED WHEN I WAS ABOUT 6 YEARS OLD, THE ONE THAT OTHER HBBS. USE A LIFETIME IF THEY DO NOT DO SOMETHING TO LEAVE AWAY THE INFANCY SELF AND UTILIZE THE ADULT ONE. THAT IS WHY WE CAN BE LIVING IN A DANGEROUS WORLD, AND THAT WHY SPIRITUAL DEVELOPMENT IS ALMOST ALWAYS SOMETHING TO PROMOTE, EVEN THOUGH IT DOES NOT HAVE TO BE DONE THROUGH A RELIGION, AND WHY THE PUBLICATION OF THIS WORK IS JUSTIFIED, FOR THE PARADIGM AT SCHOOL NOWADAYS IS RATHER SCIENCE AND TECHNOLOGY ABOVE ALL THE COMPUTER SCIENCE"

In my comment of the DP in 2000, I do not mention

Amanda because at that time she was non existent for me. I realize this only now how much the events in my life of that year are linked to the ones that I am living presently, and even causing them somehow. I realized, also, that it's nearly impossible to get all the details of the meaning of a DP immediately after we have it. We may never be able to get them all in a lifetime.

Yesterday (April 30, 2003) I did go to Vancouver Public Library where I borrowed "Motivation, Theories and Principles", a book of Robert C. Beck, and 3 videos: "The Lives of a Bengal Dancer" "Love Laughs at Andy Hardy" and "The Long Goodbye". So, I do not read the book nor see the videos yet. In my schedule for the day, today, it is written reading 11: 45 AM to 1:45AM. Now it's only 9: 25 AM. Later I am going to start reading the book. I do not know yet when I am going to see the videos.

The self leaves the body frequently at night. During its absence, we can still have dream according to Jane Roberts. It is not clear which part of the self she is referring to: the body the soul, or the spirit. Un the other hand we know that at night the the 3 are separated, each following its own schedule except in certai cases where all 3 are united.

CHAPTER XXII

Saturday May 20, 2000

DP160 something is burning on the carpet in front of the house where I appear. I push the fire and the ash off the piece of carpet. After that, I go inside of the house where I see someone who reminds me of Monise and say something kind to her. I am just about to leave when more HBBSs enter into the house. Thinking that they know Monise is my sister and wo not imagine something, I continue my way out where I meet another person trying to take something off the ground a few times unsuccessfully.

Last year Barbara was using the washing machine, left it; went upstairs. When she came back the carpet in the living room and the kitchen was flooded. Later during the day, I have heard that there was a problem with used water pipe underground in the area. Therefore, I concluded that that was the explanation for the flooded carpet.

In 1998, at the house in 3339 west 42 Avenue, while cooking, one of my roommates who was also my girlfriend, spilled some cooking oil from a frying pan the on the stove. The oil burst in flame, part of it fell on the carpet, burnt that part of the carpet. I bought a similar piece of carpet placed it at that spot.

Nevertheless, the DP is suggesting that my businesses do not take off yet for lack of energy; my goals are not created for lack of energy.

Among the notes I wrote immediately afterward there is this: at 2:30 PM I quit analyzing my DPs, dressed up a bit, took some old playboys to sell for a few bucks. While walking on the sidewalk of Broadway Street to go downtown, a woman asked me if I know where is Ash Street. I tell her that she was in the wrong direction, to cross the street, go to a bus stop, take the bus to go to Ash street, in the opposite direction, which was a little bit far from where I met her, and I tell her to ask the bus driver to let her down at Ash street to make sure she gets there. Was the fire on the carpet a premonition of what was going to happen in the same afternoon?

I just want to have these comments of this DP that this woman I saw in it is a real one, sometimes a woman or a man may symbolize an animal or a thing in a DP by the use of disguises. She is Momoko of Japan, but studying tourism in New Zeeland this year, in vacation in Vancouver this month. I placed an ad at bulletin boards at the University of British Columbia looking for HBBs. to whom to tutor oral French. She called last Thursday. I started tutoring her, last Friday May 2, 2003. As I am not teaching presently, and as I have no other way to do some activities in French, and as I will have children I want to speak at least English and French from birth, I think I should keep being active in these languages all the time for now. That's why I placed the ad.

The DP may be, consequently, saying something about monism, this philosophical doctrine according to which only the mind exists. I may come back to it later.

Psychic Faculty and Research is the name of my company with one worker: me. It reminds me of something I have read somewhere, which says that when we are familiar with the psyche, intellect and intuition unite to form a faculty. It is how I created Psychic Facilty and Research. True that I had many falls, not because I like women in the love relationships, but for not knowing who I really am. In that case I would stand for my values. keep believing in my self, in the capacity of the psyche, of the soul more precisely. The fall in 1991 2000 and 2009, would not be as disastrous as they where in terms of my economic and psychic progression.

> DP161. Richard comes to my house, puts food in a pot, the pot on the fire element on the stove. While leaving, he asks me to take care of it. When I go near the pot and look inside I see peas that have become a thick sauce.

There is a Richard the son of my cousin Andre Eli living in Montreal. His grand father, Justin Éli, left some wealth for his father in Haiti. Monise my sister is managing part of the wealth. Justin was a sugar cane "weigher" very big quantity for 6 months. That is how he made his fortune. He worked at a place called Lepine. I used to go there with the past away ant Celina to see Justin, the reason why I felt very sad when I've heard that Lepine killed himself and a group of women at the university of Montreal some years ago.

The other Richard was another roommate in the house at 3339 west 42 Avenue. He was going to Langara College and were a base player, was very good at it though. His bedroom was next to mine. He used to annoy me for playing his base too loud. I did not say anything about it for fear of inhibiting his talent. And apparently he was very good in the courses he was taking at Langara College as well.

The other roommate with the first name Richard was among the first group of roommate in 3339 W 42nd Avenue, Vancouver British Columbia. In a way, he was one the best group of roommates I had, very understanding and willing to help. It is unfortunate we could not be friends for ever, because of our fundamental differences in sexual orientation.

There is also a club called Richards on Richards in Downtown Vancouver. It used to be the hottest spot in town at one time. I met Kristin in the place, we went out for a while. The last time I've been to a club was in 2001. So it is not clear to me how the club is doing now in terms of popularity or it still exists.

Of course, this DP is about richness, and I consider myself as being a rich person for being born in a rich universe. In that sense, everybody like me is rich. The problem is to make it so that this natural richness is reflected in one's complete life. Most of the time we do not succeed in doing that for we have learned, explicitly or not, that only a few can be rich as if we were living in a poor universe, as if poverty was natural. How ignorant can we be sometimes! Where does the idea of natural poverty come from? The world of ego in which we are living is keeping us from becomoing ourselves, from becoming what we really and who we really are.

> DP162. I say to someone "Because
> of you I am going to loose a whole
> year, a whole year,
>
> Dam it."

It expresses the times I lost during 2 falls mentioned above. . It took years to recover from the one in 1991 when I lost the teaching position. Actually I should say that I will never recover from it completely. It left an indelible scarce in my psychological make up, in the structure of my character, my personality. The other one was at the end of the year 1999, when the business folded, because the supposed owner owner of the house on 3339 42nd Avenue. I was literally sick in bed for days.

> DP163. Walking in the street with
> this woman, she inserts one hand in
> her pocket, withdraws some papers.
> She shows them to me and asks me
> to pick one. The one I pick is a plane
> ticket. Continuing talking with her
>
> I say: "What are you going to do?"
>
> She names a place where she is going
> to be.
>
> I ask again "to work?"
>
> "Of course! What else could it be?
> "Are you putting ideas in my mind?"
> she advances.
>
> "I meant work. It is you who are
> putting ideas in my mind", I
> replied.

Would a woman buy some plane tickets to her lover in

other to be able to cheat on him? It did not happen exactly as described in the DP. I went to a party with her. When I arrive in the house where the party will be, she asks me to take her car and her child to go and get something forgotten at home. I never droved her car before. Previous to that she said her father did not want someone other than her to drive her car for insurance purposes. I did not drive a car for years before then; I came close to have an accident in busy street in the city of Burnaby. If she did not have a plan to cheat with her friend's husband, the host, why would she ask me to leave with her son? On the spot I did not have time to put it all in perspective. One of those behaviors that show they do not come from persons really having a good time in their lives, not really accepting having a good time in their lives. They choose the most twisted way to have fun. The fear of being cut, busted, how fun can it be? In a romantic love or real love all sexual maladies disappear. In a romantic love all sexual acts are as new, love renew itself with all its appendages.

I may have said it before, it seems to me only HBBs in Hollywood know the advantage there is in being married. They divorce many times but still get married again. It is not so much for the marriage itself, for they do divorce. It is rather for the benefits of romantic love, which dissolves all sexual psychosis, and make them the person they are, stars.

The DP may not be about cheating. It may be literal in the sense that what is described there is what it means, someone giving a plane ticket to travel to his here lover or beloved ro travel. But some how it wakes up in me the negative feeling of cheating.

In complete life , there was a woman who called me once and said she wanted to give me a both ways ticket with hotel to go to London. Not knowing why she was giving it to me, not knowing her, I refused. At that time I used to watch porn in the computer and even contacted a porn star once. I thought she wanted me to go to London to make porn films

> *DP164. There will be a marriage ceremony. The king is a woman. There is a woman invited but she is not there yet and everybody is waiting for her. She is mad at her driver, but she ends up going with her anyway.*

King in the DP is related to me may be, for my last name is Prince . I will get married some day, when I have the financial situation that allows it, especially when I am about to have children. The king is a woman. What does that suppose to mean? Is a woman is saying that I am a woman because she invites me in her life but I do not show up? She is going out with her driver. Who is this woman"?

> *DP165. Something related to cellular telephone.*

Here is the bad situation in which I find yourself today. There is a message in my cellular telephone. I cannot even listen to it, for I have 50 cents of antena time left in it. It costs 30 cents per minute to read the message. I do not know how long is the message. Before I read it I make sure I have more antenna time than that. The DP was predicting what was going to happen to me 3 years before the actual event. Then, was it a prediction or predetermination? Is the DP the cause of what is happening to me today about the telephone or was it just predicting it? No one can tell, but reminds me of this saying "the ultimate function of prophecy are not to tell but to make it."

Is this comprhension a diversion of the actual suggestion in the DP?

Sunday May 21, 2000

> *DP166. The HBBs, from Quebec I see are complaining about the fact that things are going bad for them, for their population is decreasing. There is a truck ready to leave in front of them. There is one Quebecois, who is going to go in the truck, but taking his time to talk to the others, the truck starts to leave without him, and he has to run to catch it. It is a two-passenger compartment truck. He climbs to the top one.*

If persons from Quebec were like me they would be very different in comparison to persons from the English Canada. But Quebecois are not like me, although I speak the same native language, which is French. HBBs from Quebec have been living close to English HBBs in Canada for years(Enfland and France are not very . They live close to each other even in Europe any way. So are the frog and the square head very different? Not really. The French Canadian finds himself in an awkward situation of having to fight for their survival as francophone. They are like a small island of French HBBs in a sea of Anglophones. The threat of disappearance is a real factor to take into account. The proportion is not to their advantage not only in numbers, but also in that the other culture is not an insignificant one, I mean, is very preponderant, very absorbing in regard to other cultures everywhere in the world. If we are not careful in one or two centuries from now everyone on the earth will be Anglophone. Imagine, living a life where everyone is

Anglophone. There is nothing wrong with Anglophone, but there is with a whole earth with only one culture.

So the Quebecois ends up having an acute sense of nationalism that the rest of Canadians and in the rest of the world can learn from.

I do not know for my fellows in Quebec, other immigrant fellows from the rest of the world, but I still feel like a stranger in Canada, as it said above. The truck in the DP brings to the surface of my mind a bus that carries tourists in Vancouver and this feeling of being a stranger in my own country, not so much because of the kind of life I am living here, but rather because of your feeling of living in a round planet, not a flat small part of it we call Canada, but the whole thing. I feel and think like a citizen of the whole world.

Just before moving to the werst part of Canada I was driving trucks and cars own by Louise.

DP167. The soil on my father's land has been turned recently. I have just finished taking care of the grass on it, when I hear music and see somebody dancing in the neighborhood.

He asks why has the soil in this land been turned?

I answer him by saying something like "it's to attract more customers".

Then, a couple appears and explains to me exactly why the soil has been turned. "It's because your father had a good deal on it, took advantage

of the situation to turn it around"
says one member of the couple.

There is allusion in this DP to the way the Europeans came in North America and change it into a rich continent in terms of standard of living. I do not see this fact as a put down to the Indians who where living here before the Europeans. They are different HBBs with different interest, different values. If the Europeans did not come they would survive. Life here would be different but they would not just disappear for any reason. What is to be feared now is that the Indians become too much like the Europeans. There are Indian doctors, physicians, and Indians with a PH. D. There are Indian businesspersons, Indian lawyers. There are Indian professionals in all human activities in the continent. There is the risk they become too much like the Europeans, loosing then their distinctiveness.

I think my true parents are the infinite, the Creator so I inherit the infinite, the abundance of the universe, which does not give me any right to go to another country and say "Hey, I inherit the infinite, so here is my place too, I am taking this portion of land". I would not be able to behave like that even in my own country, let alone in another already inhabited country.

DP168. Free intellect left.

Todd and Barbara have a shed in an island somewhere around greater Vancouver where they spend vacation time every year since I have been living here, this house on 16th Avenue. The DP suggests I do not feel free when they are in the house which is not theirs but which they have rented before I come to live here. I know Barbara had or was about to have a diploma in architecture when she got married. I do not know what is Todd working at, he has a permanent position in which he is working since I have known him.

In this house I do not feel as I felt when I was at the one on Manitoba Street neither as I felt in the one in 3339 west 42nd Avenue. I felt so bad in the one on Manitoba Street that I had to move the hell out as quickly as possible. I was attacked by a homosexual African. There was a white man who used to come in my bedroom and lied on the floor face doun suggesting homosexual act. In the one on 3339 west 42 Avenue, there was bit of that too, but there when I was overly annoyed with a person, I let him go, for I was the renter. In this house on 16th Avenue it is not as bad as in the on Manitoba street, not as good as the one on 3339 west 42 Avenue where I was the renter.

There is this idea that after being familiar with the psyche, the intellect and intuition unite to form a new faculty. The DP has triggered it in you. We have already seen that. By now it should be clear for everyone that the Soul Exposed id about the intellect and the intuition, the individual development, the neaning of HBB, human being becoming, the world and the Creator.

CHAPTER XXIII

Monday May 22, 2000

> DP169. Sitting on tree near a house, an HBB appears, gives me some coins, continue to walk toward another house beside which my sister is cooking some food. After that, I see many persons coming from where my sister is cooking. As they are walking strangely, I decide to go and see if sister is ok. Reaching that side of the house and not seeing my sister, I cross a veranda to go where she is living.

In the notes taken right after the DP it is written: Sitting on the tree near this house, it was like I was waiting for the person who gave me the money. It is not the first time a person or the same person gives me money in a DP. Despite the allusion to Monise, my sister, the DP is not really about her, but may rather be about Moneta, this Roman goddess which was used the first time on coin money, when the world was about to pass from barter to exchange economy. It is a DP I already have many times during the research that I am doing. I did not have enough information yet to make the connection with Moneta.

I have started to have the DP at the same time when I started the research, when I had the desire to enrich myself, but these DPs instead have contributed to my apparent poverty, because I did not understand them, and because there were not a lot of money in these hands full of coins(compare to paper money).

I must admit that sometimes there were cash in the DPs also, meaning bills.

I am sitting on a log when money is given to me; the experience of money is almost complete in this DP in the sense that this kind of money is made of paper from wood. Only gold is missing to make it complete, what will probably happen in ulterior DPs and in complete life.

Of course I would not comment it the same way today. Two years have passed already, I at least suppose to know better although as Jane Roberts would say "Knowledge, never old never new, never better, in the depth of things". Any way, I will add what follows: I am sitting while they give me money, something I will hardly see in waking life if not ever(despite that what was written at first). My attitude about the subject was wrong. The DP was indicating that there was a flaw in my personality. I might unconsciously think that I am a real prince. I am not, in waking life, although everybody is in reality. In complete life I should have a go- and -get-it attitude, especially when the object is money.

Is it the right attitude?

Some dream observers say that during DPs everything comes toyou, that is another matter, a different level of life anyway. If it is trie I accept it, welcome it. I want to enrich myself, my family and some HBBs around me.

The original comments were in French t "Assis sur un tronc d'arbre" could mean sitting on a standing tree or sitting on a log. If it were sitting on a standing tree, the DP would be indicating to me that after I have raised my consciousness, money would come to me. If it were sitting on a log like we do at English Bay beach, then the meaning would be to relax in other to have money, not so much as is Wall Street where time is money where we have to be always "à la va vite"m, more in a hurry than time itself.

Tuesday May 23, 2000

> *DP170. It is like I am at home. In the house there are my sister and a woman. She is totally nude; I am caressing her body. When things get too hot, I enter in a room with her, but because there are a lot of things in the room, I become worried. Then I hear someone talking with my sister in the living room, a person who comes to see me.*

One thing is that I say my sister without naming her, because in DP the images are not always clear and they are a lot of metaphors. In other words I am not sure she was my sister Monise.

The second thing is that, yes, Monise shows up many times during my sexual encounters with women, with Britney once, in DP, of course. I do not understand yet why it was like that.

This DP may be advancing some explanations as to why I am not in love while I am living in this house. In the bedroom there is a closet where I have cloth and many boxes of utensils. In the bedroom itself there is a sofa, a TV/ receiver/ video/stand, a chest of drawer, two small table on one there is a facsimile machine, and the like, on the other there are an alarm clock and a thermometer, a desk, and two chairs. There are lots things in a 15X15 feet room as indicated in the DP. Would that distract a couple in love and prevent them from getting intimate with each other?

There is the stereotype that black men are good in bed, but not so good or not as good as men in other race in intellectual domain for example(Is that a quality? the intellect without intuition is not a quality, can bring the whole world to oblivion). I recently come to the conclusion that it hasn't been easy for me in going out with a woman since I started the research because of the stereotype. I am saying to myself unconsciously that I cannot be with a woman who's thinking, unconsciously or not, I am not able to be to think well while I am at the same time I am writing the Soul Exposed. In other words, there is an unconscious conflict in me related to most of the women available for me to go out with. I was more or less in love in 1992 to 1993 and in 1997 to 1998, while doing the research. One of the women is black; the other one is oriental. So I conclude, also, that the unconscious stereotype conflict is with white women, as far I personally am concerned.

I am not trying to prove my intellectual prowess but. I am trying to save the world addicted to external power and dominance. to the detriment of having a self, autonomy and intuition.

DP171. I am walking with a woman with a revolver in my hand that I put in one big pocket of my blazer. I see some HoBBs agitating close by. The woman with me looks worried. I ask her not to be like that and continue to walk toward destination with her.

This is an experience I could make in the future, but have not lived something like that in the past in complete life. The day before the DP I have learned that there was an election in Haiti, it may be the trigger this DP. The man in the DP may be Eddy, Monise's who is in elemental state now and who was ambushed and killed in that country two weeks before September 11, 2001. I have just learned, also, that he just got married. Apparently he was about to become the head of the police in Port-au-Prince, what created competition, envy and his death. The DP was warning me of the dangerous situation in which he was and of what could be resulted from that. At that time, in May 2000, I did not have a clue on the meaning of the DP. If I did, I would immediately go in Haiti to tell him where he was headed.

DP172. Near a river, I appear hooked on a bouncing branch o n top of thin, tall tree. I bounce to the ground, a man appears behind me. I have a piece of wood like a fork with two branches in my hand; I threaten to hit him with it. At the same time a woman is telling him that the order they were supposed to receive did not materialize. Another man asks "what did you learn at school?" "Nothing" is my answer to his question. Suddenly the water in the river swells overflows in the streets, carrying with it cars and everything. I am asking myself what if we were able to use all the water. I bounce up on top of the tall, thin tree. There

I see some women waiting; some among them have blond hair.

Would it not be nice to have a few houses to rent for shared accommodation, a tower to rent for office purposes and a few town houses to rent for family living purposes? I remember the first month I moved in the house on 3339 west 42nd Avenue, there was a party. Sitting on a coach with a few girls they were telling me how expensive it was to live in that area, in that house. I told them some psychological blah, blah I have heard related to faith in themselves and ability to live anywhere regardless of the cost of living in that particular area. Later I have learned that the owner wanted to sell the house and that the asking price was. $730 000. That was an enormous amount of money in relation to my minimum financial possibilities. 5 months later, you did not own the house, but it was close, I could do anything with it except selling it. In other words, there is some truth to the psychological blah, blah I've heard.

Furthermore I always thought that something like a piece of land is a good thing to possess. I can develop it, leave for future generation. Leaving money for future generation is an uncertain inheritance, unless it frozen forever in an investment institution. On this piece of land, or these pieces of land I will create a tall building and a series a small houses. With the earthquake and big accident detector, the book on relationships, the one personal development, the circle of my goals would be closed, basically.

The sounds of the words "gaule" and goal in French and in English are similar, but gaule in French does not here refer to Charles de Gaule, is a long branch of tree used to harvest fruit in tall tree like mango tree in hot countries. Then, the two words goal and gaule are pronounced the same way, may have similar meaning: instrument to arrive at an objective in French, an objective to attain in English. The DP is about my goals that I will create from nothingness, called sometimes, the whatness. Placed in the context of the DPs of the day, I can draw only one conclusion. If I create my goals, they are going to make some HBBs envious; I can end up as the nephew Eddy. At least, the possibility that what happened to him to happen is very unlikely, but unconscious fearmay t prevent me from creating my goals yet. It is only an unconscious fear, because in Canada no one has such a fear. There are many millionaires and billionaires here. I do not even here of them often. Nobody attempts to kill them. Nobody really cares about someone else wealth in Canada, and probably in all the western and rich countries. One billion dollars in asset, 2 billion dollars in asset, who cares?

The other reason why I do not create goals yet, according to the DP, is a fear of starting to create wealth and being unable to stop it afterward(the fear of the "Un-numerable". That is the way the flood should be interpreted, don't you think?

The DP reminds me of Levinson and his belief that "during the midlife transition in particular, success and failure must be assessed in more complex, life size terms, if a man is to be at peace with himself, otherwise, as with the especial woman, a man dream may become his worst nightmare." I have had many nightmares since I started the research, I am still having some once in while now. There is some truth in Levinson's thinking.

How many times for me to come back to this book again. Not finding a publisher I have a tendency to work at it again and again, and each time the world is shaken, flood, frozen river spilled, Earthquake , political and strange events, you name it. I do not want to attract your attention on that but the DPs are fashioning the world around us. I have to publish the book and stop working on them to stop the disastrous spell.

> *DP173. In the group where I appear in a discussion with one person, there is a child with a person of lower height than I am. At the end of the discussion, I say to the person I am talking to that if he was with me long enough, he would understand what I want to say to him by seeing how I apply my own ideas. While talking to him, I pronounce the word racist instead of racism that I wanted to say. It's like he is relieved after I made the correction.*

Here is what I wrote after I had the DP in 2000 to comment it: While writing the last line of the DP I thought of unemployment. That would mean that I am unemployed because of racism. I am not ready to say that with my conscious mind, the consciousness of my body. I had made a lot of mistakes in my life. I realize that only now. I have been offered many employments that I did not accept for one reason or another. It's the total of theses mistakes which cause my actual financial situation. It is not that the world is always nice,, that there aren't some HBBs quite alien to themselves, doing actions quite non-reflected upon, with feelings quite bizarre. But I am the cause of my actual financial situation, of everything that happens to me.

I have pronounced the word racism, predicting the content of an emission of Radio Canada I was going to listen to in the evening, emission called Macadam Tribu of which Jacques Bertrand is the host, at 7 PM Tuesday May 23, 2000. In that emission, there is a literature sequence.

That night they talked about an American author, Alex Baldwin, who has racism for subject in his writing.

In the morning, during the conprehensive trial of the DP, I did not have any idea that it was about that. I only had a vague idea that a certain Alex Baldwin wrote on racism. I did not do any connection between the direct perception and the radio emission. But I always knew that often it is necessary to wait for the domplete l life events to unfold before you can really understand the DP(Bad habit).

Today is May 13, 2003, almost exactly 2 years after I had the DP and wrote the comment. I was a lot weaker then spiritually and intellectually speaking, and that is still using soft words.

Today I would say financial vacuum instead of financial situation.

Today, I would add also that it is definitely not about racism done to me at work, for, Eddy, the nephew I mentioned above is Haitian, was killed for work by Haitian equally but because of ignorance, then a mean aspect of HBBs. in general. in the blind run after external power and frustration. Racism is only a facade.

All in all, I stand by the previous comment that we are the only one responsible for what happened to us, in one way or another.

Wednesday May 24, 2000

> DP174. This person brings me a letter. At the same time he kind of invites me to something. I become mad and say: " Who told you that I am a homosexual?" For your information, I am not." Then, he claps his hands.

"Why are you clapping your hands? Where is the glory? I ask".

He goes back upstairs, saying something I do not understand.

At this time a guide appears, translates for me "they should have never sent me to a private school."

It may be saying that I am accusing HBBs of homosexuality, for not being one myself, it would not be easy for me to say who is homosexual or not.

It may be saying, also, that not being invited in a letter to an act of homosexuality , I have no hard proof of homosexuality.

But it is not necessary to have this kind of hard proof to know who is a homosexual or not. I , personally, after having met so many men who arebisexual, I will tell who are a thousand miles away. I was living in a bedroom on Harwood street in west-End downtown. I went to the laundry room to watch my cloths. I met a man there who is living in the same building. He invited me to his apartment. I thought he was just friendly went to his place. He had for at least $500 of liquor on a small table in his apartment. He gave me many drinks. After that he started to look funny. When I asked him what is happening, he says he wants to f you. I went to the door, opened it, and left. I never saw him again. So, even though the homosexual does not invite me to homosexuality in a letter, sometimes, they will tell me exactly what they are about.

The DP suggests that private school is at the root of homosexuality, I have no knowledge of that, may be you, the reader, knows about that. Or it is , may be, an irony, for I was thinking of sending my kids to -private school, exactly to avoid homosexuality in public school.

I did not go to private school, but the Lycée Toussaint

Louverture, equivalent of secondary school that I attained to was for boys only, no girls. It is not clear to me if that has something to do with my character, my personality in the context of sexuality.

Identification with father who likes woman, identification with mother who likes men. I like whom?

> DP175. Sleeping on a bed with a child beside me who reminds me of Allan, it is like a snake has bitten him while sleeping in the bed. His mother gives him a shot of antibiotic. While talking to me, she tries to make me touch the syringe. I tell her that I do not want to touch it in order not to disturb the child. She thinks that you are accusing her of transmitting an incurable disease to her child. You can tell by her reaction.

It is about the another ex-nephew, ex because he is no longer living. He was in early 30ies, when he past away. I am puzzled and some how emotionally affected by this event, for many reasons, but mostly because he was of an age when we do not die so to speak and because he was an orphan. He was the son of my ex-sister, Siliane, who was a single mother. I thought I let my sister down by not doing something to help her to survive. So I was expecting to make up for it by helping her children, especially Allan of an unidentified father to survive. That made the news of his passage to elemental life even harder for me to accept.

Anyway, the DP is alluding to a genetic sickness from his mother or more specifically; she had aid and passed it to him. You do not know that, may be. There is, also, allusion to homosexuality; having HIV from man to man homosexuality, but this one is to be a dismissed consideration.

It would not be the case. I think that being an orphan, living in poor country were the major factors in the causality of his return to atomic state.

Here is how I put the trigger of the DP, immediately after having it: Yesterday night, at "2-7-5 Allo" at Radio Canada, the children told that they sleep in the same bed than their parents, sometimes. One child said that he was going to quit sleeping with his parents. he was 13 years old. Another one said that he would stop doing it when he will be 8 years old. It is without a doubt the trigger of the DP. In Haiti, the situation is similar, but adolescent males sleep together in the same bed until they are of 20 years old. I remember having done that myself, sleeping in the same little house of one little room with many brothers and half brothers around 19 years of chronological age.

> DP176. *She is going to go away. Each one of us and some friends write her a letter; She meets me to have them. When she is about to leave, I notice the enormous ass that she has.*

She reminds me of Tammy, the roommate who was living in this house. I like Tammy very much. I could not explain why I did not have intimate relation with her. The attachment with my sister, meaning I was attached to her for not seeing her for along period of time before her death, who looks like Tammy in physical shape, was the unconscious motive.

This idea of a person no longer living attached to some one who is still living is new to me. I came to that conclusion because there is no event in my life to which to connect the dream to. There was a friend visiting Tammy the time of the DP who was annoying me with his homosexual advances. He might thought like that (I noticed his huge ass) about me.

That was two years ago. Yesterday, May 15, 2003, I went to a walking-in-clinic in the west-end, Downtown of Vancouver. There is a certain doctor Ned junior, junior because his father is working there too, the fouder of that place, Ido not know their first names. Younger Ned was a bit aggressive toward me at first. That reminds us of Alfred Adler who said this "He(Ned junior) is one of these men who approach another individual, feels attracted, but immediately assumes an aggressive attitude that destroys the very contact they wanted to establish." When I was there yesterday, I noticed he has a big ass, because he came to the waiting room, faced the secretary behind her desk, at the same time turning his back to me, the only way I would notice a man's ass. He is a black person, shaped in a way that make his ass appear big, especially if he is not a thin person.

Amanda left on the first, replaced by a new roommate, Michael. On the first of May, he said to me at night he was tired and that he was going to sleep early. I thought it was strange for him to tell something like that to me, for a man to say that to another, concluded he meant to say "To night I am not available, but tomorrow, I will be." He, then, put 6 exotic beers in the fridge; I took it as a homosexual temptation. He started to rearrange the living room since sometime, Yesterday night around 9:30 PM, he displaced a chair, put it right in front of my bedroom where I was sitting and watching TV. At ten PM, while going to the wash room to brush my teeth, you said hi to him talk to him a little bit, came back in my bedroom, closed the door behind me and listen to Rhona, the radio show hosted by the person of the same name. I thought if he just wanted to talk to me he would just come to my room and talk, without any arrangement. This incident reveal his homosexual intension, and that he will move out in the near future, for finding out that I am not quite the person he thought I was.

When I had the DP two years ago, I was the object of the same homosexual advances. The situation will repeat itself again, unless I live in an apartment alone, or if I have enough money to place an ad in the newspaper and can wait until you find a woman roommate. Last month I could not wait, had to take the first offer, which was Michael. Two men are not supposed to live in the same house in this culture, it is like. That encourages homosexuality.

Heather wrote me a letter when she was about to move out and go back to Calgary. I do not see the relevance of her letter to the events of my life presently.

The DP is probably about future events that I cannot know now.

CHAPTER XXIV

Thursday May 25, 2000

DP177 A group of HBBs and I are going somewhere. A lot of strange things happen during the voyage. This guy only "bottomly"

dressed is traveling in the mid air with his kite, let himself down so hard that a man wearing a costume has to catch him before he hit the ground and hurt himself. Then, itis time to eat. We cannot start to eat yet, because Paul is missing and we are waiting for him.

Paul is the first name of the Canadian Prime Minister before Steven Harper. I had some Psychic communications and experiences with Paul or Mr Martin(I find him so friendly), because in grade 4,5 and 6 I had a friend with first name Paul. He was lot more mature than I was at that age.

He was a musician, created a group of musicians making dances at night.

Paul Martin the Canadian Prime Minister abandoned his position as Chief of the liberal party abruptly. I fell a little bit guilty about that thinking that our psychic experiences may have been in the causality of his action. I think of him as the best Minister of finance Canada will ever have.

Paul in the DP may also be an allusion to Jean Paul Sartre, the French author and activist. He was also very good at psyche in the sense that that he was very familiar with it. I liked him for that.

DP178. "Anse d'Hainault achete on ti billet"

This sentence from Creole to English means: Anse "d'Hainault, buy a little ticket." It seems to be a put down on the fact that I play lottery.

I am reminded of the psychotherapist Rhona Raskin, radio talk show host as said above. When callers ask her about her thought of HBBs who play lottery, her answer invariably was that the lottery players unconsciously want to loose their money. That is her opinion, which may be true, may be untrue. The question I ask myself then is "Psychologists are supposed to be HBBs of moral superiority. Is this an eye blinder sometimes?" I ask myself the question because I think her answer reflects the idea that we all supposed to spend our time to contribute to the society, and that playing lottery does not directly contribute something to society, for there is no product consequential to this particular activity. This idea is somewhat true in regard to lottery game, but it is the same for football, baseball, hockey, etc. Ehat do the society gets from those games? DNBBS fudilling their dreams may be, there is no concrete and immediate product as in the lottery game .

We have to accept our pitiful, miserable life, because we will be re compensated in heaven. Right?

In the other hand, when someone thinks like that he or she will eventually be in opposition to a very basic psychological law, namely "It is misguided to be too intent toward life, for being so we deny reality the creativity on which it rests" The playful attitude toward life that one gets from liking to play any game is more basic to life, more beneficial to HBBs than the opposite attitude. That does not necessarily contradict Rhona's advice, but we must be careful not to throw away the "bad and the good" at the same time.

I suppose behind this sort of reaction to gaming there are many unconscious operatives such as frustration from not being able to win big money from the game, envy of big cash winners, the fear of the big number of probable winning sets involved in the lottery game, 21 million in Super Seven, the fear of neglecting the so called productive work in favor of "hazardous" game, the fear of addiction to "hazardous" games, etc. The fear of neglecting work is not rational, for in every country we have to deal with unemployment but not the contrary, meaning lack of some kind of occupation in replacement of "real work" is rather what should be feared.

Obviously, I do not think quite like Rhona does for many reasons such as human psyche should be pushed as far as possible, many HBBs are winning millions of $ in the world everyday from lottery and many other games. So to can you and I.

The second comment about the little DP or a flash is in regard of the word Anse d'Hainault, which is really a city in southwest (Where the English people tried to establish themselves unsuccessfully between 1453 to 1804) in Haiti.

One of my sisters in law's father was from there. Fernande used to go there every year to visit her father's family. When she came back, she brought with her food that was exotic for me. There was a light alcoholic beverage, similar to vodka; she used to bring it back. There was a certain Gerald, equally from there. One day, him and me drank a good deal of this liquor together until my ideas became liquorish. Gerald was sent to the la la land by a "macoute"(Duvalier's secrete police), apparently.

Fernande's father and her and her sister Germaine are about 4'tall or less, one of the reasons for the adjective "ti" or "petit" in French or small in English. Did you guess that? Of course you did.

Then, this little one sentence DP, in other words, this flash, suggests to me that the unconscious fear of getting killed by a macoute to get what I have, prevented me from winning big cash in the ppk game. Consciously, I would never thought of that, made such a link. All facts or events are accountable at the deeper level of mind, it is like.

As it is question of winning in lottery game the word Anse in Anse D'Hainault is a suggestion that I need to to find a mind hook in order to focus enough on the game and in order to win. Like in a class room, the first thing to do before presenting a lesson, Hop you up for some "rambling", is to find something that wake the student minds up, to keep their attention, the meaning of hook here, anse in French.

> *DP179. We are somewhere on a terrain with things we do not want, which we want to leave for HBBs who need them? We are worried a little, not knowing where exactly on the terrain to live them. A child appears and say "Please, do not be so preoccupied by*

them. Simply let them right where they are on the terrain now."

I wish I would be a rich person some day. A lot of money would pass through my hands. I would like that, for money, this tremendous force, as they say, would make life pleasurable for me, would help me to contribute to mankind, will help me to reach my higher life purposes. I am not quite rich now, although since the year 2002 I am almost completely in control of my time, which means to all practical ends that half way of the road toward wealth is already done.

However, I did give things I do n't need many times in my life, one the best ways of self-organization anyway. The first time I made the experience of giving was when was living in Montreal and had to go to work in Manitoba. Jacques was one of my best friends living in Montreal presently and probably. He invited many of his friends at my place. I gave most of the household goods that you had, TV, stereo, ustensil, sleeping necessities, etc. Many other times when I was living in the house in 3339 West 42nd Avenue, I gave bag of cloth left in the basement house by tenants who moved out to Big Brother most of the time. When one an ex-girlfriends left the house to go to live in the United States, she left a big bag of women cloth. The Salvation Army called, I asked them to come and pick them up.

The DP alludes to garbage, I ca not make sense of that in in my personal experiences. But today May 21, 2003, besides SARS, the name of a contagious new disease, and mad cow diseases that are the big tittles in the news of the day in Canada, Some documents to implicate an alleged criminal were found after a search on a garbage terrain in Toronto, these events are related to the DP more or less.

The day she was moving out of this house, Amanda left a basket full of her old belongings in front and beside the door of her ex-bedroom. I displaced it, thinking she was going to come back for it. When she came back, I asked her about it, she said she did not need the content of the basket, you promise to dispose of it for her, having the impression that she did not know what to do with them, equally related to the DP more or less.

May be she wanted to say to me that I am garbage.

There is also allusion to field theory, one of the first psychological approach to motivation theories.

The DP is about they future which is not possible to know entirely right now.

> DP179. A few persons and I am in a voyage, going somewhere looking for something. Once there and trying to take what I come for, a man attack one of the persons with me, fight with him. Then another appears behind and is getting ready to attack and fight with my friend also. I hit this one with something; he lost his balance and falls down. After that, I hear the call of a woman whose voice is familiar to me to give me what I am looking for. Further than where the call came from, I hear another familiar voice telling me to be careful of a group of bizarre HBBs coming my way.

Is it telling me something about war and about my goals or that it takes somewhat a surplus of energy and aggression to create my goals? For I need some kind of aggression to create something, an object, and a car for example, that was not already there, changing metal to electrical cord, etc., there is a transformation, which is a sort of aggression but directed toward matter, the metal in this case, but not toward HBBs. Another way to say that war is not necessary to create. Some HBBs seem to confuse the two kinds of aggression.

In creation itself there may be aggression, but not toward HBBs.

We would like to know whom are these bizarre HBBs coming our way? Someone who hugely successful may have that fear, but in my case, there is no such a thing and probably there will not be in the future either, for I am no gearing that way. I would be glad if the books were sold all over the world. That would be satisfying enough for me.

> *DP180. In pajamas at home, I see a black ant; I smash it by the mean of cord. Itis like the servant is in the living room also, but busy with something. Then, arrives from another room, a woman who looks like my wife or my fiancée. Looking for something, she says words like "the downer".*

> *Not understanding, I continue to question her. "Touch down" she adds.*

> *At the end she touches a baseball bat leaning against a wall in the living room to show me what she is looking for.*

Baseball bat is something I keep in my room since I started to live in shared accommodation, just in case an intruder would want to force his way in my bedroom. Some guys did try to force their way in my bedroom. I push them back some how without to have to use the baseball bat. I punched one in his face and went to get the baseball. He run down the stairs to his bedroom fell down while doing so. One other tried too; I push him by grabbing him in his neck. The black ant, it is not clear why it is there. It may be a way some other think of a black HBBs, but I've never heard of that in complete life. It's not clear who the woman is either.

DP181. In bed with my wife or a woman, I turn upside down in the bed. When she wakes up and notices my opposite position in relation to hers in the bed, she gets up, ready to leave, I say "It is nothing my love, nothing at all, my love". Then, she lies down again and falls asleep.

Here is what I wrote after having the DP. At that time I thought that may be this DP was about Craig who came to visit Tamara the roommate from Australia. For, last Monday or Tuesday, I found 2 knives side by side beside the sink in the kitchen. I became familiar to homosexual language and sexual invitation. I've learned it when I was living in the house on 3339 west 42nd Avenue. There were sometimes 7 men living there at the same time. I have finished by understand some of the clues men use to invite another to homosexua act. Sometimes, they leave one fork in the sink. One homosexual told Me once that there has been a skunk around the house.

Mike told us last week there were a smell near his toilet. Barbara is naive in regard to this subject. She washed the carpet, sprayed the spot with some chemical product. I didn't bother that much thinking it would be related to homosexuality.

Another man said to me once that he has seen a wasp nest in the fence between his house and mine near the gate. Before, I used to get mad, wanting to fight with them after seeing one of the clues in the house. One man made it clear to me that it was not something illegal. Nowadays, I decide to take the fight to its own ground by using the same clues to counteract. After seeing the two knifes in the same sense near the sink, I changed the sense of one of them in a way that they become a head and queue pair (That was the trigger of the DP, you think). That has created a sort of unspoken treaty pact between Craig and me for some time (letting him know not to bother me with his strange subliminal homosexual messages).

But before he left, or the day he was leaving Vancouver, he started the ritual again by telling me repeatedly that he was going to lie down on his bed.

I noticed the ritual also from men and women, when I was about to play in the ppk game. They invited me to love at that moment. Then because I am a hetero who prefer to the wild thing when in love with a woman, it was an upsetting behavior to me, I became mad and unable to perform according to my best skills, giving 100% of myself, then unable to win at the game. I do not really care to tell the morbid sexual part, but it is important to underline all the reasons for not winning in the game, although I am the only one responsible for anything that happens to me.

The note misdirected me a bit for the DP is only about a couple living together, or more exactly me living together with a woman. It Happened 3 times. I lived with Paulette(Introduced in a preceding DP in which there is Paul). I lived with her for about a year. Once or twice we made love for more Than 4 hours at a time(Soul Exposed). I lived also with Georgette for about a year also. She is a very nice looking lady , came from Baie Comeau and was living in Montreal when we met. With Debbie we were not completely living together, we were going out for 6 years, I slept at her place many times each weak. All that time I sill had an appartment.

DP182. A woman gets out of the room. When she gets back she sits near my feet on the bed.

What is it? I ask.

There is nothing dear, she answers.

Then I think of a certain Gilbert who has not been able to find pappy.

Yesterday, one woman was very kind to me at the Toronto Dominion Bank *She* was of an average age, her hair was almost white, pink going to white. I like this kind of hair color in general. I used to have a chat with her when I go in the bank where she works to cash a cheque. Another woman was very kind to me at Shoppers Drug Mart. Another one was also kind to me at Stongs (Choices' Safeway, and Buy-Low- Food are not very far either), one of the closest supermarkets in the area in which I am living. Two of these women are in their teen age; the others were in her 40ies. Then I went to the library. This branch of Vancouver Public Library and the pharmacy are very close to each other in what could be called the little downtown of Dunbar area. In the library a woman reading a book facing me leaning toward me from about 10 feet. I automatically started looking at her breasts, before I noticed she could be a young teen. When she saw me looking at her, she closed her top with her hand, continued reading. When she got up, I got the freight of my life, thinking she was going to complain about me to the librarian. The fear was rather caused by the fact that I was objectifyung her. I know I should not, but I did that often and I am still doing it.

Another woman, an oriental one, was very well dressed in a navy blue skirt, plus a top. She was helping her daughter with her homework. Finding the mother somewhat attractive I look at her a few times. She got up and went toward the librarian Thinking she went to complain of me, I was afraid again(I am excesssively sensitive about being accused of stalking what I find very unattractive). But when she came back, she told her daughter that what she was looking for was in a web site. Then I calmed down. After that another woman arrived looking at two racks of novels. I was looking at her between the two racks. She looks at you me for a while. A man came, told her something I did not quite decipher. I thought he knew I was looking at his wife or girlfriend, I was very afraid again.

The freighting day, isn't it?

That day, at first many women were kind to me. Later, I experienced many fears because of women. There was probably some guilt feelings working at me that day, reminds me of sentence I had in a recent DP which says "Women are my weakness." In one hand, a compulsion is a very idiotic thing. Why would women be my weakness? This sentence has been floating in the repressive society, especially in my own family. Of course I do not know how many women my ex-father was in a sexual relationships with. I just know he had 27 children born from 10 mothers. He probably felt guilty about it, felt women were a problem for him, somehow passed the idea to me by genes.

Recently, a polygamist HBB admitted to father 123 children in his polygamist camp around the greater Vancouver. He has children with underage girls. Apparently no one can do anything about it.

On the other hand, Woman is your weakness might just mean I like woman, don't you think?

There was Gilbert I met in elementary school. Se is in the deepest level of my memory. I cannot recall any incidence about him or her relevant to me, to this work. The name sounds a little like Beth, the physician(made me undresse completely once) who helps me when I was sick or who helps me prevent sickness. Sometimes the way she behaves with me makes it look l as if we were married . I do not know if she is married or not. I know she has one child for seeing the picture on the wall of her office. I ca not make any sense of her either, but there might be a transference love between us two.

She always referring to young woman roommate I have as if itis why I do not connect with her romantically, for she is less younger than they are. Then the sense of Gilbert would be Pervert. She may think like that about me out of frustration for the same reason. The roommates are young adults. Other HBBs can think of me this way for the same reason. Worse, I might think of me this way at the cellular level. Worse, because it would be the root cause or one of the sickest causes of the involuntary sexual abstinence that pervades my life presently.

> *DP183. The meal is served HBBs are eating, I do not see some vegetables in the dishes. When I enter into the kitchen where I have heard them talking everybody stops.*

This is about future self, also. It is one of my desires to have a long table in the dining room of the house that you will buy. I saw a batman film once. In one sequence, the main actor was shown eating alone at the edge of very long table. The contrast was very captivating. It gave me the idea of having a very long table, but I will not want to eat alone at it. I will invite many friends then to eat at the table, during holidays, especial occasion's etc. It reminds me of Maxim, a Roommate I had in 1972, 1973. She was a 75 less young woman at the time, but because of her up bit personality, I had a pleasant life when I was living in her house. During each holiday she invited her daughter and her son, another tenant and me to diner. During Christmas Eve, lot more HBBs were invited or just dropped by, it was party all night long.

This DP really reminds me my first work experience in a foreign country. It was in San Maarteen, a very small Island in the Caribbean Sea, not very far from Haiti. I worked at a hotel called Mullet Bay Beach. I did different type of task in the kitchen, dining room, drove a van. The hotel was spread on vast terrain on which there are many little small houses, instead of one big building. I use the van to bring food in the kitchen from the storage room. The salary was small, but I was having a real good time working there, for I did not pay for food, neither for a room to sleep. There was a sleeping building especially for workers of the hotel.

There was many HBBs from Germany working there, although the hotel itself was part of Ford's companies. The chief in the food service was Elmunt Smith, one of the impeccable HBBs I may never meet again. In Haiti, I used to go to the Warf and watched from afar pleasance boat and Americans getting out. In Mullet Bay Beach it was practically my first experience with white HBBs, for having been working with Smith who left me with such good impression of human species. Adding to that, the fact that it was always nice and hot in the island, the fact that I was always working, satisfying all my basic needs and more, it was almost like living in paradise.

* * *

DP# 180 practically terminates this volume of The Soul Exposed. In it I have tried to do a little bit of my personal therapy\World therapy in order to motivate myself in the creation of goals that I have, hoping to inspire HBBs in the rest of the world to do the same while and after reading this volume. I hope that has pleased you. Au revoir! Chao! Ouf vidersen! So long, Hasta la vista!

25 juin 2003

Arnoux Prince

CopyRight, Vancouver, 2003

> DP20. A few people and you are sitting on a grass. You have hot discussion with a young man who is there too. There is a young woman sitting beside you. Someone comes to talk to her. After the talker's departure, the young woman leans her head on you. Then you notice that she is completely nude. Another person that you don't see says that she is born beautiful.

There is another hearing imagining in this DP. You barely saw the scenery: the people and the grass on which you were sitting. You cannot conclude from this observation that the sense of hearing is more important than the other 4 senses.

You use to read playboy regularly like a bible, not only for the article, but also to look at picture of women with nothing on their body. You don't know if this one of your habits contributes to your unwanted sexual abstinence. Even the ones you see in the Playboy picture are not quite the same in waking life. In the magazine they are not moving like being dead. You have dip on women in elemental life many times. You had a DP on Marilyn Monroe. She appeared in Playboy too, but it is not the reason why she presents herself to you in DP. The phenomenon is puzzling. It's like in that state people still know people who are alive and tries to communicate with them sometimes. You would never in your conscious waking live tries to communicate with dead women, even Marilyn Monroe. What you're trying to say is that the first move was from her.

Your mother and one of your entire sisters are in elemental state. So, in a way, you used to think of women in that state, when you think of them.

Of course, every woman looks nice and attractive to you now. Sometimes you see a woman; you feel you would have to eat her flesh to be completely satisfied in making love with her. This emotion is the result of a long unwanted sexual abstinence. You were watching The Practice, a series of film on TV. In one episode, there was a man arrested and killed, He was on trial for eating the flesh beautiful dead woman. You don't quite remember the part. But you were surprised to find your feeling on TV. The behavior of the criminal wasn't explained. The writer of the series probably didn't know the explanation. They probably get the vague feeling from you without the whole picture, another phenomenon.